Beyond Neutrality

Beyond Neutrality
Perfectionism and Politics

GEORGE SHER

RICE UNIVERSITY

CAMBRIDGE
UNIVERSITY PRESS

PUBLISHED BY THE PRESS SYNDICATE OF THE UNIVERSITY OF CAMBRIDGE
The Pitt Building, Trumpington Street, Cambridge CB2 1RP, United Kingdom

CAMBRIDGE UNIVERSITY PRESS
The Edinburgh Building, Cambridge CB2 2RU, United Kingdom
40 West 20th Street, New York, NY 10011-4211, USA
10 Stamford Road, Oakleigh, Melbourne 3166, Australia

First published 1997

Printed in the United States of America

Typeset in Palatino

Library of Congress Cataloging-in-Publication Data
Sher, George.
Beyond neutrality : perfectionism and politics / George Sher.
p.   cm.
ISBN 0-521-57068-9. – ISBN 0-521-57824-8 (pbk.)
1. Political ethics. 2. Values. 3. Autonomy. 4. State, The.
I. Title.
JA79.S42   1996
320 – dc20   96-9217
                                                                              CIP

A catalog record for this book is available from the British Library.

ISBN 0-521-57068-9 hardback
ISBN 0-521-57824-8 paperback

For Emily

Contents

Preface

I am ambivalent toward contemporary liberalism. On the one hand, I believe that many of today's liberal thinkers are waging a necessary and courageous battle on behalf of certain vital but embattled Enlightenment attitudes – attitudes that include a willingness to abstract away from differences of background and culture to defend universally applicable standards of fairness and right; a commitment to such familiar liberal values as civility, toleration, and respect for others; and, most important, a confidence in the power of reason to resolve our disagreements. Without such confidence, we are at the mercy of the postmodernist tendency to reduce all political and intellectual disagreement to so much jockeying for power and advantage, and to regard the exchange of ideas as a continuation of war by other means. We are, I think, all indebted to those who resist this corrosive trend.

But, at the same time, contemporary liberal thought has taken a turn I find deeply problematic. For some important reason – I am honestly not sure what – many liberals have concluded that reason's scope is drastically limited. Though still confident about our ability to reach universally applicable conclusions about justice and rightness, these thinkers are much less sanguine about the prospects for reaching reasoned conclusions about goodness or value. There is, in their view, some sort of important asymmetry between what reason can hope to show us about what persons are morally obligated to do and what it can hope to show us about how it is best to live.

These doubts can take various forms. In some cases, they are expressed as outright value-skepticism; in others, as the subjectivist view that what counts as a good life for a person depends entirely on his own preferences or choices; in yet others, as the view that even if some ways of living really are better than others, such considerations should play no role in determining our political decisions. Under each variant, the result is a familiar sort of political theory that is exquisitely sensitive to the imperatives of choice, but is resolutely indifferent to all the gradations of better and worse among which agents seek *to* choose, and concern with which alone makes agents' choices meaningful. I suppose it is possible that the best political theory may require, as a matter of principle, that governments simply not concern themselves with either the civility and quality of public discourse or the character and achievements of their citizens; but the more I have thought about that idea, the stranger and less defensible it has come to seem. What follows is my attempt to explain why.

Because these matters have occasioned so much recent discussion, I have incurred many more intellectual debts than I can hope to discharge. Still, two books have affected my thinking more than others, and I want at least to acknowledge their influence. One, predictably, is John Rawls's magisterial *A Theory of Justice*. Although it has now been in print for a full twenty-five years, that work continues to set the standard for contemporary moral and political theorizing. The other book that has had the greatest influence is *The Morality of Freedom*, by Joseph Raz. Although Raz's arguments are substantially different from mine, I find his views about politics and the good exceptionally congenial, and I have learned a great deal from his work.

I have learned even more from the many friends, colleagues, seminars, and audiences who have read, listened to, and commented upon sections of this manuscript. Those who generously read and reacted to all or part of it include Baruch Brody, David Christensen, Amy Gutmann, Chad Hansen, Istvan Hont, Hilary Kornblith, Arthur Kuflik, Patrick Neal, Derk Pereboom, Bob Taylor, Larry Temkin, Michael Walzer, and Alan Wertheimer. I am very grateful for their efforts and the many insights these have yielded. I owe a debt of a different order to my wife, Emily Fox Gordon, who as always has provided both patient support and invaluable stylistic and substantive advice. Needless to say, none of these people are responsible for any of the errors, omissions, or oddities that the book undoubtedly still contains.

Much of an early draft was written at the University of Vermont, where I taught until 1991, and I want to thank that institution, both for its sustenance over the years and for the research fellowships it provided in the summers of 1987 and 1990. I am also grateful to the

Institute for Advanced Study for allowing me to spend my 1987–8 sabbatical in surroundings that managed to be both tranquil and intellectually charged, and to the National Endowment for the Humanities for the financial support that it provided during that year.

Parts of the book were first published elsewhere. Much of Chapter 7 originally appeared in *Philosophy and Public Affairs* 18 (Spring 1989), pp. 132–57, under its present title "Three Grades of Social Involvement." Some of Chapter 6 appeared in "Knowing about Virtue," in *Nomos XXXIV: Virtue,* edited by John W. Chapman and William A. Galston (New York: New York University Press, 1992), pp. 91–116. Chapter 3 was first published in *Social Philosophy and Policy* 12 (Winter 1995), pp. 136–59, under the title "Liberal Neutrality and the Value of Autonomy." Part of Chapter 5 appeared in *Law and Philosophy* 14, 2 (May 1995), pp. 185–201, as "Rights, Neutrality, and the Oppressive Power of the State" (copyright 1995 Kluwer Academic Publishers, reprinted by permission of Kluwer Academic Publishers). I am grateful to the editors and publishers of these journals for their permission to use this material here.

Chapter 1

Introduction

In this book, I shall present a view about government and the good life, one intermediate between two familiar extremes. At one extreme are views that the connection between government and the good life is internal – that living well requires governing as well as being governed, as Aristotle thought, or that the state exists to realize some other vision of the good. At the other extreme is the view that there is *no* connection between government and the good life – that the state should simply be neutral toward all conceptions of the good. Between these extremes, there is room for a third type of view, one that does not seek to *ground* the state in any particular conception of the good, but nevertheless holds that a government may legitimately *promote* the good. The view that I shall advance is of this third sort. To defend it, I must defuse the main reasons to deny that the state may seek to promote the good; to motivate it, I must develop a conception of the good that is worth promoting. These, accordingly, are the book's two main aims.

I

In recent years, many who call themselves liberals have maintained that the state should not favor, promote, or act on any particular conception of the good. Instead, it should simply provide a neutral and just framework within which each citizen can pursue the good as he understands it. To provide this framework, a government must sometimes interfere with liberty. It must restrict its citizens' options in order to insure security and stability, promote prosperity and efficiency, and make available various public goods. Also, if justice requires more equality than unconstrained markets can provide, the

1

state must intervene to equalize opportunity or resources. But, according to the view under discussion, this is *all* that government should do. If in addition it tries to make citizens more virtuous, to raise their level of culture or civility, or to prevent them from living degraded lives, it oversteps its bounds. Even if some traits or activities are genuinely better than others, no government should promote the better or suppress or discourage the worse. About all questions of the good life, the state should remain strictly neutral.[1]

Even in summary statement, this neutralist picture is instantly recognizable. It is, indeed, a picture that no contemporary Westerner can altogether escape. Although barraged by competing ideologies and social schemes, we have all absorbed, by a kind of cultural osmosis, the ideas that self-expression, choice, and diversity are paramount, and that how a person lives is less important than whether he lives as he prefers and chooses. We also worry, unfortunately with justification, that by tolerating departures from official neutrality, we risk allowing the state's coercive apparatus to be captured by fanatics, bullies, or worse. Neutralism also draws support from our uncertainty about where our deepest values lie and which ways of living really are best – an uncertainty that is the inevitable by-product of our (on the whole extremely salutary) critical attitude toward all belief. Given this confluence of factors, there is a strong sense in which all, or all but a very few, contemporary Americans and Europeans must feel the pull of neutralism. Thus, while my stance will be critical, my criticism will embody many of the liberal assumptions, and more of the spirit, of the view I criticize.

Nonetheless, I do think it is important at least to trim back some of liberalism's more extravagant claims, and so I must explain why. The

---

1. Because the neutrality principle has been so widely discussed, I cannot exhaustively enumerate the works in which it is defended. However, a partial list includes John Rawls, *A Theory of Justice* (Cambridge, Mass.: Harvard University Press, 1971); Robert Nozick, *Anarchy, State, and Utopia* (New York: Basic Books, 1974); Bruce Ackerman, *Social Justice in the Liberal State* (New Haven: Yale University Press, 1980); Ronald Dworkin, *A Matter of Principle* (Cambridge, Mass.: Harvard University Press, 1985); Charles Larmore, *Patterns of Moral Complexity* (Cambridge: Cambridge University Press, 1987); D. A. Lloyd-Thomas, *In Defence of Liberalism* (Oxford: Basil Blackwell, 1988); Will Kymlicka, *Liberalism, Community, and Culture* (Oxford: Oxford University Press, 1989); Richard Arneson, "Liberalism, Distributive Subjectivism, and Equal Opportunity for Welfare," *Philosophy and Public Affairs* 19, 2 (Spring 1990), pp. 158–94, and "Primary Goods Reconsidered," *Nous* 24, 3 (June 1990), pp. 429–54. In addition, closely related theses can be extracted from such important works as John Stuart Mill's *On Liberty* (Indianapolis: Bobbs-Merrill, 1956) and Thomas Nagel's "Moral Conflict and Political Legitimacy," *Philosophy and Public Affairs* 16, 3 (Summer 1987), pp. 215–40.

most straightforward reason, of course, is that it is important to believe truth and avoid falsehood, and – so I will argue – there is good reason to believe that neutralism *is* false. But quite apart from this, reliance on untenable principles and bad arguments is unlikely to help the liberal cause. Like Mill – himself the quintessential liberal – I believe that truth (and error) have a way of emerging; and I believe, too, that overstated claims tend to backfire. Thus, the best way to protect what is true and important about liberalism is to distinguish it clearly from what is exaggerated and untrue.

Even by themselves, these considerations would amply warrant a close examination of neutralism. But there is also a further and, to my mind, still more important reason – namely, that any truly neutral state must needlessly cut its citizens off from important goods. If, as I believe, some traits, activities, and ways of relating to people really are superior to others, and if there are no defensible reasons for governments *not* to promote these, then many citizens of neutral states will end up with lives that are not as good as they could be. Conversely, by combining some state efforts on behalf of the good with some liberal strictures against state excess, we may hope to increase significantly the likelihood that many citizens *will* live genuinely good lives.

II

But how, exactly, can we accomplish this, and what are the costs and risks? My full answers must of course await the discussion to follow; but some initial discussion is in order. Hence, in this section, I shall simply state, without defense or much nuance, a few of the book's main claims about government. In the next section, I shall similarly sketch the book's claims about value.

REASONS IN POLITICS

Consider first an objection that, if sound, would make short work of neutralism. To warrant serious consideration, the neutralist ideal must be one that governments can at least approach, even if not fully attain. But many believe that no government *can* even approach neutrality, since every law, policy, and political institution must automatically favor many conceptions of the good while disfavoring many others. For example, even an institution as necessary as a police force or army must require and reward traits like discipline, courage, and respect for authority. In so doing, it must favor all conceptions of the good that prize these traits over (say) spontaneity, gentleness, and compassion. This, it seems, is an obvious breach of neutrality. Moreover, the case is not isolated: governments also favor specific conceptions of the good by adopting particular tax structures, zoning laws, and environmental policies, and by taking countless other actions. But if breaches of neutrality are so pervasive and inevitable, then isn't neutralism doomed from the start?[2]

If this objection succeeded, there would be little point in going on. But most neutralists believe it does not, and their reasons are instructive. The standard response is to distinguish a stronger and a weaker version of neutralism. The stronger version asserts that governments may not adopt any laws or policies that *have the effect of* promoting any particular conceptions of the good, whereas the weaker asserts only that governments may not take any actions *in order to* promote any such conceptions. In Will Kymlicka's useful terms, the stronger version demands consequential, the weaker only justificatory neutrality.[3] This distinction is important because the current objection – that *any* government action must favor some conceptions of the good over others – tells only against the possibility of consequential neutrality. Hence, the obvious way to meet it is to interpret neutralism solely in justificatory terms. Under this interpretation, neutralism is exclusively a thesis about the *reasons* for which governments may act.

Like most neutralists, I believe the fundamental issue is one of justification; but, unlike them, I do not believe that any kinds of reasons are in principle inadmissible in politics. Instead, I believe it is no less legitimate for governments than for private individuals to try to promote the good. I believe, as well, that such efforts remain legitimate when made by individuals seeking to influence their government's laws, policies, or basic structure. In saying this, I do not mean to imply either that the reasons provided by the good can never be overridden or that role-related duties, such as the duties of the police to enforce the law or of diplomats to implement official policy, can never preempt reasons that otherwise would be decisive.

2. For argument along these lines, see Brian Barry, *Political Argument* (New York: Humanities Press, 1965), pp. 74–97.
3. Will Kymlicka, "Liberal Individualism and Liberal Neutrality," *Ethics* 99, 4 (July 1989), p. 884.

I do mean, however, that in our prior deliberations about which laws and policies to adopt, questions about how it is best to live may never simply be "taken off the agenda." In public as well as private life, the operative distinction is not between legitimate and illegitimate reasons, but rather between good and bad ones.

DEMOCRACY

Even this very partial sketch of my position is likely to set off warning bells. If governments may act on beliefs that some *ways of living* are better than others, it seems a short step to the view that they may act on beliefs that some *types of persons* are better than others. This suggests that governments may legitimately discriminate in favor of some citizens – the "better" ones – at the expense of others. Just as disturbingly, it suggests that the state's decisions are best made by a select class of overseers. In both ways, the resulting vision of politics may appear objectionably elitist.

But, in fact, both worries are groundless. To the suggestion that a nonneutral politics might sanction discrimination, the obvious reply is that even if no reasons for political action are in principle off limits, it hardly follows that all reasons are equally weighty, or even that every alleged reason must be taken seriously. It is, for example, quite clear that "reasons" of race, caste, and the like have no moral weight. They are, quite simply, bad reasons. Hence, even if arguments for (say) racial discrimination are not ruled out because they are nonneutral, they will be ruled out because their premises are indefensible. We can therefore admit the legitimacy of nonneutral political reasoning without worrying about legitimizing abhorrent forms of discrimination. Indeed, to show that a form of discrimination is *illegitimate*, the best strategy is publicly to consider, and decisively to refute, the best arguments advanced on its behalf.

Nor, second, does admitting nonneutral arguments require a decision-making elite; for the question of which grounds for political decisions are legitimate is quite different from the question of who should *make* those decisions. Because these questions are so different, the view that governments may adopt policies on the grounds that these will promote the good has no special link to the view that governments must be run by elites. To forge a link, one would have to argue that only an elite few can know enough about the good to make informed decisions about it. But, at least offhand, this is no

5

more plausible than the comparable claim about (say) international economics or nuclear deterrence. Because even neutralists agree that government must address these issues, the charge of elitism is not one that they can easily press.

Because this book is not about political authority, I shall not try to decide among the competing theories of decision making. Instead, I shall simply assume that our own system of representative democracy is at least among the legitimate options. Thus, I shall argue that a democratic polity may, through its representatives, induce or even compel its own members to live what it collectively judges to be good lives. Although the idea of collective self-compulsion is, as always, faintly paradoxical, it is no more paradoxical when the aim is to promote the good than when it is (say) to maintain public order or protect the environment.

PROTECTIVE ARRANGEMENTS

I have just suggested that a nonneutral state need not be elitist. But in urging that nonneutral policies be adopted democratically, I may seem only to replace one danger with another. The new danger, of course, is that the majority will deal tyrannically with those who hold unpopular conceptions of the good. As liberals have long realized, we need protection both from the depredations of dominant groups and from the conflicts that arise when no group can achieve dominance. To shield us from these dangers, liberals advocate a fixed constitution, a system of divided government, and various procedural and substantive rights. If a nonneutral state must dismantle these structures, then any retreat from neutrality will be a retrograde step.

But this fear, too, is ungrounded, since a nonneutral state can retain most, if not all, of the classical liberal protections. Such a state is obviously compatible with a fixed constitutional framework, a settled procedure for amending the constitution, and the separation of different branches of government. It is no less compatible with the full range of procedural civil rights. Even if democratic governments may adopt laws whose aim is to promote the good, it does not follow that they may enforce these laws in arbitrary or oppressive ways. Even a nonneutral state can guarantee every accused person a speedy trial, and can protect every citizen from self-incrimination, cruel and unusual punishment, and arbitrary search and seizure.

It can also guarantee most if not all of the substantive rights that liberals have traditionally favored. At first glance, this may not be obvious; for if citizens have rights to express themselves, practice their religion, travel, and own property, then governments cannot promote the good in any ways that these rights prohibit. But the ability to promote the good is not all-or-nothing, and even a set of rights that does protect some activities must leave many others unprotected. Hence, a democratic (or, for that matter, undemocratic) government can both acknowledge many substantive rights and still leave much latitude for nonneutral legislation.

The interesting question, of course, is how far that latitude should extend, and how the rights that limit it can be justified. If we reject the ideal of neutrality, we cannot say, with Ronald Dworkin, that civil rights exist precisely to disallow the policies that are most likely to be adopted for nonneutral reasons.[4] But even without this justification, there remain various reasons to protect especially sensitive or strategic areas of life. Although this approach is unlikely to validate all the rights that liberals have advocated or claimed to find in our Constitution – that, indeed, is what gives my position its bite – it is quite capable of allaying the most pressing liberal fears.

III

To say that governments may legitimately try to promote the good is to take no special position about what *is* good. Moreover, to tie the case against neutralism to any single conception would be strategically unwise, since in a pluralistic society, no single conception can be expected to command general assent. Still, even granting this, there remain two compelling reasons to take and defend a position about the good life. One reason, internal to my argument, is that some who favor neutralism do so precisely on the grounds that no such position *can* be rationally defended. The most effective way to answer them is to offer an argument of the kind that they say cannot be produced. But another, even more important reason to mount such an argument is that the neutrality debate does not take place in a cultural vacuum. It occurs at a time when long-held values of virtue, excellence, and reason are under wide attack. Although the critics' positive proposals are often unclear, their challenge to the

4. Dworkin makes this suggestion in his important essay "Liberalism," in *A Matter of Principle*, pp. 196–97.

familiar values is legitimate and urgent. In arguing for a very traditional list of the elements of a good life, I shall explore one possible way of meeting that challenge.

One way to classify substantive theories of the good is on a continuum from subjective to objective.[5] At the subjective end, we find the view that all value depends on people's actual preferences, choices, or affective states. Simply by wanting, choosing, or enjoying something, a person (somehow) *confers* value on it. A bit less extreme, but still quite subjective, is the view that what is valuable is not what persons actually want, choose, or enjoy, but what they *would* want, choose, or enjoy under (more) ideal conditions – for example, if they were more instrumentally rational, better informed, or better able to imagine alternatives. Still less subjective is the view that while the value of a trait or activity does depend on certain facts about the individual who has or engages in it, the relevant facts concern neither his actual nor his ideal desires, choices, or enjoyments, but certain broad capacities that all members of his species share. On this account, the good life for humans is the one that most fully realizes these fundamental capacities. Finally, at the extreme objectivist end of the spectrum, we find the view that the value of a trait or activity depends on nothing at all except its own nature. Because this view implies that the trait or activity would have the same value *whatever* else were the case, it alone treats that value as simply intrinsic.

This scheme is crude in various respects. For one thing, it ignores what many consider an important distinction between theories of what is good *for persons* and theories of what is good *simpliciter.* For another, it makes no mention of mixed theories, such as the view that both desire-satisfaction *and* various traits, activities, or types of relationship are good just in themselves. Still, despite these omissions, the scheme provides enough structure to allow me to introduce some definitions. In what follows, I shall call any variant of the first two views – any theory that traces all value to some combination of actual or ideal desires, choices, or enjoyments – a form of *subjectivism.* By contrast, if a view *denies* that these factors exhaust the determinants

---

5. By "substantive theories," I mean theories that single out specific traits or activities as superior to others. Thus, as defined, the continuum does not include expressivism or any other variant of noncognitivism; for the primary question that these theories seek to answer is not Which things are good? but What do we mean (or what are we doing) when we say that something is good?

of value, I shall call it a form of *perfectionism*. Because one version of what I shall call perfectionism grounds the good life for humans in the realization of their fundamental capacities, and because these fundamental capacities are distinct from any of the specific activities or traits that realize them, some whom I classify as perfectionists do not believe that any activities or traits are *intrinsically* valuable. The related form of value that they do attribute I shall instead call *inherent*. Thus, on my account, one may qualify as a perfectionist by saying that certain activities and traits are either intrinsically or inherently valuable.[6] By introducing these definitions, I imply that subjectivism and perfectionism are exhaustive categories.[7] I imply, too, that if someone holds the mixed view that some value is conferred by actual or ideal desires, choices, or enjoyments while some is not, he counts as a perfectionist rather than a subjectivist.

Because "perfectionist" has no canonical meaning, it may be helpful to compare my definition to a number of others. Perhaps the most significant division is between those who interpret perfectionism only as a view about the good, and those who also take it to involve a view about the right. Of the latter thinkers, the most prominent is John Rawls, who defines perfectionism as the view that we should maximize human excellence.[8] (Later in *A Theory of Justice*, Rawls extends this definition to encompass the more moderate view that promoting excellence is only one duty among others.)[9] Among those who construe perfectionism only as a view about the good, some

6. My definition of perfectionism thus brings together two quite distinct ways of thinking about it; and this is an advantage because both are well represented in the literature. Vinit Haksar nicely captures the difference when he distinguishes weak perfectionism, which asserts that some forms of human life are superior to others because they "are more suited to human beings," from strong perfectionism, which says that there are x's and y's such that "whatever human nature turns out to be . . . it would still be the case that x would be superior to y" (Vinit Haksar, *Equality, Liberty, and Perfectionism* [Oxford: Oxford University Press, 1977], pp. 3–4).

7. Because the two categories are exhaustive, any substantive approach to value that I have not yet mentioned will have to fall in one or the other. Given the definitions I have introduced, the different variants of the Divine Command (or, as we might say, Divine Approval) theories will count as subjectivist, whereas a theory like Nozick's, which identifies a thing's value with its degree of organic unity, will count as perfectionist. (For discussion, see Robert Nozick, *Philosophical Explanations* [Cambridge, Mass.: Harvard University Press, 1981], ch. 5.) These classifications seem intuitively acceptable.

8. Rawls, *A Theory of Justice*, p. 25. See also Thomas Hurka, "Perfectionism," in Lawrence Becker, ed., *The Encyclopedia of Ethics* (New York: Garland, 1992), pp. 946–49, and Thomas Hurka, *Perfectionism* (Oxford: Oxford University Press, 1993).

9. Rawls, *A Theory of Justice*, pp. 325–32.

take it to equate the good with excellence or perfection itself,[10] others take it to equate the good with the advanced development, or perfection, of certain characteristically human capacities,[11] and still others take it to say only that some traits, activities, or forms of life are intrinsically better (or more "perfect") than others.[12] Although my definition differs from all of these, it coincides roughly with the conjunction of the last two. Also, although I do not include any of the other claims in my definition, I do agree that excellence is one (though not the only) perfectionist good and that both individuals and the state ought to promote (though not maximize) such goods. Thus, in the end, my view will incorporate much, though far from all, of what most perfectionists have wanted to say.

One need not, of course, be this or any other kind of perfectionist to be opposed to neutralism. Instead, even someone who believes that only enjoyment or desire-satisfaction has value can take the position that some activities, traits, or relations are more conducive to it than others; and he can say, further, that the state should promote these value-conducive activities and traits while discouraging or suppressing others. Such a person would clearly be a subjectivist rather than any kind of perfectionist; but because he would believe that the state should promote (what he takes to be) the good, he would, on at least some readings, not be a neutralist.

Still, despite this possibility, the affinities between neutralism and subjectivism remain clear and close. Other things being equal, each person can be presumed to know his own desires and tendencies best, and each can be presumed to care more than others about his own satisfaction and enjoyment. These facts give subjectivists special reasons to doubt that governments can effectively promote the good. Also, because the (criminal) law affects behavior by attaching penalties to some choices, it is not a promising mechanism for promoting any values that stem *from* people's choices. For both reasons, it is easiest to hold that governments should not try to promote the good

---

10. This, for example, is the view of the good that Rawls sometimes seems to associate with perfectionism; see *A Theory of Justice*, p. 325 (though for remarks that may imply a different view, see p. 331).
11. One contemporary philosopher who understands perfectionism in this way is James Griffin in *Well-Being* (Oxford: Oxford University Press, 1986), ch. 4. The classic theory of this sort is of course Aristotle's.
12. This view is what Vinit Haksar calls "strong perfectionism" (see note 6). Another philosopher who seems to accept this definition of perfectionism is Arneson in "Liberalism, Distributive Subjectivism, and Equal Opportunity for Welfare."

if one traces all value to enjoyment, desire, or choice.[13] Conversely, it is easiest to hold that governments sometimes *should* try to promote the good if one believes that at least some value is *independent* of enjoyment, desire, and choice.

And that is what I do believe. In what follows, I shall defend the view that some activities, traits, and types of relationship are inherently valuable because they are implicated in certain very abstract goals that (virtually) all humans unavoidably seek. I shall argue, further, that the inherent value of these activities, traits, and types of relationship imposes significant normative demands on various political agents. Because I shall not insist either that all inherent value is hierarchically ordered or that pleasure, desire, and choice are not additional sources of value, my brand of perfectionism will be less extreme than some others. Even so, however, it will be problematic and controversial enough to require extended defense.

In recent years, perfectionism has enjoyed something of a revival. Inspired by Aristotle and Hegel, various writers have returned to the theme that humans are social animals whose flourishing must itself be understood in social terms.[14] In developing this theme, these "new communitarians" have advanced recognizably perfectionist views of both virtue and the good life, and some have explicitly brought these views to bear in arguments against neutralism.[15] To avoid any misunderstanding, I want to stress at the outset that my version of perfectionism is very different from theirs. For one thing, I am extremely skeptical about the idea that civic participation, solidarity with others, or engagement in common projects is even a necessary condition for living a good life. For another, I cannot see why society or its history, conventions, or practices must supply, ratify, or undergird whatever (other) perfectionist values there are. I shall return to these matters later. For now, the point is simply that even though I accept some of the communitarians' value-claims, their basic approach is decidedly not mine.

13. Two neutralists who do hold what I call subjectivist theories of value are Rawls and Arneson; two who appear not to are Dworkin and Kymlicka.
14. This theme is developed, among other places, in Alasdair MacIntyre, *After Virtue*, 2d ed. (Notre Dame, Ind.: University of Notre Dame Press, 1984); Michael J. Sandel, *Liberalism and the Limits of Justice* (Cambridge: Cambridge University Press, 1982); Charles Taylor, *Philosophy and the Human Sciences: Philosophical Papers 2* (Cambridge: Cambridge University Press, 1985); and Roberto Unger, *Knowledge and Politics* (New York: Free Press, 1975).
15. See, for example, MacIntyre, *After Virtue*, especially ch. 17, and Taylor, "What's Wrong with Negative Liberty?" in his *Collected Papers 2*, pp. 216–29.

IV

Not mine, even more emphatically, are certain other antiliberal views that have achieved a degree of currency. Although liberalism is often attacked from both the political left and the right, many common arguments against it – and, in particular, against its neutralist and subjectivist strands – fall somewhere between the superficial and the intellectually disreputable. To define my position further, I want to dissociate it from some of the worst offenders.

We all know the litany of complaints. By stressing the moral importance of freedom and insisting that it be protected by rights, liberals are said to enshrine insularity and selfishness. They are accused of favoring private, hedonistic, consumption-oriented lives at the expense of solidarity and concern for others. In addition, by opting for official neutrality, the deluded liberal is said to seek what cannot be had. Indeed, true neutrality is held to be impossible for two reasons: first, because in refusing to take sides, governments merely favor the already privileged, and, second, because the liberal values of choice and autonomy are themselves substantive and hence nonneutral.

But whatever we finally say about subjectivism or neutralism, these surely are bad arguments. Let me briefly review their errors, beginning with the charge that liberalism presupposes a (meta)ethic of selfishness. On one reading, what this charge amounts to is that when liberals treat individuals' desires, choices, or enjoyments as the sole (or even a main) source of value, they ignore the bonds of attachment that alone are said adequately to ground (or motivate) duty and responsibility to others. This personalistic approach to duty has been criticized, in my view justly, for its failure to explain how we can have duties toward acquaintances, strangers, and others to whom we lack close ties.[16] However, in the current context, the problem is simpler: the objection manages to get the liberal position almost exactly backward. It is precisely *because* liberals regard each individual and his preferences, choices, and enjoyments as so morally important that they insist that each individual has rights that strictly limit the ways in which others may treat him. By arguing that

16. Indeed, as Christina Hoff Sommers notes in "Filial Morality," *Journal of Philosophy* 83, 8 (August 1986), pp. 439–56, an approach that stresses care and concern to the exclusion of impersonal duty cannot even do justice to what we owe to parents and others with whom we *share* close personal ties.

individuals have such rights, liberals imply that each person has many negative duties toward others. Moreover, this same regard for the individual leads liberals to insist that goods must be distributed justly *among* individuals; and that leads many to postulate additional positive duties. Taken together, these ideas lie near the heart of liberalism and are among its deepest sources of strength. Hence, whatever their other failings, even wholehearted subjectivists can account for duties and responsibilities to others.

They also can avoid the implication that they view individuals *as* selfish; for even if individuals' preferences, choices, or enjoyments are the sole sources of value, nothing at all follows about *what* anyone prefers, chooses, or enjoys. When someone cares about the well-being of loved ones, the alleviation of suffering, or some elevated moral, aesthetic, or scientific ideal, he is not selfish in any interesting sense. Of course, when critics link subjectivism to selfishness, they may mean not that the truth of subjectivism *entails* that people are selfish, but rather that *believing* subjectivism tends to *make* people selfish. But quite apart from its irrelevance to whether subjectivism is true, this causal claim is neither supported by evidence nor plausible on its face. When someone comes to believe that all persons are sources of value, he acquires a (further) reason to advance each person's interests and aspirations. Hence, far from promoting selfishness, the acceptance of subjectivism seems likely, if anything, to promote *un*selfishness.

And just as many common objections to subjectivism rest on confusions, so too do many common objections to neutralism itself. One confused objection is that what passes for neutrality is merely conservatism or unthinking resistance to change. Much as the "neutral" university has been said to enshrine the values of dominant groups, the "neutral" state is sometimes said simply to perpetuate inequalities of wealth and power. By not taking a position about how goods should be distributed, we are said merely to rationalize the prevailing (unjust) distribution. And because it only perpetuates the status quo, the state's alleged neutrality is said to be a sham.

Like the earlier objection that no government can avoid favoring some conceptions of the good over others, this objection takes a government's neutrality to depend on the consequences of its actions rather than their justifications. In so doing, it makes a mistake that has already been dealt with. But because it takes the fundamental issue to be the distribution of wealth and power, this objection also commits a further error. In fact, the alternatives toward which official neutrality is urged concern not the *distribution* of wealth and power but their *use*. The neutralist ideal is a society in which each citizen has access to a defensible share of the available resources to use as he sees fit.[17] If achieving this ideal requires rectifying distributive injustice, then neutralists are quite willing to disturb the status quo. It is, indeed, precisely their willingness to do this that links neutrality – in itself a doctrine of restraint – to the activist programs of the welfare state. Thus, whatever its other failings, neutralism surely embodies no conservative bias.

Nor, finally, is neutralism self-defeating in any other obvious way. It is true that some neutralists object to nonneutral policies on the grounds that these make it hard(er) for citizens to live autonomous lives.[18] It is also true that some neutralists take this line precisely because they believe that autonomous lives are best. But even if someone does thus ground neutralism itself in one particular conception of the good – and many neutralists do not – his position is only superficially inconsistent. To restore consistency, he need only acknowledge that the neutrality he advocates is incomplete – that, in his view, the state should be neutral toward the different options among which persons may choose, but not toward the value of self-aware, autonomous choice itself.[19] Of course, without further discussion, we may well wonder *why* self-aware, autonomous choice should have this special status. However, anyone who appeals to autonomy must in any case say far more about it; and when he does, an explanation of its privileged position may fall out as a by-product.

V

These, clearly, do not exhaust the bad arguments against either neutralism or subjectivism. But it should by now be clear that no quick refutation of either is likely to succeed. What is needed is a careful and extended discussion of both views, and I shall develop my own alternatives through just such a discussion. Here, by chapter, is how the argument will run.

17. It is the open-endedness of the idea of a defensible distribution that explains how philosophers as different as Rawls and Nozick can both be neutralists.
18. For a clear statement of this position, see David McCabe, "Liberal Education *Is* Moral Education," *Social Theory and Practice* 21, 1 (Spring 1995), pp. 83–96.
19. For a similar reply to the proposed objection, see Jeremy Waldron, "Legislation and Moral Neutrality," in Robert E. Goodin and Andrew Reeve, eds., *Liberal Neutrality* (London: Routledge, 1989), pp. 80–81.

Although much has been said for and against neutralism, its exact content has received relatively little close attention. Thus, in Chapter 2, I shall explore some of its ambiguities and unclarities. There I shall discuss both the different political levels at which neutrality is possible and the different ways in which governments can act on conceptions of the good. Also, and most important, I shall ask exactly what a conception of the good *is*. Despite wide agreement about the justifications that neutralism allows and forbids – appeals to justice, prosperity, health, and safety are clearly in, whereas appeals to high culture, salvation, and particular sexual moralities are out – the distinction's exact basis is surprisingly obscure. After examining several attempts to clarify it, I shall conclude that no single rendering is privileged, but that several are coherent, practicable, and prima facie plausible.

With these analytical tasks discharged, I shall turn to more substantive matters. As I have already suggested, this book has two main aims: first, to lay the groundwork for democratic perfectionism by criticizing each main argument for neutralism, and, second, to defend a version of perfectionism that I take to be appealing and plausible. The first task is undertaken in Chapters 3 through 6, the second in Chapters 7 through 9. A brief tenth chapter brings the two themes together.

Broadly speaking, neutralism can be defended in three main ways. It can be argued that nonneutral governmental decisions (1) violate the autonomy of citizens, or (2) pose unacceptable risks of oppression, instability, or error, or (3) rest on value-premises that cannot be rationally defended. Because the appeals to autonomy are morally if not historically the most important, I shall begin with them. The idea that only a neutral state can satisfy the demands of autonomy informs the work of classical liberals such as Mill and Kant and important contemporaries such as Rawls, Ackerman, and Dworkin. Reduced to its essentials, this idea asserts that when governments promote particular conceptions of the good, they invert the proper relation between the person and his ends. To qualify as autonomous, a person must formulate, execute, and monitor his *own* life-plan. He must make his *own* decisions about what is valuable or best for him. But when the state promotes a conception of the good, it channels citizens in directions they have not (yet) chosen, and so preempts their autonomous choices. Thus, indefensibly, it substitutes its judgment about how they should live for their own.

Although this argument is important, it is also ambiguous, for it can be taken to appeal either to the great *value* of living autonomously or to a stringent obligation to *respect* autonomy. On the first reading, the argument asserts that the best way to live is freely and reflectively to shape one's own destiny, but that governments which act on specific conceptions of the good prevent their citizens from doing this. On the second, it asserts that even when the value of someone's autonomous choice would be outweighed by the disvalue of what he would wrongly or foolishly choose, the state remains obligated to leave the choice exclusively in his hands. For convenience, I shall call the argument's first version *the appeal to the value of autonomy,* and its second *the appeal to respect for autonomy.* Because the two versions have such different underlying structures, each must be dealt with separately.

Clearly any attempt to assess the appeal to the value of autonomy must presuppose some account of what autonomy is. Thus, in the first half of Chapter 3, I shall develop such an account. My strategy will be first to draw together a number of important intuitions and beliefs about autonomy, and then to propose an analysis that integrates them. I believe this analysis has considerable independent merit, but my criticism of the appeal to the value of autonomy will not depend on its correctness. Instead, I shall maintain that the dependency works the other way – that it is only by relying on some such analysis that the appeal to the value of autonomy can hope to succeed.

Once this analysis is in place, I shall examine the argument's (other) key premises. These I take to be, first, that it is never reasonable for governments or their agents to sacrifice any of their citizens' autonomy to promote a greater amount of some other value, and, second, that some autonomy always *is* sacrificed when governments try to promote other values. My conclusions will be that there is a (controversial) view that makes the first premise true, but that we need not evaluate that view because the second premise is so plainly false. Given its falsity, no appeal to the value of autonomy can justify neutralism.

Nor, I shall continue in Chapter 4, can neutralism be justified by any principle of respect *for* autonomous choice. Although neutralists do not always distinguish between the two sorts of autonomy argument, it is this second sort that appears the more popular. Moreover, one reason for its popularity is surely that it promises to avoid the problem of trade-offs between autonomy and (other) values. Yet just because the appeal to respect for autonomy promises this, its central principle requires more defense than it is generally given. It is, to say the least, not self-evident that even the weightiest of perfectionist reasons – reasons that should and often do guide our personal conduct – should have *no weight at all* in our deliberations about law and public policy. Moreover, this idea is far more often presupposed than reflectively defended. However, pertinent and influential arguments have been advanced by John Rawls and Ronald Dworkin; and I shall devote the bulk of Chapter 4 to them. After a rather extended discussion, I shall conclude that the case for neutralism has again not been made.

As many have noted, Rawls's recent work is a rich blend of pragmatism and principle. But neutralism can also be defended in more starkly pragmatic terms. To do so, one can stress either the acrimony and turbulence that result when different factions vie for control of the state's coercive apparatus; the ease with which that apparatus can be turned to oppressive or acquisitive purposes; or the danger that the state will act on a conception of the good that is indefensible or simply false. Of these dangers, each is clearly real and important. However, as I shall argue in Chapter 5, making the state neutral is neither a necessary nor an effective means of avoiding them. By contrasting this device with other, more effective mechanisms, I shall try to show how we can have a nonneutral state without compromising either safety or stability.

That leaves only the third, broadly epistemological class of arguments for neutralism. These arguments assert that the reason the state must not try to promote the good is simply that no one can know, or know well enough, which ways of living *are* good. However strongly such beliefs are held, they are said to lack sufficient rational warrant. When someone takes this line, his skepticism may extend either to all beliefs, to all beliefs about normative matters, or only to beliefs about the good as opposed to the right. However, as I shall argue in Chapter 6, the argument's first two variants are pragmatically inconsistent; and, though the third escapes this objection, its highly selective version of skepticism is implausible in light of at least one widely accepted and appealing conception of knowledge.

With the failure of the epistemological argument(s), there is no further reason to deny that governments may take an interest in the goodness of their citizens' lives. But by itself, this conclusion is too abstract to be satisfying. Having come this far, we will naturally want to know *which* conception(s) of the good the state should promote. The three following chapters address this substantive question.

In recent years, the most influential challenges to liberalism have been mounted by communitarians. For this reason, I shall begin by asking what approach to the good life, if any, can be extracted from their position. Although much about communitarianism remains obscure, one of its most prominent themes is that each person's identity is somehow bound up with his society's practices, conventions, and history. According to many communitarians, society's involvement in the self means that what constitutes a good life for a person cannot depend on his own preferences or choices. Instead, this must depend on certain "constitutive" ends that are supplied by the society's culture, history, or shared understandings. In Chapter 7, I shall distinguish a number of connections between society and the individual and a number of normative inferences that might be drawn from these. In the end, I shall conclude that none of these arguments either discredits subjectivism or supports any form of perfectionism.

But other arguments seem more promising, and in the next two chapters I shall turn to these. In Chapter 8, I shall argue that no variant of subjectivism can easily be reconciled either with many of our standard beliefs about the good or with the ordinary structure of practical deliberation. I shall argue, as well, that what appear to be certain important advantages of subjectivism – that it can explain how value motivates, what makes value-claims true, and how value comes into existence – either are no advantages at all or else are available also to some forms of perfectionism. Although these arguments do not settle the issue, they significantly raise the cost of being a subjectivist. In so doing, they prepare the ground for a positive perfectionist account.

And, in a lengthy Chapter 9, I shall develop just such an account. My strategy there will be, first, to canvass the various activities, traits, and forms of relationship that perfectionists most often take to be intrinsically or inherently valuable; second, to identify certain very general goals that few can avoid pursuing, and that are intimately linked to the various perfectionist goods; and, third, to argue, on independent grounds, that those near-universal and near-inescapable goals are the most plausible *sources* of the goods' inherent value. The resulting theory is perfectionist because it asserts that some activities and traits are valuable for reasons independent of any individual's subjective states; it is pluralistic because it provides only an (unordered) *list* of inherently good activities and traits; it is mixed because it includes pleasure and other subjective states among its significant goods; and it is open-ended because some of the entries on its list can be realized in a wide variety of ways. Although the theory is in some obvious ways Aristotelian, it avoids any commitment to Aristotle's metaphysical essentialism.

With the development of this theory, the book's main argument will be complete. Its most important conclusions are, first, that governments may and should take an active interest in the goodness of their citizens' lives, and, second, that many of the value-claims that have long been regarded as fundamental – claims about the importance of excellence, knowledge, certain preferred modes of interaction among persons, and the traditional virtues – really are so. Taken together, these conclusions imply that both governments and individual political agents often have good reason to promote the favored traits and activities. In a short concluding chapter, I shall consider the range of political decisions to which perfectionist reasons are relevant and their relations to reasons of other sorts.

Chapter 2

The principle of neutrality

Although the principle of neutrality has been much discussed, it has less often been carefully formulated. Thus, before we can evaluate it, we must clarify its scope and meaning. This means asking which agents the principle constrains, at which political levels it applies, and which ways of promoting the good it forbids. It also means asking what, in this context, a conception of the good *is*. In the current chapter, I shall say something about each question. Although I shall not settle on any single set of answers, I shall try at least to lay out a manageable range of plausible alternatives.

I

First, though, I want to convey a bit more of the flavor of neutralism, and to make explicit the principles that will guide my analysis. Here are five representative formulations, the first two by supporters Ronald Dworkin and John Rawls, the last three by critics Alasdair MacIntyre, Michael Sandel, and Joseph Raz:

[P]olitical decisions must be, so far as is possible, independent of any particular conception of the good life, or of what gives value to life.[1]

Justice as fairness . . . [does not] try to evaluate the relative merits of different conceptions of the good. . . . There is no necessity to compare the worth of the conceptions of different persons once it is supposed they are compatible with the principles of justice. Everyone is assured an equal liberty to pursue

1. Ronald Dworkin, "Liberalism," in *A Matter of Principle* (Cambridge, Mass.: Harvard University Press, 1985), p. 127.

whatever plan of life he pleases as long as it does not violate what justice demands.[2]

[A] community is simply an arena in which individuals each pursue their own self-chosen conception of the good life, and political institutions exist to provide that degree of order which makes such self-determined activity possible. Government and law are, or ought to be, neutral between rival conceptions of the good life for man, and hence, although it is the task of government to promote law-abidingness, it is . . . no part of the legitimate function of government to inculcate any one moral outlook.[3]

[S]ociety, being composed of a plurality of persons, each with his own aims, interests, and conceptions of the good, is best arranged when it is governed by principles that do not *themselves* presuppose any particular conception of the good.[4]

[I]mplementation and promotion of ideals of the good life, though worthy in themselves, are not a legitimate matter for government action. . . . Government action should be neutral regarding ideals of the good life.[5]

As even this short list of quotations suggests, the neutral-framework view is a very common topic of philosophical discussion.[6]

Yet just because it is, its clarification is a matter of some delicacy. Although neutralism has been formulated in remarkably consistent terms, philosophers notoriously use the same words in subtly different ways. Thus, instead of relying on any canonical text, we must seek the interpretation that allows us to give the principle its most sympathetic hearing. But on what basis are we to select that interpretation?

2. John Rawls, *A Theory of Justice* (Cambridge, Mass.: Harvard University Press, 1971), p. 94.
3. Alasdair MacIntyre, *After Virtue*, 2d ed. (Notre Dame, Ind.: University of Notre Dame, 1984), p. 195.
4. Michael J. Sandel, *Liberalism and the Limits of Justice* (Cambridge: Cambridge University Press, 1982), p. 1.
5. Joseph Raz, *The Morality of Freedom* (Oxford: Oxford University Press, 1986), p. 110.
6. In addition to Rawls and Dworkin, other contemporary defenders of neutralism (or closely related views) include Robert Nozick, Bruce Ackerman, Thomas Nagel, Charles Larmore, Will Kymlicka, Richard Arneson, and D. A. Lloyd-Thomas. For references, see Chapter 1, footnote 1. Other contemporary critics include Charles Taylor, *Philosophy and the Human Sciences: Philosophical Papers 2* (Cambridge: Cambridge University Press, 1985); Roberto Unger, *Knowledge and Politics* (New York: Free Press, 1975); William Galston, *Liberal Purposes* (Cambridge: Cambridge University Press, 1991); Amy Gutmann, *Democratic Education* (Princeton: Princeton University Press, 1987); and Stephen Macedo, *Liberal Virtues* (Oxford: Oxford University Press, 1990).

There are at least three factors to consider. First and most obviously, a good intepretation must accommodate most of our firm intuitions about neutrality. It is, for example, intuitively clear that laws against rape and murder do not violate the principle, but that laws against homosexuality and pornography often do. Hence, there must be a strong presumption against any interpretation that fails to yield these results. Whatever we say about borderline cases, a good interpretation must account for most if not all of our confident intuitive judgments.

Second, a good interpretation must avoid the twin pitfalls of construing the principle of neutrality as too weak to be interesting and too strong to be practicable. Thus, faced with a choice between taking neutralism to impose more or less stringent requirements, we should, all else being equal, adopt the stronger interpretation. On the other hand, if an interpretation implies that no government can possibly *satisfy* all the requirements of neutrality, then that interpretation is too strong and should be rejected.

Even by themselves, these constraints would eliminate many interpretations of neutralism. But the field is further narrowed by the fact that some versions are more *defensible* than others. This is important because our aim is precisely to find out whether an interesting version of neutralism can *be* defended. Given this goal, we must acknowledge a third constraint: other things again being equal, we must prefer whichever interpretation(s) mesh best with the strongest argument(s) for neutralism.

II

Guided by these constraints, let us now turn to the task of interpreting neutralism. We may begin with a fundamental point that has already been made: that any acceptable interpretation must construe neutrality as a property of the *justifications* of laws, policies, or institutions rather than their effects. The reason, clearly, is that however we interpret "conception of the good," all laws, policies, and institutions, and a fortiori their effects, are bound to conform to many such conceptions while failing to conform to many others. Thus, if someone were to insist on neutrality of effects, his proposal would be doomed from the start. Recognizing this, most on both sides accept Kymlicka's claim that the relevant form of neutrality is justificatory rather than consequential. In Charles Larmore's alternative terms, most agree that "[the liberal state's] neutrality is not meant to be one of *outcome*, but rather one of *procedure*. That is, political neutrality consists in a constraint on what factors can be invoked to justify a political decision."[7] In what follows, I, too, shall accept this prevailing view.

But while this much is (close to) common ground,[8] much else about neutralism remains unclear. An initial difficulty is that any law, policy, or governmental structure, and hence also any decision to implement it, can be justified in many ways. For example, if a government has decided to build a new network of interstate highways, its possible justifications may include the facts that the roads will further commerce, that they will facilitate troop movements in times of emergency, and that building them will provide work for a depressed construction industry. Of these three possible reasons, which one is *the* justification of the state's decision? To which one does neutralism apply?

One possible answer is that the relevant justification is just the one that actually provided the impetus to build the highways. On this account, what matters is not the justifications that an arrangement *could* be given, but only the one(s) that in fact motivated its institution. When we evaluate an arrangement's neutrality, we do so on the basis of the intentions with which it was actually adopted.

But if this were what neutralism involved, then that view would be deeply problematic. In that case, we could not assess the legitimacy of any law, policy, or other political arrangement without first reconstructing the reasoning that actually led to its adoption. Yet even when a policy has been instituted by a single person, reconstructing

---

7. Charles Larmore, *Patterns of Moral Complexity* (Cambridge: Cambridge University Press, 1987), p. 44 (emphases in original). For two further statements of the view that neutrality is a property of justifications or reasons, see John Rawls, "The Priority of Right and Ideas of the Good," *Philosophy and Public Affairs* 17, 4 (Fall 1988), p. 262, and Jeremy Waldron, "Legislation and Moral Neutrality," in Robert E. Goodin and Andrew Reeve, eds., *Liberal Neutrality* (London: Routledge, 1989), pp. 66–68.
8. The agreement is less than complete. Two dissenters are Robert E. Goodin and Andrew Reeve, who write that "[w]e shall take it . . . that the results analysis of neutrality is the correct one in the context of the state. Even if there is a plausible reason to be concerned with motives or dispositions in the case, say, of education, when we move to problems of institutional design we do not want to produce the right motives or attitudes in people. Instead, we want to produce the right pattern of results" ("Do Neutral Institutions Add Up to a Neutral State?" in Robert E. Goodin and Andrew Reeve, eds., *Liberal Neutrality* [London: Routledge, 1989], p. 202).

his motives can raise immense empirical and conceptual difficulties.[9] Also, of course, most laws and policies are implemented not by single individuals but by many people acting in concert, and most agents have a variety of reasons for what they do. Thus, on the current proposal, the legitimacy of most political arrangements will be very difficult if not impossible to ascertain.

The problem is most acute when an arrangement has been in place for a long time. On the proposed account, the key question about a long-standing law, policy, or institution is what motivated the original legislators or policy makers (or, in the case of the Constitution, the original framers). But whatever we think of "original intent" as a criterion of legislative or constitutional *interpretation*, we surely must reject it as a criterion of current *legitimacy*. If we did not, the status of many perfectly acceptable laws and institutions would be hopelessly obscure. Just as troubling, we would then be able to sanitize any questionable laws by first repealing them and then passing them again for (more) neutral reasons. To avoid these difficulties, we must reject the suggestion that the legitimacy of a well-entrenched law or political structure depends on the mental processes of long-dead persons. This must depend, instead, on some aspect of that law or structure *as it now exists*.

Because every possible justification of a given law or structure is equally an "aspect of it as it now exists," this conclusion returns us to our starting point. Before we can assess the neutrality of any political arrangement, we still must determine which of its possible justifications is the relevant one. But perhaps this way of putting the problem gets it just backward. Instead of first asking which of an arrangement's many possible justifications is relevant and then asking whether that justification is neutral, perhaps we should first ask whether any of the ways of justifying an arrangement are neutral and then simply count any that emerge as relevant. Perhaps, in other words, we should accept

---

9. Suppose, for example, that a legislator says (and thinks) only that he supports a proposed law because it will shore up the traditional family. What determines whether he favors supporting traditional families for the presumably neutral reason that they maximize the opportunities and well-being of children, or for the presumably nonneutral reason that they are intrinsically better than other domestic arrangements? This obviously depends on what the legislator would think, say, or do under certain alternative conditions; but how these conditions are to be specified is far from obvious.

(N) A law, institution, or other political arrangement is neutrally
     justifiable if and only if *some* possible argument for it has only
     neutral normative premises.

According to (N), the crucial question is not whether any *particular*
argument for a law, policy, or institution can satisfy the neutrality
constraint, but only whether *at least one* of them can.

Because (N) detaches an arrangement's neutrality from its historical origins, it represents a major step forward. But as it stands, (N)
makes neutrality far too easy to achieve. To demonstrate the neutrality of an arbitrarily chosen law or policy, (N) allows us to introduce some uncontroversially neutral value-premise – say, the premise that health or economic growth is a good thing – and then add
that the relevant law or policy promotes the valued end. The resulting justification will automatically qualify as neutral because (N)
does not require that its premises be either true or plausible. Also con-
spicuously absent is any specification of *how strong a reason* a neutral
justification must provide. Thus, taken at face value, (N) will count
any road-building policy as neutrally justifiable as long as the roads
will reduce the travel time of even a few commuters by a few seconds.

To avoid these difficulties, we obviously must strengthen (N)'s
requirements. The simplest way to do this is to stipulate that to be
neutral, a justification must contain only true premises and valid
inferences and must be stronger than any countervailing justification. Thus augmented, (N) becomes

(N') A law, institution, or other political arrangement is neutrally
      justifiable if and only if at least one possible argument for it
      (1) has only neutral normative premises, and (2) contains no
      falsehoods or inferential mistakes, and (3) provides a reason
      for adopting the law, etc., that is stronger than the reasons
      provided by any arguments for any alternative arrangement.

By replacing (N) with (N'), we will decisively avoid the objection that
all political arrangements can be neutrally justified.

In so doing, however, we will move too far in the other direction;
for because (N') requires an argument that is both sound and
decisively strong, it implies that the only legitimate political arrangements are those that are best, all things considered. (N') thus col-
lapses the distinction between an arrangement's not being sup-

ported by *the right sorts of* reasons and its not being supported by *good enough* reasons. But that distinction must surely be preserved; for even a neutralist must concede that we may (and often do) legitimately support political decisions for reasons that are weak, foolish, or badly mistaken.

To arrive at a more plausible criterion, we must draw back from (N')'s uncompromising references to truth, validity, and the (objective) strength of reasons. In their place, we must incorporate references to what merely *seem* to be true premises, valid inferences, and sufficiently strong reasons. This adjustment gives us

(N") A law, institution, or other political arrangement is neutrally justifiable if and only if at least one possible argument for it (1) has only neutral normative premises, and (2) contains no implausible premises or obvious fallacies, and (3) provides a justification of reasonable strength.

By accepting (N"), we will avoid both the implication that all political arrangements are legitimate and the implication that the only legitimate arrangements are those that are best, all things considered.

The question about (N"), though, is whether it can be made precise enough to be serviceable. The difficulty is not merely that its expressions "plausible premises," "obvious fallacies," and "reasonable strength" are all very vague. It is, more seriously, that these notions all seem relative to certain background beliefs. What is plausible, obvious, or reasonable from one person's perspective may be implausible, unobvious, or unreasonable from another's. Thus, to complete our statement of (N"), we need to specify *by whose lights* an acceptable argument's premises and the rest must be plausible, obvious, and reasonable.

Before we can answer this question, however, we must get clearer about another: namely, why should any merely possible justification of a political arrangement have any bearing on its legitimacy at all? Because possible justifications are only abstract structures of propositions, they may, at first glance, seem too detached from reality to be morally significant. But on closer inspection, they *are* morally significant; for even if a possible argument has not yet influenced anyone's actions, the very fact that someone now recognizes it *as* possible makes it a potential source of motivation *for him.* Even if it tells for arrangements that are already well entrenched, and even if these were originally installed for quite different reasons, accepting the argument gives one a new motive to support their *continued* existence. Conversely, coming to believe that a political arrangement has *no* acceptable justification provides a new motive to alter or abolish it. Even if there is no immediate prospect of success, these new motives will incline one to act should the occasion arise.

Thus, to the question of how a merely possible justification can be morally relevant, the quick answer is that there *are* no merely possible justifications. Any justification, if accepted, is a potential guide for action. But if all justifications are potentially action-guiding, then so are all higher-order principles that tell us which justifications are legitimate. Thus, in particular, the principle of neutrality is itself action-guiding; for it limits the first-order reasons for which persons may act to establish, preserve, alter, or abolish any actual or possible political arrangements. And once this is made clear, we can easily answer the question about whose background beliefs should supply (N″)'s standards of what is reasonable or plausible; for as long as (N″) is a component of an action-guiding neutrality principle, the relevant standards will obviously be those of the persons whose actions will be guided. Thus, to the question "By whose lights must an argument's premises and inferences be plausible and reasonable?" the obvious answer is "Whoever is considering that argument with an eye to assigning it a role in his practical deliberations."

Although I know of no philosopher who has analyzed "neutral justifiability" in just this way, the action-guiding dimension of neutralism has not gone unnoticed. Jeremy Waldron, for example, has put it this way:

Perhaps the doctrine of liberal neutrality ought to be understood primarily as a basis of political morality in a narrow sense – that is, as a basis for each law-maker to evaluate her own intentions – rather than as a doctrine for evaluating legislation as such. Or perhaps it can be seen as a constraint on the reasons *we* deploy in our reconstruction of the justification of some rule we support (whatever its original intention was). We should not think of political morality simply as a set of principles for judging outcomes. Its primary function is to guide action and to constrain practical thought.[10]

Because this practical interpretation resolves some otherwise intractable problems, I shall accept it in what follows.

10. Waldron, "Legislation and Moral Neutrality," p. 67 (emphasis in original).

27

III

But other problems remain. Precisely *because* neutralism is best understood as a constraint on practical political decisions, we need to know more about both the decisions it constrains and the constraints it imposes on them. To be a bit more specific, we need to answer (at least) the following questions:

1. To which sorts of *agents* does the proposed practical principle apply? Does it apply only to governments, or also (or instead) to individuals? If also to individuals, then to which ones?
2. At which political *levels* does the principle apply? Does it constrain efforts to sustain or modify entire constitutional systems? Legislative and policy decisions made within such systems? The administration and enforcement of specific laws?
3. Which *methods* of advancing conceptions of the good does the principle forbid? Does it rule out only coercion and force, or other methods too? If other methods, which ones?
4. Just what *is* a conception of the good anyhow? How broadly should this notion be understood? What distinguishes conceptions of the good from other normative claims?

To complete my analytical discussion of neutralism, I shall take up each (set of) question(s) in turn.

Let us begin with the question of whom the principle of neutrality constrains. The answer that is suggested by many of the principle's formulations is simply "governments themselves." This, for example, is a natural reading of both Raz's already quoted formulation ("government action should be neutral regarding ideals of the good life") and Larmore's claim that "so long as a government conforms its decisions to this constraint . . . it will be acting neutrally."[11] Moreover, whatever else we say, the idea that there are limits to the reasons for which governments may legitimately act is far from absurd. For because governments are corporate entities that can intelligibly be said to hold beliefs, weigh options, and act for reasons, it must also be intelligible to say that they should *not* act for certain sorts of reasons.

11. Larmore, *Patterns of Moral Complexity*, p. 44.

Still, while this is clearly intelligible, it is unlikely to be the whole story; for every government decision supervenes on many individual ones. More precisely, it seems to be true both that every government action is a complex function of the *actions* of many individuals and that the reasons for every governmental decision are a complex function of the *reasons* of many individuals. This makes it unlikely that governments could refrain from acting for nonneutral reasons unless many individuals refrained as well. As a consequence, it is unlikely that any plausible principle of neutrality could constrain governments without also constraining individuals.

Unlikely, but not impossible; for we can imagine legal or political structures whose function is precisely to *transform* the nonneutral acts of individuals into neutral governmental ones. These structures, if they existed, would take as inputs all the efforts of individuals to influence governments, including any that were undertaken for nonneutral reasons, but would yield as outputs only government actions with appropriately neutral justifications. In so doing, they would (partially) resemble the "invisible hand" that is said to transform the myriads of self-interested economic transactions into a collectively beneficial process. But while there does seem to be conceptual space for such transformative structures, no neutralist has carefully developed the possibility, and so I shall not pursue it either. Instead, when I say that neutralism prohibits governments from trying to promote the good, I shall indeed take its prohibition to extend to at least some individuals.

Individuals can influence governments in many ways. They can do so, inter alia, by voting for persons to represent them as legislators or in the executive branch, by representing others in turn, by acting in various administrative and bureaucratic capacities, by trying to amend the Constitution, and by advising or lobbying persons in each of the other roles. Thus, by interpreting the principle of neutrality as applicable to individuals, we may seem greatly to have complicated our task; for now we must explain *which* of the many political actions of individuals the principle should constrain.

Fortunately, the general outlines of an answer are implicit in the rationale for extending the principle to individuals at all. That rationale, to repeat, was simply that if no individuals were prohibited from acting for nonneutral reasons, then governments could not effectively be prohibited from doing so either. But given this reasoning, the individuals to whom the prohibition must apply are clearly the ones whose reasons will become (or stand a great enough likelihood of becoming) the sorts of governmental reasons that the principle rules out. This means, for example, that if the principle of neutrality applies at the legislative level, it will constrain at least the legislators themselves and probably also the aides and advisors who will (most) directly influence their reasoning. Also, even when an individual's influence on his government is far less direct – even when, for example, he is simply voting for a legislator to represent him – he may at least be obligated to minimize the *likelihood* that his government will act for nonneutral reasons.[12]

These constraints on individuals, which draw their force from a constraint on government, should not be confused with the constraints imposed by political roles. Confusion is possible because many political roles also impose restrictions on the reasons for which their occupants may act. For example, the broadly political role "police officer" allows its occupants to use their powers to enforce the law, but not to advance their merely private ends. This greatly limits, if it does not altogether eliminate, the freedom of the police to promote the good as they see it. Yet even if the police must never act for nonneutral reasons, this prohibition has no special connection to the political nature of their role. Many people in private life, such as physicians and teachers, are similarly restricted by the roles they occupy. Hence, even when a given role *is* political, its requirements will raise different issues, and will require different treatment, than the requirements of neutrality.

---

12. I have argued that any plausible neutrality constraint is likely to extend to at least some individuals. But how effective can such a constraint be? In general, constraints on individuals tend to be ineffective when (1) each would put himself at a disadvantage by complying if others did not, and (2) each lacks assurance that (enough) others *will* comply (see Rawls, *A Theory of Justice*, sec. 42). A neutrality constraint on individuals is open to this objection because when someone complies with it while others do not, he increases the likelihood that the state will act on one of their conceptions of the good rather than his.

This problem is yet another aspect of neutralism that has been insufficiently addressed. To meet the objection, a neutralist could take any of several tacks. He could argue that (1) under the right circumstances, a stable and well-understood convention of neutrality is sufficient to assure individuals that (most) others will comply; that (2) we have, or can devise, mechanisms to filter out the most egregious violations; that (3) we have, or can devise, mechanisms to elicit or encourage neutral decision making by individuals; or that (4) the neutrality principle is a political ideal whose ability to enlist compliance is beside the point. Which answer is the most promising, and whether any succeed, are again questions beyond our present scope.

IV

At which political *levels* does the principle of neutrality apply? This is a question about which neutralists themselves disagree. Some take their principle to apply primarily to legislative and administrative decisions, whereas others take it to apply primarily to decisions about the larger framework within which laws and policies are made.

The leading proponent of neutrality at the framework level is of course John Rawls. In *A Theory of Justice,* Rawls's topic was precisely the justice of "the major social institutions [which] distribute fundamental rights and duties and determine the division of advantages from social cooperation."[13] These institutions include "the political constitution and the principal economic and social arrangements."[14] According to Rawls, a society's basic institutions are just when they conform to principles that would be chosen by free and equal rational persons in a suitably constrained situation. To be suitably constrained, the parties must be kept ignorant of all bias-inducing facts – including, significantly, all facts about their own conceptions of the good. Thus, for Rawls, any adequate justification of a set of basic principles must indeed be neutral, since the "veil of ignorance" will filter out all specific premises about how it is best to live.

At least in *A Theory of Justice,* Rawls also seemed to endorse neutrality at other political levels. For example, in the "four-stage sequence" that bridges the gap between the abstract principles of justice and the concrete decisions of political life, the parties are to remain ignorant of their own conceptions of the good until the final stage "of the application of rules to particular cases by judges and administrators, and the following of rules by citizens generally."[15] This implies that no conception of the good can be a basis for deliberation at either the second stage, where the parties select the just constitution that is most appropriate to their own society's circumstances, or the third stage, where they legislate and set policy as permitted *by* the chosen constitution and the principles of justice. Moreover, later in the book, Rawls explicitly added that "the principles of justice do not permit subsidizing universities and institutes, or opera and the theater, on the grounds that these institutions are

13. Rawls, *A Theory of Justice*, p. 7.
14. Ibid.
15. Ibid., p. 199.

intrinsically valuable, and that those who engage in them are to be supported even at some significant expense to others who do not receive compensating benefits."[16] By contrast, in his later work, Rawls appears to have drawn back from the uncompromising requirement that all legislative and policy decisions must be neutral. In his recent book *Political Liberalism,* for example, he writes that "[c]itizens and legislators may properly vote their more comprehensive views when constitutional essentials and basic justice are not at stake."[17]

Even in his earlier work, Rawls was most concerned about neutrality at the framework level. But many pitch their versions of neutralism at far less deep levels. Some debate the neutrality of the (often very particular) decisions of public administrators and civil servants,[18] whereas others – at least if we judge by their illustrations – seem mainly interested in the justification of specific laws. Among the latter, Thomas Nagel has claimed that laws should not be based on premises about the morality of "abortion, sexual conduct, [or] the killing of animals for food,"[19] and Jeremy Waldron illustrates neutralism by reminding us of Mill's claim that "the fact that a law against Sunday trading would accord with the requirements of a sabbatarian faith is not a good reason for having such a law; but the fact that it is necessary to prevent shop employees from being overworked may be."[20] And, finally, we can also imagine versions of neutralism that apply at yet other intermediate levels – for example, the somewhat higher level at which legislatures redraw political boundaries or establish new systems of family courts.

16. Ibid., p. 332. What Rawls says in this passage is subtly different from what he says about the four-stage sequence. The difference is that when he discusses the four-stage sequence, Rawls represents the parties at the legislative and policy-making stages as both bound by the principles of justice *and* still ignorant of their own conceptions of the good. Because their continued ignorance would be otiose if the principles themselves forbade appeals to conceptions of the good, this implies that, at the legislative and policy-making stages, the requirement of neutrality is *distinct from* any requirement of justice. By contrast, in the arts passage just quoted, Rawls implies that at the legislative stage, the requirement of neutrality is imposed precisely *by* the principles of justice.

17. John Rawls, *Political Liberalism* (New York: Columbia University Press, 1993), p. 235.

18. See, for example, Adrian Ellis, "Neutrality and the Civil Service," in Robert E. Goodin and Andrew Reeve, eds., *Liberal Neutrality* (London: Routledge, 1989), pp. 84–105.

19. Thomas Nagel, "Moral Conflict and Political Legitimacy," *Philosophy and Public Affairs* 16, 3 (Summer 1987), p. 233.

20. Waldron, "Legislation and Moral Neutrality," p. 67.

Given this array of possibilities, at which level(s) should *we* take neutralism to apply? One obvious option is to take it to apply at all of them. In defense of this maximally inclusive reading, one might argue that neutralism becomes more interesting as it becomes more ambitious. One might argue, as well, that at least some selective readings appear arbitrary and unmotivated. For example, it seems anomalous to say that legislators are forbidden to act on their conceptions of the good, but that unelected civil servants – whose charge, after all, is to implement the legislature's will – may indeed act on theirs.

Still, despite these advantages, the maximally inclusive reading is hardly forced upon us. As Mark Sagoff rightly observes, "[t]here seems to be no necessary connection . . . between the aspect of equality that is expressed in the neutrality of social institutions and the aspect of equality that may be reflected, for example, in policies liberals pursue, with or without success, in those institutions."[21] Moreover, in support of a more selective reading, one might argue that some defenses of neutralism are not *effective* at all political levels. This, if true, would be significant; for as we saw, it is ceteris paribus preferable to adopt whichever interpretation(s) of neutralism mesh best with the strongest defense(s).

To see why the best defenses may not succeed at all levels, we need only run through a few possibilities. Suppose, first, that the best defense of neutralism is an appeal to skepticism about the good. In that case, the relevant version of the principle probably *will* apply at all political levels. But suppose, instead, that the best defense is the argument that in a pluralistic society, government efforts to promote the good are bound to lead to instability and conflict. In that case, the relevant version of neutralism will apply only at those levels at which nonneutral decisions are in fact destabilizing. Or, again, suppose the best defense is an appeal to the value of autonomy. In that case, the relevant version will prohibit only those nonneutral decisions which are in fact threats to autonomy.

All this, of course, is extremely sketchy. To work out the details, we would have to look more closely both at the different defenses of neutrality and at the effects of deviations from it at different political levels. Because these topics will be dealt with later, no conclusions can be drawn now. Still, we have made progress simply by discover-

21. Mark Sagoff, "Liberalism and Law," in Douglas MacLean and Claudia Mills, eds., *Liberalism Reconsidered* (Totowa, N.J.: Rowman and Allanheld, 1983), p. 13.

ing where the answers lie. Although it is an overstatement to say that "[j]ustificatory argument in political theory and jurisprudence must precede conceptual analysis, not the other way round,"[22] it is no overstatement to say that interpretation and justification are so intertwined that they must be pursued together.

V

In its generic formulation, neutralism asserts that the state should not promote any particular conception of the good. However, governments can promote what they take to be the good in a variety of ways, so a further analytical question is, Which *methods* of promoting the good does neutralism rule out?

Not surprisingly, the most common answer cites the use of force and threats. Whatever their disagreements, all neutralists agree that persons should never be punished merely because their activities are (regarded as) unsavory, base, or unworthy. All neutralists agree, too, that governments should not compel citizens to do things merely on the grounds that they are elevated, valuable, or fine. When these claims are conjoined with a prohibition against the use of coercion to prevent persons from harming themselves, they yield the familiar view that as long as an activity does not harm others, each agent should be free to decide whether to engage in it without fear of legal, economic, or (organized) social sanctions.

Although this view has often been expressed, its locus classicus remains Mill's *On Liberty*. In a much quoted passage, Mill wrote that

the only purpose for which power can be rightfully exercised over any member of a civilized community, against his will, is to prevent harm to others. His own good, either physical or moral, is not a sufficient warrant. He cannot rightfully be compelled to do or forbear because it will be better for him to do so, because it will make him happier, because, in the opinions of others, to do so would be wise or even right.[23]

More recently, Ronald Dworkin has given the point a contemporary gloss:

Government must be neutral in matters of personal morality, [and] must leave people free to live as they think best so long as they do not harm others.

22. Waldron, "Legislation and Moral Neutrality," p. 69.
23. John Stuart Mill, *On Liberty* (Indianapolis: Bobbs-Merrill, 1956), p. 13.

But the Reverend Jerry Falwell, and other politicians who claim to speak for some "moral majority," want to enforce their own morality with the steel of the criminal law. They know what kind of sex is bad, which books are fit for public libraries, what place religion should have in education and family life, when human life begins, that contraception is sin, and that abortion is capital sin. They think the rest of us should be forced to practice what they preach.[24]

Because threats are so direct and intrusive, their salience in these discussions is not surprising.

But salient or not, threats are hardly the only effective ways of influencing behavior. Just as penalties make activities less attractive, rewards can make them *more* attractive. Hence, a second important way of encouraging a favored mode of behavior is by providing suitable incentives. As Ronald Dworkin has noted, one way to do this is to manipulate prices:

Suppose the limited demand for books, matched against the demand for competing uses for wood pulp, would fix the price of books at a point higher than the socialist managers of the economy will charge. . . . It might be said that in a socialist economy books are simply valued more, because they are inherently more worthy uses of social resources, quite apart from the popular demand for books. But the liberal theory of equality rules out that appeal to the inherent value of one theory of what is good in life.[25]

Because the state could not manipulate prices if it lacked a monopoly on force, libertarians sometimes treat this second way of influencing behavior as equivalent to the first. But while it is indeed salutary to recall the omnipresence of force, assimilating the two methods would be a mistake. If we ran them together, we would obscure a number of important differences – for example, in the persons to whom the threats are addressed, the ways they produce the desired results, and the psychological effects of the two methods.

Although price regulation is practiced in many places, it has long been unpopular in the United States. But our government has been far more willing to offer incentives of other sorts. It has, for example, offered tax deductions to encourage charitable and religious con-

24. Ronald Dworkin, "Neutrality, Equality, and Liberalism," in Douglas MacLean and Claudia Mills, eds., *Liberalism Reconsidered* (Totowa, N.J.: Rowman and Allanheld, 1983), p. 1.
25. Dworkin, "Liberalism," p. 195.

35

tributions, and has made aesthetic and cultural activities more affordable by subsidizing art, literature, and scholarship. Also, if certain perennial proposals are ever adopted, our public assistance programs will be restructured to give all recipients more incentive to work and to give male recipients more incentive to remain with their families.

Threats and incentives both influence behavior by altering what would otherwise be its predictable effects. But whether someone engages in an activity depends not only on its expected effects, but also on whether he *likes or approves of* the activity and its effects. This means that we can also influence people's behavior by altering what they like and approve of. Notoriously, what someone likes and approves of is often determined less by his exposure to reasoned argument than by the attitudes and actions of those whom he admires and wishes to imitate. It also often depends on the (positive and negative) reinforcement that the person has received. And, hence, a third way in which governments can influence behavior (and character) is precisely by manipulating these nonrational determinants of preference.

This sort of nonrational manipulation has occasioned much controversy, and, for obvious reasons, much of it has centered on the public schools. Here many on the right complain that sex education legitimizes promiscuity and that teaching evolution replaces religious faith with "secular humanism," while some on the left argue that grading promotes competitive or "elitist" attitudes and that civics classes foster uncritical patriotism. Moreover, outside the schools, we hear similar complaints: that welfare prevents the formation of good work habits, that the ready availability of abortion encourages sexual irresponsibility, and that the prevailing stereotypes socialize women into a narrow range of "traditional" preferences. In each case, remedial state action is demanded.

One further method of influencing behavior warrants brief mention. Thus far, I have discussed only ways of influencing choices among fixed options. But governments also exercise considerable control over which options their citizens *have,* and so a fourth way of promoting the good is just to provide the right sorts of options. Our government shapes our options by sustaining museums, theaters, universities, and other institutions that make cultural activities and open intellectual inquiry possible. It also does so by deciding which agreements it will and will not enforce – for example, by recognizing monogamous heterosexual but not homosexual or polygamous marriages, and agreements to sell auto parts but not bodily parts.[26] Such selective enforcement, indeed, affects our options both by insuring that certain agreements will be kept, and thus increasing their attractiveness, and by adding emphasis and gravity to what would otherwise be merely informal commitments.[27]

To sum up: a government can induce its citizens to live what it takes to be good lives in at least four ways. It can (1) threaten to punish them for not living as it thinks best; (2) offer them incentives to live in the desired ways; (3) nonrationally cause them to prefer to live in those ways; and (4) create the conditions under which they *can* live in those ways. Correspondingly, the most sweeping version of neutralism must also *prohibit* all four methods of promoting the good. But here, as previously, the most sweeping version of neutralism may not be the most plausible. If one or more of these methods are not ruled out by the best defense(s) of neutralism – if, for example, the best defense appeals to a principle of respect for autonomy that the selective creation of options does not violate – then the most plausible version of neutralism will not be the most inclusive. Thus, here again, our final interpretation of neutralism must await our normative discussion.

VI

So far, we have discussed several questions about the neutrality principle's scope. However, a final important question concerns not its scope but its meaning. How are we to understand the key phrase "conception of the good?"

Taken literally, that phrase means something like "belief about what makes people better off, or what makes their lives better." But in the current context, this interpretation is both too narrow and too broad. It is too narrow because some normative claims that are often treated as conceptions of the good – for example, claims about what God requires of us, or the moral status of abortion – are really about what is right rather than what is good. It is too broad because many

26. The selective enforcement of agreements typically involves both threats (of punishment for failure to perform) and incentives (since enforcing an agreement can make entering into it more desirable). However, because both elements enter only indirectly, this method of promoting the good still warrants separate treatment. I owe my appreciation of its importance to Alan Wertheimer.
27. Thus, despite some recent slippage, there remain important qualitative differences between marriage and mere cohabitation.

views about what makes people better off are not, in the relevant sense, conceptions of the good at all. For example, people are obviously better off when they are healthy, prosperous, and secure, yet even neutralists agree that governments may legitimately promote these goods.

As these examples suggest, the extension of "conception of the good" is better understood than its intension. In general, while such conceptions are taken to include religious doctrines, ideals of character and virtue, aesthetic and cultural values, and norms of sexual behavior, they are not understood to include claims about health, economic prosperity, security, freedom, equality, or social justice. Hence, the best way to understand the notion is to ask what distinguishes these lists. And here one obvious answer is that the entries on the first list seem far more controversial. Virtually everyone agrees that health, freedom, and safety are good things, while there is no similar consensus about the value of (say) chastity, salvation, or communal solidarity. Thus, one tempting interpretation of "conception of the good" is simply "a controversial normative claim."

This interpretation represents one prominent strain of neutralist thought. It seems to be implicit in Larmore's claim that "so long as some view about the good life remains disputed, no decision of the state can be justified on the basis of its supposed intrinsic superiority or inferiority."[28] Something like it may also underlie Rawls's claim that "in a constitutional democracy the public conception of justice should be, so far as possible, independent of controversial philosophical and religious doctrines."[29] Still, despite its prominence, the proposed reading of "conception of the good" – I shall refer to it as "the sociological interpretation" – remains vulnerable to two kinds of counterexample.

For, first, some extremely controversial normative claims do *not* seem to express conceptions of the good. This is true, in particular, of many claims about freedom, justice, and rights. Notoriously, there is no consensus about whether inheritance is just, what equal opportunity requires, or whether noneconomic liberties should take precedence over economic ones. As Rawls himself puts it, we share only a concept, but not a conception, of justice.[30] Thus, by the proposed

28. Larmore, *Patterns of Moral Complexity*, p. 47.
29. John Rawls, "Justice As Fairness: Political Not Metaphysical," *Philosophy and Public Affairs* 14, 3 (Summer 1985), p. 223.
30. Rawls, *A Theory of Justice*, p. 5.

criterion, these claims should also count as conceptions of the good. Our intuitions, however, suggest that they do not.

Different responses to this challenge are possible. Larmore, for one, seems willing to tolerate at least some redrawing of boundaries. He writes, for example, that "just as ideals of the good life are a permanent object of dispute, so too are more substantial ideals of freedom, and so it cannot be the concern of the state to promote these."[31] By contrast, Rawls responds by downplaying surface disagreements and stressing the need to find some deeper consensus. He writes that "we must find a new way of organizing familiar ideas and principles into a conception of political justice so that the claims in conflict, as previously understood, are seen in another light."[32] Although I shall not pursue them, it is possible that one of these responses, or some combination of them, may succeed in disarming the first set of counterexamples.

Other counterexamples, however, remain, for there are also normative claims which *do* seem to express conceptions of the good despite the *lack* of controversy about them. These claims include both the taboos against polygamy and incest that prevail in our society and the shared belief of many Islamic societies that it is best to live in accordance with the Koran. Although such claims are not controversial, and so do not satisfy the proposed definition, each would be considered an improper basis for state action by at least some neutralists.

So far, I have considered only attempts to understand "conception of the good" in terms of controversy or disagreement. But perhaps these attempts focus too much on *the numbers of persons who accept* a normative belief and not enough on *the reasons for which* those persons accept it. A bit more specifically, perhaps the crucial point about salvation, culture, and sexual behavior is not that normative claims about them tend to be controversial but, rather, that the controversies cannot be rationally resolved. Perhaps, in other words, the notion of a conception of the good is, at bottom, not sociological but epistemological.

Let us try to make this suggestion more precise. What can it mean to say that a dispute cannot be rationally resolved? One thing it might mean is that the dispute persists even among persons of goodwill who have shown themselves to be reasonable in other contexts.

---

31. Larmore, *Patterns of Moral Complexity,* p. 47.
32. Rawls, "Justice As Fairness: Political Not Metaphysical," p. 229.

On this interpretation, a conception of the good is simply a normative claim about which reasonable people can disagree.

But, once again, this will not do. The problem is not merely that the proposal replaces the imprecise notion of a dispute that cannot be rationally resolved with the equally imprecise notion of a reasonable person. It is, more seriously, that on *any* plausible rendering of "reasonable person," the proposal fails to draw the line in the right place. For, as Thomas Nagel correctly observes,

[r]easonable persons can disagree not only over religious doctrines and ultimate conceptions of the good life, but over levels of public provision of education and health care, social security, defense policy, environmental preservation, and a host of other things that liberal societies determine by legislative action.[33]

Hence, if we do define a conception of the good as a normative claim about which reasonable people can disagree, our definition will again be far too inclusive.

To avoid this danger, Nagel proposes a further distinction. He points out that when reasonable people hold opposing views, their disagreement can take either of two forms. In some cases, the dispute is "open-ended in the possibility of its investigation and pursuit, and [does] not come down finally to a bare confrontation between incompatible personal points of view."[34] By contrast, other disagreements are intractable in the deeper sense that the disputants cannot reach any such "objective common ground."[35] And, Nagel in effect suggests, a more adequate epistemological interpretation will take a conception of the good to be a normative claim that engenders disagreements that are intractable in this second, deeper sense.

Does *this* interpretation do justice to our intuitions? In Nagel's view, it does:

My sense is that the sort of liberal restraint I have been describing should apply, in the present state of moral debate, to certain matters besides the enforcement of religious views. I would include abortion, sexual conduct, and the killing of animals for food, for example. . . . Of course there are reasons and arguments on both sides, but they come to an end in a different

33. Nagel, "Moral Conflict and Political Legitimacy," pp. 231–32.
34. Ibid., p. 232.
35. Ibid.

and more personal way than arguments about welfare payments or affirmative action, for example.[36]

Unfortunately, Nagel provides no argument to back up these impressions, and they are far from obvious. Even if some political disputes do "come to an end with moral instincts which are simply internal to the points of view of the opposed parties,"[37] do these really always include disputes about abortion but not affirmative action, or religion but not welfare? Isn't it more plausible to say that where a dispute ends depends less on the disputed topic than on the thoughtfulness and sophistication of the disputants? Don't some people express merely personal points of view when arguing about *any* of the topics Nagel cites, while others conform just as consistently to requirements of public justification?

If, as I suspect, the answer to these questions is yes, then Nagel's suggestion, too, will fall short. But what should we conclude from this? One possible conclusion is that we cannot define "conception of the good" in either sociological *or* epistemological terms. But another possibility, which I now want to explore, is that any adequate account must incorporate elements of *both* approaches.

To combine the insights they afford, we need only replace Nagel's variant of the epistemological question – roughly, Can the relevant normative claim be defended from a point of view on which all reasonable people might converge? – with a variant that asks whether that claim can be defended *from the points of view of certain specific persons.* Of course, to make this change, we must explain who these persons are; but because our broader topic is the justification of political arrangements, we may naturally identify them with the persons who will be affected *by* the relevant arrangements. When we do, we define a conception of the good as a normative claim about the effects of certain political arrangements on certain persons that is not defensible from those persons' own perspectives.[38]

36. Ibid., p. 233.
37. Ibid.
38. In section II, I argued that those who supply (N")'s standards of plausibility are just the persons who engage in political deliberation. This suggests that it may also be political agents, and not the parties whom their policies will affect, who should be taken to supply the perspective that determines whether their normative claims count as conceptions of the good. However, if we took this line, then very *few* normative claims would qualify as conceptions of the good; for even claims about the value of (e.g.) high culture, communal solidarity, and sexual abstinence are generally defensible from their proponents' own perspectives.

41

This definition correctly captures the difference between claims about the value of religious, cultured, and chaste lives, on the one hand, and claims about the value of health, safety, prosperity, and freedom, on the other. To apply the definition, we begin by assuming that each claim attributes value to the effects of some political arrangement on some persons, and we go on to ask whether its attribution of value is defensible from the affected parties' own points of view. When we do, we immediately see that claims about the value of religion, chastity, and culture are not likely to pass the test; for to someone who is to be made more religious, more cultured, or more chaste, the change will hardly seem an improvement. Indeed, from his point of view, it is apt to look more like a harm than a benefit. However, and in stark contrast, claims about the value of health, safety, prosperity, and freedom almost certainly *will* pass the test; for (virtually) everyone takes it to be in his interest to become healthier, safer, more prosperous, and more free. In this way, the combined approach nicely explains why the value-claims on the first list, but not those on the second, express conceptions of the good.

But the combined approach is less successful in other contexts; for here again, there are counterexamples in both directions. To find a normative claim that satisfies the definition yet intuitively does *not* express a conception of the good, consider the claim that justice requires the redistribution of wealth or power. Because any redistribution will worsen the situation of some who benefit from injustice, such a claim is not likely to be defensible from the perspective of all the affected parties. Hence, by the proposed definition, it will qualify as a conception of the good; but few neutralists would so regard it.[39] Conversely, to find a normative claim that fails to satisfy

Should we then revise our earlier interpretation of (N") to square it with our current suggestion? To do so, we would have to take (N") to require that every premise and inference of a neutral justification be plausible, not from the perspective of the person advancing the justification, but rather from the perspective of every person who would be affected by the proposed political arrangements. However, this requirement would be so stringent that virtually every political argument, and certainly every controversial one, would violate it. Thus, if we accepted this proposal, then (virtually) no argument would qualify as neutral.

Taken together, these considerations suggest that the persons whose perspectives determine (N")'s standards of plausibility and those whose perspectives are best taken to determine what counts as a conception of the good are simply not the same. Just why this is so is an interesting question which I will not pursue.

39. I can envision two ways of trying to meet this objection. One is to argue that what is just or unjust is not the way an arrangement affects individuals one by one, but rather its distribution of goods *among* them. If this claim can be sustained, the

the definition yet *does* seem to express a conception of the good, consider an agent who supports a policy simply because it will enhance *his* ability to pursue some cultural or religious activity. As long as such an agent does not care about the policy's effects on others – as long as his normative claim concerns only its effects on *his* life – the only perspective from which that claim needs to be evaluated is his own. And from the agent's own perspective, the normative claim is indeed defensible. Hence, on the proposed account, it will *not* qualify as a conception of the good. But in fact, the claim that one's life will be improved by greater access to opera or the theater, or by the granting of official status to one's religion, is close to a paradigm of such a conception.[40]

This last difficulty is as serious as any that beset our earlier proposals, and is not eliminable through any obvious further refinement. Hence, like each previous interpretation of "conception of the good," the current proposal leaves important intuitions unaccounted for. And because no further proposal seems any more promising, it seems that no single intepretation can accommodate all of our intuitions about what does and does not qualify as a conception of the good.

VII

But what are we to make of this? One possibility, of course, is that the notion of a conception of the good is simply incoherent. Another possibility, however, is that our intuitions reflect several different but partially overlapping notions each of which *is* internally coherent. This suggestion, moreover, draws important support from the fact that each of the three notions that we have discussed is presupposed by one of the three main arguments for neutralism.

individuals who benefit from injustice may not be affected parties in the relevant sense. Alternatively, and perhaps more plausibly, one might concede that those who benefit *are* affected parties, but might insist that unjust arrangements will be indefensible even from their perspective once it is purged of all morally irrelevant features. To be effective, this rejoinder must be backed by a non–question-begging account of which features of a person's perspective are morally irrelevant. Also, given the intuition that appeals to many different principles of justice can all count as neutral, the rejoinder must explain how a variety of incompatible principles can all be defensible from a single perspective. While I am not prepared to dismiss this rejoinder, I am not hopeful about its prospects for success.

40. This difficulty was brought to my attention by Derk Pereboom.

The reasoning here is straightforward. Suppose, first, that some-one wants to defend neutralism primarily as a device of accommoda-tion for persons who hold radically different ideals and values, but who nonetheless all wish to live harmoniously together. In that case, he will naturally say that a normative claim expresses a conception of the good whenever it *is* a matter of controversy among the relevant parties. This, however, was precisely our first interpretation of "con-ception of the good."

Suppose, next, that someone wants to defend neutralism primarily on the grounds that the premises of nonneutral arguments are im-possible or very difficult to know. In that case, he will naturally say that a normative claim expresses a conception of the good whenever its truth *is* impossible or very difficult to establish. This, however, was precisely our second interpretation of "conception of the good."

Suppose, finally, that someone wants to defend neutralism on the grounds that it is important or obligatory to give each citizen maxi-mal leeway in shaping his own life. In that case, he will naturally hold that a claim about how someone should live expresses a concep-tion of the good whenever it is not acceptable from that person's own perspective. This, however, was precisely our third interpretation of "conception of the good."

Because each main interpretation is dictated by one of the three main arguments, the hypothesis that each is valid in its own sphere, but that none dominates, is strikingly confirmed. Just as strikingly, we are again reminded that any full analysis of neutralism must await the results of our normative inquiry. Let us therefore set aside any remaining analytical questions, and turn without further ado to that inquiry itself.

Chapter 3

Autonomy and neutrality (1)

The first normative argument to be considered is an appeal to the value of autonomy. This argument asserts that each person has a preeminent interest in living an autonomous life and, hence, that government can promote (the most) value by not acting on any particular conception of the good. Because the notion of autonomy is so elusive, there is an obvious risk that any formulation of this argument will be tendentious. Fortunately, however, the very analysis of autonomy that seems to me the most plausible is also the one that gives the argument its best chance of success. In the first half of this chapter, I shall defend that analysis and explain why the argument must presuppose it. In the second, I shall ask how autonomy, so conceived, is affected by the different methods of promoting (other) values. These, it will turn out, are far less inimical to autonomy than is generally supposed.

I

Although autonomy figures prominently in many discussions, there is little consensus about what it involves. Hence, an important first step is to survey the main approaches to it. These can usefully be grouped in three categories.

1. Perhaps the first thing that comes to mind about autonomy is its close connection to freedom. Indeed, in some discussions, these notions are simply equated. Thomas Hurka, for example, seems to treat them as interchangeable when he writes: "This, then, is the challenge to the value of autonomy: if free choice is intrinsically good, it should be better to have one good option and nine bad options than just to

45

have one good option. And why should this be so?"[1] Moreover, even when freedom and autonomy are distinguished, they are often (and rightly) taken to be closely linked.

Their linkage complicates our task because the conditions for freedom are themselves complex. As Hurka's remarks suggest, a person's freedom depends in part on the number and quality of his options. But a person may also act unfreely because he lacks the information to evaluate his options or because he lacks the ability to process what information he has. In addition, we deny that people choose freely when their choices are coerced by threats of harm and when they are subject to "alien" internal forces such as compulsion and irresistible impulse.

Given the close connections between freedom and autonomy, it is not surprising that many conditions necessary for freedom have also been taken to be necessary for autonomy. For example, Joseph Raz has written that "autonomy is opposed to a life of coerced choices."[2] Raz also writes that an autonomous person "must have the mental abilities to form intentions of a sufficiently complex kind, and to plan their execution,"[3] and that he must have "an adequate range of options to choose from."[4] But while these claims are not clearly wrong, they are also not all clearly correct. It is not obvious that a person can never autonomously surrender his money to avoid being shot by robbers. It is also not obvious that persons can never autonomously choose from restricted ranges of options or exercise autonomy despite their ignorance of relevant features of their situation.[5] Also, of course, there are hard questions about which proposals *are* coercive, which internal forces *are* alien, and which ranges of options *are* adequate.

2. Although autonomy may in some respects demand less than freedom, in other respects it demands more. Someone who makes an informed, uncoerced, noncompulsive choice from an adequate range of options may be choosing freely; but his choice is not autonomous

---

1. Thomas Hurka, "Why Value Autonomy?" *Social Theory and Practice* 13, 3 (Fall 1987), p. 363.
2. Joseph Raz, *The Morality of Freedom* (Oxford: Oxford University Press, 1986), p. 371.
3. Ibid., p. 372.
4. Ibid., p. 374.
5. To be fair to Raz, it is not clear how much of this he is committed to denying; for he is concerned less with understanding when a *particular choice or action* is autonomous than with specifying the conditions under which someone lives an autonomous *life*.

if it is the result of certain sorts of past manipulation. For example, persons are thought not to act autonomously when they are motivated by preferences that were shaped by systematic indoctrination or "brainwashing." More subtly, they are often said to be deprived of autonomy by certain forms of *unintended* conditioning. To recall a useful cliché, we would consider someone nonautonomous if, as a result of lengthy past involuntary servitude, he now opted to remain a slave when he might go free. Here again, there are hard questions about which forms of conditioning undermine autonomy; but we need not be able to answer them to say that some forms of conditioning clearly have this effect.

3. Yet even together, freedom and the absence of a history of objectionable conditioning may not exhaust the prerequisites for autonomy. In addition, many believe that agents are not autonomous unless they have subjected their ends to rational scrutiny. Subjecting one's ends to scrutiny involves considering the reasons for and against doing what one prefers, and acting only on the preferences that survive. It also involves trying to modify any preferences that one finds good reason to abandon. As William E. Connolly describes the process,

[a] person may want to follow a particular career simply because his parents and friends expect him to pursue this path. He might, however, adopt the same goal after deliberately canvassing the expectations others have of him, reassessing his previous tendency to adopt unreflectively the hopes those others have for him as his own, critically exploring the contours of the profession under consideration in the light of his own capacities, strengths, and weaknesses, and comparing the career in question to other alternatives that might be open to a person with his interests, capacities, and opportunities.[6]

Though somewhat more controversial than the others, this critical-reflection requirement, too, is widely accepted. Also like the others, it is in need of further specification – in this case, of the standards that agents should use when thinking critically about their preferences.

Taken together, these three sets of conditions (or some subset of their elements) may indeed be sufficient for autonomy. Yet even if they are, difficult questions remain. Given the diversity of its prereq-

---

6. William E. Connolly, *The Terms of Political Discourse,* 2d ed. (Princeton: Princeton University Press, 1983), pp. 150–51.

uisites, is autonomy really a single notion? If so, how are its elements related? If not, which form(s) of autonomy are morally important?[7]

II

Despite its apparent fragmentation, I believe that autonomy is a strongly unified notion. In this and the next section, I shall sketch and briefly defend the account that I take to integrate its elements.

That account is a variant of the familiar idea that autonomous persons are self-directing; but it differs from other variants in its understanding of "self-direction." On many readings, this means only that an agent's goals, plans, and decisions originate in his own will. By contrast, on the reading I favor, autonomous agents are self-directing in the more stringent sense of exercising their will *on the basis of good reasons.* A bit less cryptically, I shall argue that we can make the most sense of what most of us believe about autonomy – our disagreement as well as our agreement – if we adopt the hypothesis that in this context "self-directed activity" means "activity that is motivated by an agent's appreciation of reasons provided by his situation."

The idea that autonomy is responsiveness to reasons is of course not new. A version of this idea is central to Kant's ethical theory, and the idea is presupposed by all who believe that "moral autonomy means doing what is right and good *because* it is right and good."[8]

7. One way of responding to these questions is simply to identify autonomy with one or another of (what I have presented as) its necessary conditions. Interestingly, this has been tried with all three sets of conditions. Thus, as we have seen, in "Why Value Autonomy?" Hurka focuses exclusively on (an aspect of) the first condition when he identifies autonomy entirely with the freedom to choose among important life-options. By contrast, Irving Thalberg focuses exclusively on the second when he suggests that to be autonomous is to have received the sort of socialization that men, but not women, currently get; see Thalberg, "Socialization and Autonomous Behavior," *Tulane Studies in Philosophy* 38 (1979), pp. 21–37. And in addition to Connolly, various philosophers have fastened on the third condition, and have held that the essence of autonomy is critical scrutiny of one's goals and values. See, for example, Danny Scoccia, "Autonomy, Want Satisfaction, and the Justification of Liberal Freedoms," *Canadian Journal of Philosophy* 17, 3 (September 1987), pp. 583–601, and Adina Schwartz, "Against Universality," *Journal of Philosophy* 78, 3 (March 1981), pp. 127–43. Although I shall not examine any of these accounts, the obvious worry about them is that each fails to accommodate the intuitions that motivate its rivals.

8. Amy Gutmann, *Democratic Education* (Princeton: Princeton University Press, 1987), p. 62.

But as the quotation illustrates, the idea is most often confined to discussions of autonomous *moral* decisions. By contrast, I want to generalize it to apply also to nonmoral decisions; I mean it as an analysis of personal as well as moral autonomy.[9] Also, while many Kantians appear to believe that acting autonomously is responding to what is *objectively the strongest* (moral) reason provided by one's situation, I shall allow that persons may act autonomously in response to reasons that are less than the strongest. To defend this account, I shall argue that it explains (1) why autonomy imposes the requirements that it does, (2) why autonomy is morally important, and (3) why so much of what we believe about autonomy is unclear or indeterminate.

Consider, first, the question of how any univocal notion can impose requirements as disparate as (some of) the prerequisites for freedom, the absence of a history of (certain forms of) conditioning, and a critical attitude toward one's own ends. If autonomy is responsiveness to reasons, the answer is straightforward: each requirement rules out a way in which responsiveness to reasons can fail. Thus, the explanation of why autonomous agents must have various cognitive abilities is that otherwise they could not recognize their reasons for acting. The explanation of why they must have control over their impulses is that otherwise they could not respond to whatever reasons they recognize. The explanation of why a history of brainwashing, indoctrination, or oppressive servitude undermines autonomy is that it diminishes one's current ability to respond to reasons. And the explanation of why autonomous agents must subject their ends to critical scrutiny (or at least be open to reasons to initiate such

---

9. For two discussions that explore related conceptions of freedom, see Susan Wolf, "Asymmetrical Freedom," in John Martin Fischer ed., *Moral Responsibility* (Ithaca: Cornell University Press, 1968), pp. 223–40, and Robert Nozick, *Philosophical Explanations* (Cambridge, Mass.: Harvard University Press, 1981), pp. 291–362. Wolf does not quite say that an agent acts freely when he acts in response to a good reason. Instead, she asserts that "[i]n order for an agent to be morally free, . . . he must be *capable of* being determined by the Good" (p. 236, emphasis added). By contrast, Nozick does consider the possibility that acting freely "is (to be determined) to do the action that is the best of those available to us; moreover, that this doing what is best or most valuable not be an accident, like true belief, but rather that the action tracks value or bestness" (p. 317). However, he concludes that "we are left with the feeling that the notion of 'tracking bestness or rightness' has not gotten to the heart of the free will problem" (p. 332). Whether Nozick would also say that "tracking bestness" fails to illuminate autonomy is unclear.

scrutiny)[10] is that otherwise they would be apt to overlook important reasons for acting.

The responsiveness-to-reasons account thus makes at least rough sense of various necessary conditions for autonomy. But it also explains why we may feel ambivalent toward other (alleged) necessary conditions. As we saw, acts performed under threat, such as surrendering one's money to a gunman, are clearly unfree; but they do not always seem nonautonomous. The explanation, we can now see, is that unlike other factors that undermine freedom, a threat does not prevent an agent from responding to reasons. Instead, it restructures the situation that *provides* his reasons. This means that an agent can have, and respond to, a good reason for complying with a threat. Similarly, the explanation of why having few options does not necessarily undermine autonomy is that even someone with few options may have a good reason for choosing one course of action over others.

Consider, second, what the responsiveness-to-reasons account implies about the moral importance of autonomy. If autonomy were simply arbitrary choice, there would be no obvious basis on which to claim either that it is good to be autonomous or that our legal and political system should protect and foster autonomous choice. Mere self-assertion uninformed by reason appears to have little value. But if autonomy is *reasoned* self-direction – if it consists precisely in recognizing and allowing oneself to be guided by rational considerations – then its normative significance is much easier to grasp. In that case, its value is essentially that of (practical) rationality itself. This, of course, does not explain *why* autonomy is valuable; but since rationality is widely considered one of our most precious attributes, it does place autonomy's value effectively beyond dispute.

Consider, finally, how the responsiveness-to-reasons account illuminates what we find unclear about autonomy. There are, as we saw, a number of unresolved questions: about what sorts of impulses, mental capacities, and so on render agents nonautonomous, about what forms of conditioning lead agents to make nonautonomous choices, and about what standards an agent should use in evaluating his ends. If autonomy is responsiveness to reasons, the

10. The idea that (moral) autonomy need not involve ceaseless self-scrutiny, but requires only "continuous but essentially passive receptivity to particularly significant developments" together with "periodic full-scale reviews," is advanced by Arthur Kuflik in "The Inalienability of Autonomy," *Philosophy and Public Affairs* 13, 4 (Fall 1984), p. 274.

existence of these questions is easy to understand. They arise because our basic concept of autonomy is schematic and, hence, requires completion by a substantive theory of reasons and how they move us. Because these matters are obscure, the lacunae in our understanding of autonomy are just what we should expect. Moreover – a separate point – while the proposed account does not itself answer the questions, it does at least tell us how to approach them. To find out which impulses and mental incapacities subvert autonomy, it directs us to ask which impulses and incapacities prevent reasons from getting a motivational grip. To find out which forms of conditioning undermine (later) autonomy, it directs us to ask which influences cause us to develop preferences that later resist rational alteration. And to establish the criteria for evaluating one's ends, it directs us to ask which aspects of an agent's situation are relevant to his deliberations.

III

Because our topic is neutralism and not autonomy, most of these issues are beyond our scope. But before I resume the discussion's main thread, I must consider some objections to the proposed account. There are, it seems, at least two important difficulties.

The first is that agents often make (nonmoral) choices which seem autonomous despite the absence of objective reasons to choose one option over another. When someone must make a moral choice – when, for instance, he must choose between self-interest and fairness, or between promoting the general welfare and keeping a promise – at least one available action always has moral value, so there is always some moral reason to which he can respond. But when someone must make a *non*moral choice – when, for instance, he must choose between marrying and remaining single – the possibility of his recognizing and responding to an objective reason may seem less clear. Against this possibility, one might argue that neither being married nor being single has inherent value and, hence, that the agent has no objective reason to choose one over the other. Nor, to vary the example, does there appear to be anything about collecting stamps that makes it objectively better or worse than, say, birdwatching. Because such choices can nonetheless be autonomous, one might conclude that autonomy cannot be responsiveness to reasons.

This objection would be too quick, however. One way to resist it is simply to challenge its assumption that the world contains too few objective values to guide all nonmoral choices. Certainly the fact that being married does not *always* have objective value does not entail that it *never* does. And, more generally, the worry about the paucity of nonmoral values may reflect only an unwarranted suspicion of perfectionism.

But although I am sympathetic to this reply, I need not press it here; for there is a much easier way to show that there are always enough reasons to guide nonmoral choices. Even if the world is far less rich in values than I take it to be – indeed, even if *no* outcomes are intrinsically better or worse than any others – an agent's own desires and aversions, as well as his past decisions and psychological makeup, are surely themselves important sources of reasons. More-over, while a desire is in one sense a subjective state, its existence is no less objective than any other fact. Hence, the easiest way to secure an ample stock of nonmoral reasons is to include an agent's desires, history, capacities, and traits in his reason-generating situation. Once these factors are included, we no longer need fear the inference from "no fact external to X gives X a reason to marry Y" to "X cannot choose to marry Y in response to an objective reason"; for X's want-ing to marry Y will itself provide just such a reason. If X lacks count-ervailing reasons (and is aware of this), his desire-based decision to marry Y may indeed satisfy the requirements for autonomy. More-over, in other cases, agents may satisfy those requirements by re-sponding to reasons provided by their second-order desires to be, or not be, specific sorts of persons.[11]

---

11. It is, indeed, an additional important virtue of the responsiveness-to-reasons ac-count that it assigns a significant yet subordinate role to the idea that agents only act autonomously when they are motivated by desires by which they want to be motivated. This idea is often put forward as yet another rival approach to auton-omy. (For some important statements of it, see Harry Frankfurt, "Freedom of the Will and the Concept of a Person," *Journal of Philosophy* 68 [January 1971], pp. 5–20, Gerald Dworkin, "Acting Freely," *Nous* 4 [1970], pp. 367–83, and Wright Neely, "Freedom and Desire," *Philosophical Review* 83 [1974], pp. 32–54.) Yet as many have noted, we cannot simply identify acting autonomously with acting in accor-dance with one's higher-order desires; for, among other things, one may be brain-washed to acquire higher-order as well as first-order desires. But if autonomy is responsiveness to reasons and if desires sometimes provide reasons for seeking their objects, then higher-order desires will fall into place as important sources of reasons for retaining, revising, or implementing lower-order desires. They will thus at least partly determine the criteria an agent should use in critically evaluat-ing his ends.

Thus, however we understand nonmoral reasons – whether we take them to stem from perfectionist values, from psychological facts about agents or others, or from some mixture of the two – there plainly are enough of them to guide choice whenever autonomy is possible. Indeed, there probably are few acts that are *not* supported by one or another reason. But just because of this, the responsiveness-to-reasons account now raises a very different question: namely, to *which* of the many reasons provided by an agent's situation must he respond to qualify as autonomous?[12]

The simplest answer to this second difficulty, of course, is that he must respond to the *strongest* reason provided by his situation. This proposal would forge the tightest possible link between autonomy and practical rationality. It would also account adequately for our intuitions about some cases. For example, we might well doubt the autonomy of someone who refused to undergo lifesaving surgery merely because he feared postoperative pain. Here the explanation may indeed be that self-preservation is much more important than avoiding transient pain, and hence that anyone who declined the operation would not be responding to the strongest reason provided by his situation. But the same proposal that yields this explanation also has many less welcome implications. Suppose, for example, that a second agent also needs surgery to survive but, unlike the first, has no way of knowing this. If autonomy were responsiveness to the strongest reason provided by one's situation, then this agent, too, would fail to act autonomously if he chose not to undergo surgery. Yet if someone is unavoidably ignorant of his need for surgery, then his failure to submit to it surely does *not* affect the autonomy of whatever else he does.

To block such counterexamples, we must at least relativize the reasons to which autonomous agents must respond to what they know (or, perhaps, can reasonably be expected to know) about their situations. Yet even when so relativized, the proposal that acting autonomously is responding to one's strongest reason remains problematical. For consider, next, a case in which X not only has a strong desire to marry Y, but also knows that their marriage will fail unless he gives up his career. Suppose, further, that X knows that his talents are modest and that his career is not promising in any event. Knowing all this, X may well have more reason to marry Y than to pursue

---

12. I owe my appreciation of the issues discussed in the remainder of this section to the constructive bullying of Derk Pereboom and David Christensen.

his career. Yet while X certainly can autonomously choose to marry Y and give up his career, we must concede that he also can autonomously choose the career over the marriage. More generally, we must concede that persons can and often do exercise their autonomy by acting *against* their strongest reasons.

To allow for this, we might try further relativizing the reasons to which autonomous agents must respond. Those reasons, we might now say, depend not only on what agents know about their situations, but also on their beliefs about which aspects of their situations are reasons and how strong these reasons are. We might suppose, in other words, that an agent acts autonomously whenever he acts in response to *whichever reasons appear strongest to him.*

But this proposal will not do either; for while it would account for the intuition that X could autonomously choose either to marry Y or to pursue his career, it would do so at the cost of making the conditions for autonomy so weak that virtually all actions (except, perhaps, some that result from weakness of will) could satisfy them. It would imply, indeed, that even a madman acts autonomously as long as he acts reasonably by his own lights. Worse yet, if acting autonomously were acting merely on what one *regards* as one's strongest reasons, then one could act autonomously without making any contact at all with one's actual reasons. This would eliminate the very connection between autonomy and practical rationality that promised to explain why autonomy is valuable.

To avoid these difficulties, we must hold fast to the idea that acting autonomously is allowing oneself to be guided by one's actual reasons. The question, though, is how we can both do this and still make the needed concession that an autonomous act need not be supported by the agent's *strongest* reasons.

To work our way toward an answer, let us return to X's decision to pursue his career. That decision, we said, could qualify as autonomous despite the fact that X's reason to pursue his career was less strong than his reason to marry Y. But here it may be relevant that even if X's reason to pursue his career is not his strongest, it remains both reasonably strong and reasonably close to its competitor in strength. Even if we disagree with X's choice, we must admit that, given the central role that careers play in life-plans, there is a good deal to be said for it. In this respect, choosing a career over a marriage is very different from deciding to forego lifesaving surgery merely to avoid postoperative pain.

Could an act's autonomy depend on the *relative* strength of the reasons for performing it? Because we are taking autonomy to be *responsiveness* to reasons, the only reasons whose relative strength can count are those that actually influence the agent. Hence, if we adopt this suggestion, we will have to say that agents can be influenced by reasons that are real but not their strongest. This may at first seem implausible. However, as Raz has noted,

I may not have a reason to prefer going to medical school to going to law school. But if that is what I do then I do it because I believe that a medical education is important and worth while for it will, for example, enable me (1) to serve others, as well as (2) to have a satisfying career, and (3) to live and work in almost any country. 1 to 3 are my reasons, and the fact that I believe that I also have reasons for choosing a legal career which are no less worthy and important does not undermine the fact that when I choose medicine I choose it for the stated reasons.[13]

Although Raz presents no real argument, I believe these remarks are correct and important. At least when one's alternatives are equally valuable or incommensurable, the fact that neither is supported by a stronger reason does not imply that neither can be chosen for whatever reason does support it. Even if B would be just as good as A, one's choice of A may still be grounded in what *makes* A good.

But once we have come this far, we can go farther. If a choice can be reason-based despite the existence of *equally good* reasons to do something else, it surely can also be reason-based despite the existence of *better* reasons to do something else. As long as A *is* supported by reasons, an agent may respond to those reasons despite his awareness of facts that provide even stronger reasons to do B. Of course, in failing to respond to the stronger reasons, the agent will fall short of *full* rationality; but falling short of full rationality is not the same as being *ir*rational. Moreover, if the reasons for A and B are nearly equal in strength, then the choice of A will at least be close to fully rational.

Although these observations are obvious, they are also liberating; for they immediately suggest an alternative to the view that acting autonomously is acting in response to the strongest reasons provided by what one knows. They suggest, instead, that an agent may qualify as autonomous whenever he acts in response to reasons provided by what he knows about his situation that are at least *strong enough.* By retreating just this far, we can retain the link between autonomy and

13. Raz, *The Morality of Freedom*, p. 304.

practical rationality while allowing that agents can autonomously choose what is less than best. Of course, to make this suggestion precise, we would need to spell out just when a reason *is* strong enough. That in turn would require deciding whether what matters is a reason's absolute strength or its strength in comparison to the agent's other reasons.[14] But whatever we say about this, any defensible threshhold seems likely to be exceeded both by X's reason to marry Y and by X's reason to pursue his career. Thus, on any reasonable interpretation, the current proposal will explain why X could make either decision autonomously.

While much more could be said, the conclusion at this point is that neither of the main objections to the responsiveness-to-reasons account is unduly damaging. Moreover, as we saw earlier, that account has the positive virtues of integrating autonomy's elements, explaining its value, and illuminating its obscurities. Even alone, these considerations would add up to a strong case for adopting the account. But in the current context, the case is far stronger. For, as we will soon see, if autonomy is *not* construed as responsiveness to reasons, the argument from its value to neutralism cannot be made even superficially plausible.

IV

To see why, let us now turn to the value-of-autonomy argument itself. At least in broad outline, that argument is very familiar. Bruce Ackerman, who characterizes it as one of "several weighty arguments in support of neutrality,"[15] summarizes it this way:

Even if you don't think you need to experiment, you may adopt a conception of the good that gives a central place to autonomous deliberation and deny that it is possible to *force* a person to be good. On this view, the intrusion of non-Neutral argument into power talk will seem self-defeating at best – since it threatens to divert people from the true means of cultivating a truly good life.[16]

14. Even if an agent's autonomy depends entirely on the relative strength of the reason that moves him, what moves him about the reason may still be its absolute strength.
15. Bruce Ackerman, *Social Justice in the Liberal State* (New Haven: Yale University Press, 1980), p. 11.
16. Ibid.

In a similar vein, David A. J. Richards first postulates "a general right of personal autonomy,"[17] but then goes on to write that "[t]he neutrality, in Dworkin's sense, of this right, among a wide number of visions of the good life, arises from its source in the value of autonomy."[18] And while Mill tends to present the case against government interference in people's lives as resting on the value of individuality rather than autonomy, similar reasoning can be extracted from various passages in *On Liberty*.[19]

Familiar though it is, however, the idea that governments can always promote the most value by allowing citizens to exercise their own autonomy is extremely puzzling. Perhaps the most obvious problem is that even if autonomy has great value, it hardly follows (and is almost certainly false) that autonomy is the *only* thing with value. Indeed, on the account of autonomy just defended – an agent acts autonomously when he acts in response to reasons provided by his situation – the claim that nothing except autonomy has value *must* be false. It must be false because an agent cannot respond to a reason for pursuing X unless there *is* a reason for him to pursue X, and there cannot be such a reason unless his pursuing or attaining X either has intrinsic value or has acquired value from its relation to something else.[20] Because one cannot respond to a reason unless there is some value that gives rise to that reason, it is inconsistent to hold both that autonomy is responsiveness to reasons and that autonomy is the only thing with value.

Yet if autonomy is *not* the only thing with value – if it is only one good thing among others – then exactly how can its value justify neutralism? Even if promoting other values invariably undermines autonomy, why must governments always resolve the dilemma in autonomy's favor? If governments or their agents have well-grounded beliefs that citizens' lives are improved by close and committed family relationships, or that the breakdown of public civility is a bad thing, why shouldn't they promote public civility or the family even at the cost of sacrificing some autonomy? Or, again, why

---

17. David A. J. Richards, "Human Rights and Moral Ideals: An Essay on the Moral Theory of Liberalism," *Social Theory and Practice* 5, 3–4 (1980), p. 474.
18. Ibid.
19. Here I have in mind not only some of what Mill says about individuality in Chapter 3 of *On Liberty* – see for example, his remarks about Calvinism – but also his emphasis in Chapter 2 on the importance of understanding the grounds for one's beliefs.
20. Here I assume, of course, that the case is not one in which *duty* supplies a reason to pursue X.

shouldn't they sacrifice some autonomy to promote such values as high culture or communal solidarity? There actually are two cases to consider, since either the value of autonomy is commensurable with these other values or it is not. But if the values are not commensurable, then nothing follows about how governments should choose between autonomy and other values; while if they are commensurable, then the conclusion seems to be that governments should *not* promote autonomy if they can do more good by promoting other values. Either way, the inference from the value of autonomy to neutralism appears to fail.[21]

Is there any way to rescue it short of retreating to the untenable view that autonomy is the only thing with value? One possibility, suggested by Ackerman, is that it is "not necessary for autonomy to be the only good thing; it suffices for it to be the best thing that there is."[22] Here Ackerman's thought appears to be that if autonomy is better than anything else – as he believes it to be – then governments can never reasonably promote other values at its expense. Yet even if autonomy *is* the best thing there is, the amount of value a government can produce by promoting it may still be smaller than the amount of value that can be produced by promoting more of something less valuable. Thus, to rule out the possibility of trade-offs, the value of autonomy must be prior in some stronger sense.

Can a stronger priority claim be made out? Although I know of no neutralist who has squarely addressed this question, one possibility, at least, seems worth exploring. This is the suggestion that autonomy is *internally* connected to the other values that appear to call for trade-offs – that, in other words, the value of superior ways of life resides not merely in (say) their intrinsic nature, but rather in their being chosen *because* of that nature. On this account, the values of family, culture, community, and the rest will not be competitors to autonomy, but rather will presuppose it; for lives involving close family ties, culture, and community will be valuable only when (or only to the extent that) they are adopted *for the reasons provided by their value.*

Is this suggestion coherent? At first glance, it may seem not to be; for it asserts both that whether a way of life is valuable depends on whether it is autonomously chosen and that whether a way of life is autonomously chosen depends on whether it has independent value.

---

21. Hurka notices this problem in "Why Value Autonomy?" p. 377.
22. Ackerman, *Social Justice in the Liberal State*, p. 368.

Given this circularity, we may seem unable to make determinations of either autonomy or value. Yet despite initial appearances, the circularity need not be vicious. To tame it, we need only say, first, that when we call a way of life independently valuable, what we mean is that it *would* have actual value if it were chosen autonomously and, second, that choosing it autonomously is choosing it precisely because one recognizes this potentiality. To mark this complication, I shall henceforth speak not simply of responding to value but of responding to (potential) value.

Like the idea that autonomy is responsiveness to reasons, the idea that only autonomously chosen ways of life have value is not new. Although Lawrence Haworth does not recognize the complication just discussed, he plainly implies that at least some values presuppose autonomy when he writes:

[W]hat is there to value in a community of shared values when the members of the community are automata? The fact of sharing or of being mutually devoted to a transcendent or collective good commands respect only to the extent that the members of the community participate autonomously – to the extent that each, by joining with the rest in a collective pursuit, is living his own life, pursuing his (procedurally) own conception of the good.[23]

Will Kymlicka makes the same point in more general terms when he writes that "no life goes better by being led from the outside according to values the person doesn't endorse. My life only goes better if I'm leading it from the inside, according to my beliefs about value."[24] Moreover, the view we are considering – that some ways of life are better than others, but that even the (potentially) best lack value if not chosen for the right reasons – is the exact structural analogue of Kant's famous view that some sorts of actions are morally better than others, but that even the (potentially) best lack moral value if not performed for the right reasons.

This view immediately opens up new possibilities. If only autonomously chosen activities can have value, then any government that tries to increase the value of its citizens' activities at the expense of their autonomy will merely destroy the conditions under which their activities can *be* valuable. Because of this, a person's activities will

23. Lawrence Haworth, *Autonomy: An Essay in Philosophical Psychology and Ethics* (New Haven: Yale University Press, 1986), p. 208. For a similar suggestion, see Hurka, "Why Value Autonomy?" p. 378.
24. Will Kymlicka, *Liberalism, Community, and Culture* (Oxford: Oxford University Press, 1989), p. 12.

always lack value when his government has induced him to pursue them nonautonomously; but they will *not* always lack value when his government has *not* induced him to pursue them non-autonomously. Under these conditions, one's chances of living a valuable life may indeed be best if one's government interferes least with one's autonomy.[25]

It should now be clear why the value-of-autonomy argument must treat autonomy as responsiveness to reasons. We just saw that that argument will not succeed if there can be trade-offs between autonomy and other values. We saw, as well, that the only way to rule out such trade-offs is to hold that no activity can have value unless it is chosen on the basis *of* its (potential) value. Since this way of saving the argument equates being chosen autonomously with being chosen on the basis of (potential) value, it in effect presupposes a responsiveness-to-reasons account of autonomy. Of course, the reasons provided by an activity's (potential) value need not exhaust the reasons for engaging in it, so this version of the responsiveness-to-reasons account does not exactly match the one developed earlier. Still, as long as the current version also requires that the reasons provided by (potential) value exceed a certain level of strength, it can be viewed as an especially stringent variant of the original.

The harder question, of course, is whether it is *true* that only autonomously chosen activities can have value. Certainly that premise is not universally accepted. Against it, some would maintain that there is value even (or especially) in unquestioning obedience to (divine or human) authority. Others would insist that certain specific ways of behaving – for example, premarital chastity and marital fidelity – are best no matter *what* the agent's reasons. Of course, the mere fact of disagreement settles nothing, since it may be the dissenters who are mistaken; but right or wrong, their view does not seem absurd. Thus, the premise that only autonomously chosen activities have value is itself in need of defense.

25. As David Christensen has pointed out to me, the reasoning of this paragraph presupposes that autonomy is an all-or-nothing matter. If instead autonomy is a matter of degree, then even policies that do diminish autonomy may increase people's chances of living valuable lives. In particular, this will be possible whenever (1) a policy does not undermine a person's autonomy enough to prevent his choices from actualizing any (potential) value, and (2) it leads him to choose activities that are much more (potentially) valuable than any alternatives. This rejoinder is significant because responsiveness to reasons (and hence, on my account, autonomy) does seem to be a matter of degree. However, in the discussion to follow, I shall forgo this objection in favor of others.

V

Fortunately, we need not decide whether it can be defended; for the argument from the value of autonomy – or, as we now might more accurately call it, the argument from autonomy's contribution *to* value – breaks down decisively at another point. To succeed, that argument must presuppose not merely that only autonomously chosen activities have value, but also that when governments try to induce citizens to choose valuable activities, the resulting choices never *are* autonomous. Yet whatever we say about the first premise, the second is clearly false.

In the remainder of this chapter, I shall argue this point in some detail. First, though, I must specify more precisely what needs to be shown. As we saw in Chapter 2, a government can promote (what it considers) a valuable form of life in at least four ways. It can (1) threaten to punish those who reject that form of life; (2) offer citizens incentives to accept it; (3) nonrationally cause them to acquire a preference for it; or (4) create institutions or social forms that make the favored way of life possible or enable it to flourish. Because the most interesting version of neutralism forbids all four methods of promoting good lives, we could block the current argument for that version merely by showing that *one* of those methods can issue in autonomous choices. But if we showed only this much, we would leave open the possibility of invoking autonomy's contribution to value to establish a weaker version of neutralism. To foreclose this possibility, I shall try to show that *all four* methods of promoting valuable lives can issue in autonomous choices.

Consider, first, policies aimed at nonrationally causing citizens to acquire or retain preferences for (what the policy makers consider) good lives. Although their actual rationales are no doubt mixed, many current policies appear to have this aim among others. These policies encompass the use of "directive" techniques of moral education, including exhortation, reward, punishment, and personal example, to cause students to acquire desirable habits and preferences. They also include employing the techniques of advertising to instill an aversion to drug use and other unwholesome activities; encouraging writers to portray women in nonstereotyped ways; hiring workers who are positive "role models" for persons with low aspirations; making work a condition of public assistance to alter the habits of recipients; and trying to reform criminals by incarcerating them.

To simplify the discussion, I shall simply assume that some such policies do nonrationally cause people to acquire new preferences. Granting this, the question is whether those preferences can issue in autonomous choices.

Given our analysis of autonomy, the answer may at first seem to be a clear no. For suppose a government's policies do nonrationally cause a citizen C to prefer a way of life W; and suppose, further, that C's choice of W is motivated by the preference that is thus caused. Because that preference is, by hypothesis, not a response to any reason for preferring W, C's choice of W must also not be a response to any such reason. However, according to our account of autonomy, an autonomous choice just *is* a choice that is made in response to a good reason. Hence, it may seem to follow immediately that nonrational conditioning cannot issue in autonomous choices.

I shall explain shortly what I take to be wrong with this argument. First, though, I want to discuss briefly a response that we should *not* make. We saw earlier that even if neither being married nor being single has any inherent value, the fact that X wants to marry Y can itself give X a good reason to marry Y. We saw, further, that if X does choose to marry Y for this reason, X's choice can indeed be autonomous. But if so, then it may seem that C's choice of W can similarly qualify as autonomous; for even if C's preference for W is not *grounded* in a good reason to adopt W, that preference itself may *provide* C with such a reason. If it does, then C's choice of W will indeed be grounded in a good reason and, hence, will be made autonomously, as long as C chooses W in response to the reason that is thus provided.

The problem with this rejoinder is that it ignores the special requirements imposed by the current context. Because our aim is to find out whether C's choice of W can actualize W's (potential) value, our question is not merely whether C's choice of W is autonomous in the sense of being a response to *some* sufficiently strong reason. Instead, it is whether C's choice of W satisfies the more stringent requirement of being a response to a sufficiently strong reason *that is provided by W's potential value.* Of course, the mere fact that C's immediate reason is his preference for W does not show that C is *not* responding to W's (potential) value; for many preferences are themselves grounded in deeper reasons. But because C's preference for W has by hypothesis been nonrationally instilled, that cannot be the case here. Hence, for present purposes, C's choice of W must indeed be nonautonomous.

This, I think, is (one of) the grain(s) of truth in the widely held view that nonrationally influencing people's preferences undermines their autonomy. But although the point is not insubstantial, it falls far short of establishing that governments can not induce their citizens to live valuable lives by nonrationally influencing their preferences. To establish that, one would have to show not merely that C's *initial* choice of W is nonautonomous, but also that its lack of autonomy infects any *further* choices to which it leads. Yet even if C does choose W nonautonomously at t_1, his resulting later choice(s) of W may surely have a different status. Precisely *by* living the life he was nonrationally caused to prefer, C may become increasingly aware of the value-based reasons for living that way. He may come to appreciate W's (potential) value "from the inside." By putting C in a position to do this, his choosing W at t_1 may enable him to respond at t_2 to the reasons provided by W's (potential) value. If at t_2 C does choose W on this basis, then C's nonrational conditioning *will* have led him to choose W in a way that actualizes its (potential) value.

This is far more than a bare logical possibility. We have all known students who were first influenced to take up a subject by a respected teacher, but who later made it their life's work because they recognized its beauty or depth, or because they were challenged by its puzzles. We also know people who at first acted truthfully and fairly to avoid punishment or to please their parents, but who now act in these ways because they recognize the interests of others. In these and many other cases, the agent's behavior eventually acquires whatever value his initial failure to respond to the appropriate reasons may have caused it to lack. Even if the later behavior is overdetermined – even if either the original nonrationally acquired preference *or* the agent's new appreciation of reasons would now be sufficient to motivate it – there is no reason to deny that it has value.[26] And the same holds, mutatis mutandis, of the behavior of citizens who have come to appreciate the reasons for continuing to live in the ways that they were nonrationally caused to prefer.

Thus, nonrationally induced preferences can indeed lead individuals to make choices that are autonomous enough to actualize the (potential) value of what is chosen. But what, next, of *incentives* to adopt (potentially) valuable ways of life? Although incentives are less widely regarded as threats to autonomy than conditioning, they

26. For pertinent discussion, see George Sher and William J. Bennett, "Moral Education and Indoctrination," *Journal of Philosophy* 79, 11 (November 1982), pp. 665–77.

too provide reasons for choosing that are unconnected to the (potential) value of what is chosen. Hence, choices motivated by incentives must also lack the autonomy that (we are assuming) is alone capable of actualizing (potential) value. Indeed, in one respect, incentives are actually *more* inimical to autonomy than nonrational conditioning; for while preferences instilled by conditioning can generally coexist with the appreciation of (potential) value, incentives are apt to divert attention from the (potential) value of what they make attractive. In this way, incentives can actively prevent agents from responding to (potential) value.[27]

Here again, however, an influence that does not at first lead someone to choose something for the right reasons may in the longer run do precisely that. Like choices based on nonrationally conditioned preferences, choices that are directed at incentives, and hence are unconnected to the (potential) value of what is chosen, may themselves put agents in a position to appreciate that (potential) value "from the inside." If as a result an agent subsequently does respond to an activity's (potential) value, the incentive *will* indirectly have led him to choose it autonomously. Moreover, while incentives admittedly can divert attention from value-based reasons, they can also cancel the effects of counterincentives that otherwise would themselves divert attention from such reasons. For example, by subsidizing artistic projects, a government can reduce the need for artists to undertake commercial ventures, and thus can free them to respond to more purely aesthetic considerations.

Our third method of promoting valuable activities – the creation and sustenance of valuable options – may seem even less threatening to autonomy. Unlike its predecessors, this method does not seem even to diminish anyone's *present* ability to respond to value-based reasons. Instead, when governments codify and enforce what they consider potentially valuable types of arrangements – when, for example, they extend official approval and protection to monogamous but not polygamous marriages – they appear only to enrich the array of value-based reasons to which their citizens may respond. Hence,

27. Compare Jeremy Waldron: "The trouble with a perfectionist tax is that it provides a reason for refraining from an activity that is not one of what I have called 'the merits' of the case. A subsidy would be objectionable on similar grounds if it were so substantial as to provide a positive inducement to an activity thought to be noble. We would then worry because people were responding, not to the nobility of the activity, but to the bribe that was being offered for pursuing it" (Waldron, "Autonomy and Perfectionism in Raz's *Morality of Freedom*," *Southern California Law Review* 62 [1989], p. 1147).

this method of promoting valuable activities may seem entirely unproblematical.

But on closer inspection, the issue is not this simple; for, as Jeremy Waldron has argued, "[t]he decision to favor one type of relationship with a legal framework but not another artificially distorts people's estimate of which sort of relationship is morally preferable."[28] To make this estimate without distortion,

[E]veryone who chooses to live with another and to make a life together has to contemplate the possibility that things may go wrong. The relationship may break up or one of the partners may die, and then property and financial entanglements will have to be sorted out. One of the partners may fall ill. . . . Even if things do not go wrong, they may be complicated. A child may be born, and questions will then arise about who should take care of it and make decisions about its future.[29]

Thus, to choose monogamy autonomously, one must do so (at least partly) because it generates fewer complications than polygamy. However, in sanctioning monogamous but not polygamous marriages, "[t]he government has decided on the basis of *its* estimate of these factors to distort the matter by making it *even easier* for monogamous couples to sort these problems out than for polygamists."[30] By thus making it more difficult to respond to monogamy's true measure of (potential) value, a government does reduce the chances that its citizens will choose it autonomously.

Although I doubt that monogamy's (potential) value has much to do with the relative ease with which monogamists can "sort out problems," Waldron may be right to say that governments that recognize only monogamous marriages provide what amount to artificial incentives to choose monogamy over polygamy. But even if he is right, this will hardly save the case for neutralism. The reason, of course, is that in that case, the same considerations that showed that *incentives* can induce citizens to respond to (potential) value will also show this about the state's attempts to create new options. Thus, even if this third method of inducing citizens to live good lives is no less threatening to autonomy than the first two, it is at least no more threatening either.

28. Ibid., p. 1151.
29. Ibid.
30. Ibid.

VI

I have now discussed three of the four ways in which governments can use their power to promote the good. The fourth way – the use of threats and force – will be considered shortly. However, before I turn to it, I must consider the objection that even if the first three methods sometimes do lead citizens to choose the good autonomously, they do not do so often enough to tip the balance against neutralism.

This objection trades on two concessions that were made earlier. I conceded above that only *some* of the persons who are induced by nonrational conditioning or incentives to adopt (potentially) valuable ways of life will eventually respond to their (potential) value. I conceded, as well, that the choices that stem more immediately from nonrationally conditioned preferences and incentives are *not* autonomous in the relevant sense. But given these concessions, can't a neutralist still insist that many people's lives will have more value if their government does *not* try to shape their preferences or provide them with incentives? And, hence, isn't the consequentialist case for rejecting neutralism inconclusive at best?

I think, in fact, that this suggestion badly underestimates our ability to make reasonable predictions. While not all incentives or nonrationally induced preferences are equally likely to increase an agent's later responsiveness to (potential) value, we can say a good deal about the conditions under which these effects are likely. Where those conditions are met, there is every reason to believe that the agent's later choices will actualize enough (potential) value to outweigh any earlier losses.

But this is not the main problem with the current suggestion. A further (and in my view more decisive) difficulty is that no government can *avoid* either nonrationally shaping its citizens' preferences or providing them with incentives. Even if governments do not try to produce these effects, they are bound to occur as unintended consequences of many political arrangements – including, importantly, many arrangements that are adopted for quite different reasons. It was, indeed, precisely this sort of fact that led us to interpret neutralism as ruling out not all political arrangements with value-promoting *effects*, but rather all political reasoning that *appeals to* such effects. By taking neutralism to forbid only the adoption of political arrangements *because* they will issue in preferences or incentives that favor certain ways of life, we can acknowledge that all political arrangements will have such effects without concluding that it is impossible to be a neutralist.

But the same considerations that compelled this reinterpretation now suggest that if a government knows which ways of living are (potentially) best, it can definitely increase overall value through the judicious use of conditioning and incentives. The reason, in brief, is that if all political arrangements do nonrationally shape preferences and provide incentives, a government will not *further* diminish autonomy simply by producing these effects intentionally. It will only further diminish autonomy if it shapes preferences or provides incentives in ways that undermine responsiveness to reasons more than it would be undermined in any event. Thus, if a government makes no effort to promote value by conditioning preferences and providing incentives, the result will be no gain in autonomy, but only a lessening in the number of citizens who live in the ways that the government considers (potentially) valuable. Since by hypothesis those ways of life *are* (potentially) valuable, this means that fewer citizens will be put in a position to appreciate their (potential) value from the inside, and hence that fewer citizens will eventually respond to it. Thus, the ultimate effect of neutralism will be to prevent at least some citizens from living valuable lives.[31]

VII

Far from ruling out all four methods of promoting valuable ways of life, autonomy's contribution to value has been found to be compatible with at least three. But we have yet to consider its bearing on what many regard as the core thesis of neutralism. This, of course, is the thesis that governments should never use force (or threats of force) to promote ways of life they consider valuable, or to deter behavior that does not harm others but is viewed as ignoble, base, or

31. In making this argument, I assume that however much conditioning interferes with autonomy, it does leave room for at least some autonomous choices. Some thinkers, such as B. F. Skinner, reject this assumption; see, for example, Skinner, *Beyond Freedom and Dignity* (New York: Knopf, 1971). If a neutralist followed Skinner in rejecting it but retained the premise that only autonomously chosen lives have value, he could recast his argument by inferring, first, that all attempts to promote valuable ways of life are doomed and, second, that any available funds should be spent in pursuit of more achievable aims. But in addition to invoking (what I take to be) an extremely implausible premise, this move would transform what began as an appeal to the value of autonomy into an appeal to its impossibility. This would entirely fail to capture the argument's original intent.

degraded. A prohibition against such "legal moralism" is sometimes regarded as the sole consequence of the appeal to autonomy's (contribution to) value, and is always regarded as its most important consequence.

It is not hard to see why. Although threats do not so much undermine responsiveness to reasons as alter the reasons to which agents can respond, threats resemble incentives and conditioned preferences in that none of the choices that they motivate are grounded in the (potential) value of what is chosen. Hence, no such choices can be autonomous in the sense that concerns us. Moreover, in addition to being just as destructive to autonomy as the other methods, the use of force is much easier for governments to avoid. While eliminating one form of conditioning only opens the way for others, and while removing one incentive may only make others more attractive, a government that decriminalizes one class of acts need not compensate by criminalizing another. Although every government needs some criminal justice system, governments may punish their citizens for wider or narrower ranges of activities. Hence, if a government does not pass laws against (what it considers) base, ignoble, or degrading behavior, it will genuinely reduce the number of reasons that compete with the reasons provided by (potential) value.

In view of this, it is not surprising that the second premise of the argument designed to ground neutralism in autonomy's contribution to value – the premise that government efforts to promote good lives do not lead to autonomous choices – is most often couched in terms of threats or force.[32] Thus construed, the premise asserts that it is either useless or self-defeating for a government to force its citizens to lead good lives because any activity that is undertaken to avoid punishment is *ex hypothesi* not undertaken because of its (potential) value. Yet while this version of the premise may be less decisively false than its predecessors, it is vulnerable to essentially the same reply: that even if a choice is not itself a response to (potential) value, it may contribute to further choices that *are* responses to (potential) value.

32. To cite just one example, Will Kymlicka seems mainly concerned with threats and force when he writes that "[s]ince lives have to be led from the inside, someone's essential interest in leading a life that is in fact good is not advanced when society penalizes, or discriminates against, the projects that she, on reflection, believes are most valuable for her" (Kymlicka, "Rawls on Teleology and Deontology," *Philosophy and Public Affairs* 17, 3 [Summer 1988], p. 186). Kymlicka suggests that similar claims are attributable to Mill, Rawls, Nozick, and Ronald Dworkin (ibid., p. 187, n. 20).

Before I elaborate the reply as it applies to threats and coercion, it may again be helpful to introduce some examples. Many laws forbid or seriously restrict activities that do not harm others in any straightforward way. These activities include, among others, copulating in public places, defecating in public, using profane language on television or radio, selling bodily organs, selling babies, gambling, and using narcotic drugs. Although some of the laws clearly have nonperfectionist aims – human waste endangers health, gambling and narcotics are said to attract organized crime[33] – they also appear to be informed by a widely shared vision of what sorts of lives are decent and worthy. Although the notion of decency can easily seem quaint or even priggish, I believe (and I will argue in Chapter 9) that it represents a deep and significant evaluative category. I believe, too, that it is a notion that few persons, either in our own age or in others, would altogether wish to discard. And while I have already conceded that anyone who is deterred by laws against the cited activities is not responding to the (potential) value of a decent and worthy life, it is not hard to see how the laws can make eventual responses to that (potential) value more likely.

For, first, if an agent avoids narcotic drugs, he will obviously not become addicted. Thus, even if his choice is not autonomous, it will protect his later capacity to respond to (potential) value – including, but not restricted to, the (potential) value of a drug-free life. If his behavior provides an example to others, or reduces the peer pressure on them, the choice that he made in order to avoid punishment may also help to protect *their* capacity to respond to (potential) value. Similarly, if an agent is in danger of becoming a compulsive gambler, his nonautonomous decision not to gamble may protect his later capacity to respond to (potential) value. By attaching penalties to such autonomy-threatening behavior, the law acknowledges that disvaluable as well as valuable activities can be most attractive "from the inside."

This, however, is not the main point; for although any activity can become a habit, most disvaluable behavior is neither especially addictive nor especially destructive of one's general capacity to respond to value. But even when the general capacity remains intact, repeated exposure to disvaluable activities can reduce one's sen-

---

33. Of course, in response to this justification, it can be replied that gambling and narcotics attract organized crime precisely because they *are* illegal; for discussion, see Ethan A. Nadelman, "The Case for Legalization," *Public Interest* 92 (Summer 1988), pp. 3–31.

sitivity to specific *kinds* of value or disvalue. Hence, an even more important rationale for laws against disvaluable behavior is that those laws create and sustain the conditions under which such sensitivity can thrive.

This, I think, is the most significant effect of laws that attach penalties to coarse and licentious activities. Where such activities abound, it becomes difficult even to envision, much less to see the appeal of, the richer but subtler possibilities of a more refined sensibility. But by creating an environment in which (at least outward) decency and civility prevail, the law can inscribe a measure of these qualities in the public culture. Moreover, since there is no clear boundary between the public culture and our inner lives, all citizens can thereby be made acquainted with the texture of decent, civil lives and the possibilities these afford. Assuming that decency and civility really are (potentially) valuable, all citizens will thus be put in a better position to appreciate their (potential) value and, hence, to choose them for the right reasons. And, although I think the argument is less promising, a similar case can be made that prohibiting the sale of bodily organs curtails commercialism while increasing responsiveness to the demands of altruism.[34]

Of course, none of this shows (or is intended to show) that governments should criminalize any major part of the behavior that most citizens consider disvaluable. Even if we assume, unrealistically, that the majority's unreflective judgments are usually correct, some disfavored activities – watching and reading pornography are standard examples – may become less rather than more attractive with repetition. These may best be allowed to extinguish or stabilize themselves. Others, such as gambling, become addictive to comparatively few. Still others, such as disapproved sexual behavior, are detectable only through massive invasions of privacy, or are preventable only by laws that are so intrusive as to elicit strong resentment. A person who is forced to curtail his sexual proclivities, or to endure religious prohibitions he does not accept, is more apt to despise than to internalize his society's way of life. Hence, threatening him with punishment is unlikely to increase the value of what he subsequently chooses.

34. See Richard Titmuss, *The Gift Relationship* (New York: Random House, Pantheon Books, 1971). For an interesting exchange on Titmuss's book, see Kenneth J. Arrow, "Gifts and Exchanges," *Philosophy and Public Affairs* 1, 4 (Summer 1972), pp. 343–62, and Peter Singer, "Altruism and Commerce," *Philosophy and Public Affairs* 2, 3 (Spring 1973), pp. 312–20.

Yet these facts demand not that governments altogether avoid using the criminal law to promote valuable choices, but only that they temper its use with good judgment. They suggest that before any government uses force to encourage the better or suppress the worse, it must ask both how successful the effort is likely to be and whether any expected gains are important enough to warrant overriding the general presumption in favor of liberty and noninterference. If there are no deeper objections, a government that wishes its citizens to live the best possible lives must neither use coercion indiscriminately nor withhold it altogether, but must consider each occasion on its merits.

The interesting question, of course, is whether there *are* deeper objections. In this chapter, I have maintained that if one argues that all departures from neutrality undermine the autonomy that valuable choices require, one makes a consequentialist argument that is defeated by the contributions of nonautonomous choices *to* autonomous ones. Yet precisely because our target has been a defense of neutralism that appeals to consequences, we may be said to have missed the real point. According to many, the real significance of autonomy is not that it is (or contributes to) a value that should be maximized, but that it is a source of rights or an object of respect. On their account, what autonomy demands is precisely that we treat each person's assessment of his own situation, and any decisions he bases on it, as decisive *whether or not* we have good grounds for expecting them to bring about a net loss of value. Autonomy thus enters not as a locus, ingredient, or prerequisite of value, but as a constraint on its pursuit.

Clearly this second version of the appeal to autonomy requires separate treatment. To assess it properly, we must investigate both the basis of the obligation to respect even wrong decisions and the exact scope and content of that obligation. To these matters, I now turn.

Chapter 4

Autonomy and neutrality (2)

The appeal to respect for autonomy is not a single, tightly focused argument, but a loosely related family of defenses of neutralism. Their central contentions are, first, that each person must be treated as a rational agent, capable of shaping his own destiny, and, second, that a government violates this injunction whenever it tries to advance any particular conception of the good.[1] Because all such arguments invoke a (near-)outright prohibition on government efforts to promote the good, they all sidestep the problem of balancing autonomy against competing values. As I shall argue, however, they win this advantage only at the cost of raising serious new problems.

1. Although this way of defending neutralism is instantly recognizable, and is very much in the air, it is often intertwined with arguments of very different sorts. For example, in the last chapter we found David A. J. Richards arguing that a "general right of personal autonomy" has its "source in the value of autonomy." As presented there, Richards's argument seemed a clear instance of the appeal to the *value* of autonomy. But a few lines later, Richards goes on to remark that "only by allowing people themselves to assume final normative responsibility in making these choices over a wide range of cases . . . can we secure the desired respect for the basic higher-order capacities of the person to accept with dignity the responsibility for her or his life as a free and rational being" (Richards, "Human Rights and Moral Ideals: An Essay on the Moral Theory of Liberalism," *Social Theory and Practice* 5, 3–4 [1980], p. 474). Again, although Charles Larmore first defends neutralism as a mere modus vivendi for people with very different visions of the good, he then wonders "why we should continue to talk with those who neither stand at least close to us in their views nor have enough power to make us pay attention" (Larmore, *Patterns of Moral Complexity* [Cambridge: Cambridge University Press, 1987], p. 60). His answer is that we have a duty to display equal respect toward all persons, and that doing so involves acknowledging that others are "capable of coherently developing beliefs from within their own perspective (although not necessarily on their own, or autonomously)" (ibid., pp. 63–64). If this is not exactly the argument that interests us, it certainly comes close. And, as I shall argue, other interesting versions of the argument can be extracted from the celebrated theories of John Rawls and Ronald Dworkin.

72

I

One obvious problem is that the argument's central notion – respect for autonomy – is very vague. We clearly fail to respect somone's autonomy when we coerce him to do our bidding. Even if we coerce him "for his own good," we show disrespect by preventing him from choosing as *he* thinks best. But does the state similarly disrespect its citizens' autonomy when, for example, it tries to shape their preferences in nonrational ways? If so, exactly what is disrespectful about taking (benign) advantage of a causal process that would occur anyhow? And what about providing incentives to make certain options more attractive? Does this disrespect an agent's autonomy by preventing him from evaluating his options on their merits? Or does it respect his autonomy by giving him more attractive options *to* evaluate?

As these questions suggest, any serviceable notion of respect for autonomy would require a good deal of clarification. But instead of trying to work out the details, I want to move directly to the notion's normative core. This I take to be its implication that in the political context, our usual reasons for promoting the good simply have *no weight*. It is not that they are outweighed or overridden, but that from the beginning they must be put altogether out of play. Though not always made explicit, this idea clearly underlies the view that autonomy is not a value to be balanced against others, but rather a constraint on the pursuit of value. And, as I see it, the fundamental question is why we should *accept* any such constraint. Why *should* considerations that have weight in most contexts have none at all in this one? Why, if it really matters that citizens live good lives, should an activity's goodness provide no reason at all for the state to promote it?[2]

At first glance, this may look like a special case of a far more general question; for *many* ways of achieving worthy goals seem morally off limits. Two familiar examples are torturing a captured soldier to extract information and killing a healthy person to obtain his organs for redistribution. Even if torturing the soldier would

---

2. In *Practical Reason and Norms* (1975; Princeton: Princeton University Press, 1990), Joseph Raz defines an exclusionary reason as "a second-order reason to refrain from acting for some reason" (p. 39). Couched in Raz's terms, my question is why the state should be thought to have an exclusionary reason for not acting on the first-order reason provided by an activity's goodness.

spare others far greater suffering, and even if killing one would allow us to save several, we remain reluctant to torture or kill. Thus, here too, what are normally strong reasons (to prevent suffering and save lives) are thought to lack their usual weight.

But, whatever their rationale, these standard deontological constraints are importantly different from the needed respect-for-autonomy constraint. To see the difference, consider one familiar attempt to justify the standard constraints. According to John Rawls, the reason we may neither torture people to extract vital information nor kill them to obtain their organs is that one person's losses cannot be offset by the gains – even the greater gains – of others. Balancing different people's gains and losses, Rawls argues, does not treat individuals as distinct and inviolable moral units, but instead traces their moral importance to their membership in some larger social whole. In this way, any view that seeks exclusively to maximize the good "does not take seriously the distinction between persons."[3]

Although this familiar argument obviously requires close scrutiny, it stands at least a chance of justifying the standard constraints. However, and in stark contrast, it stands no chance of justifying a constraint against government efforts to induce citizens to live good lives. The reason it cannot be extended is that such efforts typically do not sacrifice the interests of some to advance the interests of others, but rather seek to advance the interests of *each* affected party. Thus, against them, the charge of ignoring the distinctness of persons is obviously without weight.

Rawls's argument, of course, may not be the best way to justify the standard constraints. If some better justification exists, it may also justify a respect-for-autonomy constraint. For that matter, even if Rawls's argument is the best justification, the two sorts of constraint may still be linked at some deeper level. They may, for example, both be consequences of the single Kantian injunction to treat all persons as ends in themselves and never merely as means. But, at least if treating someone as an end involves taking his own aims seriously, the prospects for establishing this sort of linkage are called into question by a *second* disanalogy.

For unlike torture and killing, which straightforwardly *thwart* their victims' aims, a government's efforts to improve its citizens' lives are standardly related to their aims in a more complicated way. The

3. John Rawls, *A Theory of Justice* (Cambridge, Mass.: Harvard University Press, 1971), p. 27.

source of the complication is that citizens themselves often aim at what they see as good. As many have noted, agents often make choices because "[t]hey believe that the objects of their desires or their pursuits are valuable (and sometimes that the pursuit itself is valuable not merely as a means to achieve its object)."[4] This, of course, does not make any citizen's aims *identical* to those of a government that seeks to improve his life: whatever the overlap, there remains an important difference between trying to live a good life and trying to induce *another* to live a good life. But what does follow is that both aims will equally be frustrated if the citizen does not in fact live a good life. And, hence, whereas any government that tries to induce a citizen to live as it, but not he, correctly thinks good will indeed act against one of his own aims (i.e., that he not live that way), any government that *refrains* from inducing a citizen to live as it, but not he, correctly thinks good will *also* act against one of his own aims (i.e., that his life in fact be good). Just what this shows about the relation between trying to improve a person's life and taking his own aims seriously is obscure.

Needless to say, none of this shows that some strong respect-for-autonomy constraint cannot be defended. In the end, the view that our usual reasons to promote the good lack weight in the political context may be exactly right. But given the view's problematic relations to the other constraints, it cannot borrow its authority from them. In order to assess its prospects, we must ask whether it is independently defensible.

Unfortunately, that question is hard to answer because there are so many possible starting points. If certain reasons have no weight in political contexts, or if all governments or their agents must put certain reasons entirely out of play, the explanation may turn either on some special feature of the political context or on some more general consideration. If the explanation lies in some feature of the political context, the relevant feature may be either the state's monopoly on force or else one of the conditions – whatever these are – whose satisfaction makes a government legitimate. If instead the explanation turns on some more general consideration, this may be either some aspect of personhood or some requirement of practical

---

4. Joseph Raz, *The Morality of Freedom* (Oxford: Oxford University Press, 1986), p. 140. See also Charles Taylor, "What's Wrong with Negative Liberty?" in *Philosophy and the Human Sciences: Philosophical Papers* 2 (Cambridge: Cambridge University Press, 1985), pp. 211–29, and E. J. Bond, *Reason and Value* (Cambridge: Cambridge University Press, 1983).

reason. And, of course, there are many other potential starting points, many ways of developing each, and many ways of combining their insights.

Because the situation is so fluid, we cannot march through the possibilities in orderly fashion. But, as it happens, the theories of two of the most prominent neutralists both have strong respect-for-autonomy components. Despite their differences, John Rawls and Ronald Dworkin have both argued that governments should entirely disregard what in other contexts are strong reasons to promote the good. Moreover, they both ground this view not in any form of skepticism,[5] but in certain explicitly normative considerations. Taking my cue from this, I shall simply allow their theories to dictate which arguments I consider. If neither can justify the needed constraint, we may tentatively reject the respect-for-autonomy approach.

II

It has always been clear that autonomy plays some prominent role in Rawls's thought. Even in *A Theory of Justice,* Rawls emphasized that

The parties' aim in the original position is to establish just and favorable conditions for each to fashion his own unity. Their fundamental interest in liberty and in the means to make fair use of it is the expression of their seeing themselves as primarily moral persons with an equal right to choose their mode of life.[6]

---

5. Both philosophers explicitly deny that their positions rest on any form of skepticism. Thus, in *A Theory of Justice,* Rawls stated that "I have not contended that the criteria of excellence lack a rational basis from the standpoint of everyday life" (p. 328). In a more recent essay ("The Idea of an Overlapping Consensus," *Oxford Journal of Legal Studies* 7, 1 [February 1987]), he added that "[i]n following the method of avoidance, as we may call it, we try, so far as we can, neither to assert nor to deny any religious, philosophical, or moral views, or their associated philosophical accounts of truth and the status of values" (pp. 12–13). Similarly, Dworkin has written that "skepticism seems exactly the wrong answer to make, because if the moral majority is wrong, and each person should be free to choose personal ideals for himself, then this is surely because the choice of one life over another is a matter of supreme importance, not because it is of no importance at all" ("Neutrality, Equality, and Liberalism," in Douglas MacLean and Claudia Mills, eds., *Liberalism Reconsidered* [Totowa, N.J.: Rowman and Allanheld, 1983], p. 2).
6. Rawls, *A Theory of Justice,* p. 563.

In later essays, Rawls continued to stress the links between moral personhood and what is usually called autonomy:

[W]e take moral persons to be characterized by two moral powers and by two corresponding highest-order interests in realizing and exercising these powers. The first power is the capacity for an effective sense of justice, that is, the capacity to understand, to apply and to act from (and not merely in accordance with) the principles of justice. The second moral power is the capacity to form, to revise, and rationally to pursue a conception of the good. Corresponding to the moral powers, moral persons are said to be moved by two highest-order interests to realize and exercise these powers.[7]

And in his recent book *Political Liberalism*, Rawls has added that

citizens' rational autonomy is modeled in the original position by the way the parties deliberate as their representatives. By contrast, citizens' full autonomy is modeled by the structural aspects of the original position, that is, by how the parties are situated with respect to one another and by the limits on information to which their deliberations are subject.[8]

As these passages suggest (and many others confirm), the idea of a link between certain autonomy-related features of persons and the design of the original position has been a constant theme in Rawls's work.

But while this theme has remained constant, the way it is worked out, and the context in which it is embedded, have undergone important changes. *A Theory of Justice* can easily be read, and often has been read, as an extended argument for a universally applicable set of principles of justice. On this reading, the argument's premises are put forth as plausible candidates for truth; and its conclusions – the principles themselves – are said to apply to all societies that have attained a certain level of material prosperity. Because the argument includes both a defense of the original position and an attempt to show that Rawls's principles would be chosen by the persons in it, the design of the original position is one of the argument's important intermediate conclusions. Moreover, a central component of that design is precisely a "veil of ignorance" that prevents each party

7. John Rawls, "Kantian Constructivism in Moral Theory: The Dewey Lectures 1980," *Journal of Philosophy* 77, 9 (September 1980), p. 525.
8. John Rawls, *Political Liberalism* (New York: Columbia University Press, 1993), p. 77.

from knowing his conception of the good. Thus, on this reading, the neutrality that the original position imposes upon the derivation of the principles is itself an implication of the argument's putatively true premises, and so, at one remove, is the neutrality that Rawls (at some points) takes the principles to impose on the justifications of particular laws and policies.[9]

However, in his more recent work, Rawls has explicitly disavowed this interpretation. He now refuses either to affirm or to deny that his normative premises are true (or that they have any other determinate metaphysical status); and neither does he now represent his principles as universally applicable. Instead, Rawls now presents his theory only as a (favored) realization of certain fundamental ideas, including a conception of persons as free and equal and a conception of society as a fair scheme of cooperation over generations, which draw their authority from their centrality within our own political culture. What is important about these ideas is simply their wide tacit acceptance, as manifested in "the political institutions of [our] constitutional regime and the public traditions of their interpretation (including those of the judiciary), as well as historic texts and documents that are common knowledge."[10] Correspondingly, Rawls's principles of justice are now put forth only as a reasonable political morality for us here and now. In its current incarnation, justice as fairness is said to be "political not metaphysical."

Why has Rawls thus recast his theory? The reason, he says, is that he previously failed to appreciate that a "modern democratic society is characterized not simply by a pluralism of comprehensive religious, philosophical, and moral doctrines but by a pluralism of incompatible yet reasonable comprehensive doctrines."[11] Because a reasonable pluralism is inescapable in any modern democratic society, any theory that presupposes a single philosophical, moral, or religious outlook will be unacceptable to many citizens who hold incompatible but no less reasonable views. Such a theory will not be capable of gaining the assent of adherents of all or even most reasonable doctrines, and so will not be able to "win sufficiently wide support to achieve stability."[12] Hence, to find the common ground that social stability requires, Rawls now advocates "looking to the

---

9. For examples, see Chapter 2, section IV of this book.
10. Rawls, *Political Liberalism*, pp. 13–14.
11. Ibid., p. xvi.
12. Ibid., p. 39.

public culture itself as the shared fund of implicitly recognized basic ideas and principles."[13]

Because Rawls's substantive theory can be interpreted in such different ways, there must also be different ways of reconstructing its inferential route(s) to neutralism. Hence, instead of considering that theory as a (diachronic) whole, I shall examine the different stages of its development separately. This will mean discussing, first, a number of arguments that are suggested primarily by Rawls's earlier writings and, next, arguments that are suggested primarily by his later work. In both cases, I shall be less concerned with fidelity to Rawls's texts or intentions than with exploring the resources of the respect-for-autonomy argument.

III

Let us begin with *A Theory of Justice;* and let us ask why, in that book, premises about the good life are not allowed to shape the principles of justice. Because all conceptions of the good are put out of play by the veil of ignorance, this is tantamount to asking how (Rawls's version of) the veil can be defended.

The veil, Rawls says, is a device whose aim is to insure "that no one is advantaged or disadvantaged in the choice of principles by the outcome of natural chance or the contingency of social circumstance."[14] This suggests that his reason for placing all conceptions of the good behind it may be simply that they are *among* the "morally arbitrary" contingencies he wishes to exclude. That is, Rawls may wish to exclude conceptions of the good because he regards them as direct causal consequences of factors that could easily have been different, and over which agents lack control. These factors may include either each person's genetic makeup or (more plausibly) some form of social conditioning. This reading draws support from the fact that Rawls explicitly refers to conceptions of the good in the passage that contains the quoted sentence. It also draws support from one of his reasons for allowing the parties in the original position to want only primary goods – that is, for allowing them to want only those things that it is rational to want *whatever* else one wants. For at one point Rawls defends this stipulation precisely on the grounds that "the social system shapes the [more particular] wants

13. Ibid., p. 8.
14. Rawls, *A Theory of Justice,* p. 12.

and aspirations that its citizens come to have."[15] Because Rawls does not draw a sharp line between a person's wants and aspirations and his conception of the good, he may take the contingency of people's wants and aspirations to extend to, and thus infect, their conceptions of the good as well.

Still, despite these hints, the current proposal – that our beliefs about the good life are too contingent to play any role in shaping the principles of justice – is not really compatible either with all the facts or with the respect-for-autonomy strand of Rawls's own argument. For, to take the second point first, our capacity to form, revise, and pursue a conception of the good would not be morally significant if the way we exercise it were entirely a function of natural or social forces. If forming, revising, and pursuing a conception of the good did not have an important rational component – if the use of reason did not figure prominently at each stage – then the exercise of this capacity could hardly qualify as a "highest-order interest." Hence, when Rawls says that the capacity's exercise *is* among our highest-order interests, he must indeed assume that persons can reflectively assess, and on that basis alter, even desires and aims whose origins were merely contingent.

Moreover, quite apart from its role in Rawls's theory, this view is surely correct. Even a moral skeptic must concede that we often think and reason seriously about the good. There is, indeed, just as much difference between socially inculcated desires and reflectively acquired ends as there is between inherited prejudices and re-flectively acquired beliefs. Thus, whatever else we say about conceptions of the good, we cannot refuse to allow them to influence our reasoning about justice merely on the basis of their social or natural origins. If we did, then not only all conceptions of the good, but also all other (normative and nonnormative) beliefs – including, of course, any that Rawls advances to support his own "Archimedean point" – would lack any moral or practical authority.

A second possible reason for placing conceptions of the good behind the veil seems consistent with these facts. At some points, Rawls talks as though the crucial fact about conceptions of the good is not that they are *shaped by* factors external to the self, but is, rather, that they *themselves* are external to the self. This, for instance, appears to be the thrust of his assertion that

15. Ibid., p. 259.

[w]e should not attempt to give form to our life by first looking to the good independently defined. It is not our aims that primarily reveal our nature but rather the principles that we would acknowledge to govern the background conditions under which these aims are to be formed and the manner in which they are to be pursued. For the self is prior to the ends which are affirmed by it; even a dominant end must be chosen from among numerous possibilities. There is no way to get beyond deliberative rationality.[16]

Because this passage emphasizes the self's active, rational nature, it is very much in the spirit of the respect-for-autonomy argument. But in what sense, exactly, are selves "prior to their ends," and how does this justify placing all conceptions of the good (roughly, all specific ends) behind the veil?

In the quoted passage, Rawls appears to take the self's nature to be revealed precisely by the principles that it would choose in the original position. Moreover, those principles do limit the ends which the self may adopt or pursue: "[t]he principles of right, and so of justice, put limits on which satisfactions have value; they impose restrictions on what are reasonable conceptions of one's good."[17] Thus, if those principles do determine the self's nature, there is indeed a sense in which selves are prior to their ends. But because what is crucial about the principles is precisely that they *would* be chosen in the original position, this assertion of their priority must already *assume*, and so can hardly be used to *justify*, the design of that position. Hence, on this reading of the self's nature, it would be blatantly circular to invoke that nature to defend a veil that excludes all conceptions of the good.

Might some other interpretation of Rawls's view enable him to avoid this pitfall? The most promising move, I think, is to draw back from the view that the self's nature is revealed by any particular principles, and to say, instead, that its nature is revealed by its *general* capacity to evaluate its ends on a principled basis. By falling back just this far, Rawls might avoid the objection that his account of the self's nature presupposes, and so cannot be used to justify, the design of the original position. However, at the same time, he might preserve the core of the idea that the self is prior to its ends; for if the self *is* constituted by a general ability to reflect on its ends, then it cannot relinquish that capacity without ceasing to be the (kind of) self it is,

16. Ibid., p. 560.
17. Ibid., p. 31.

whereas it *can* relinquish any particular end – even one that is required by reason – without undergoing a similar transformation.

Does this revised version of Rawls's argument succeed? According to some communitarians, it fails because it rests on an inadequate ontology of the self. In particular, Michael J. Sandel has forcefully argued that each self has some commitments that *do* go so deep as to be essential or "constitutive." But although I agree that the proposed Rawlsian argument fails, I do not think its main error lies here. Instead, it seems to me that even if we do regard selves as ontologically prior to all their ends – and I shall argue in Chapter 7 that nothing Sandel says really rules this out – it simply does not follow that we may never appeal to premises about the good when we deliberate about justice.

The easiest way to see this is to generalize the argument. If someone's identity can survive even a change in his deepest views about what makes life meaningful or what is most worthwhile, then a fortiori it can survive a change in his views about other, less deep matters. We do not become different persons simply by altering our beliefs about (say) the laws of economics or psychology. But if so, and if the self's ability to remain the same despite changes in its conception of the good implies that we should not base our principles of justice on any such conceptions, then, by parity of reasoning, the self's ability to remain the same despite changes in any of its *other* beliefs must also imply that we must not base our principles of justice on any of *them.* But this last implication is plainly absurd. If we could not base our reasoning on *any* of our beliefs, then we would lack *any* rational basis upon which to evaluate competing principles of justice. Thus, here again, a natural extension of the argument would undermine Rawls's ability to defend his own "Archimedian point." Moreover, quite apart from this, the obvious criterion for whether any given belief should guide our thinking is not whether we could abandon it without loss of identity, but simply whether we have good grounds to think it true.

All in all, neither the contingency nor the mutability of the self's conception of the good provides any compelling reason for placing all such conceptions behind the veil. However, as Rawls correctly notes, any group of persons who *did* know all the particulars of their lives would find it hard to agree on a determinate set of principles. Even allowing them to know only their (perhaps radically divergent) beliefs about the good life might greatly complicate, if not altogether vitiate, their prospects for achieving consensus. Hence, to make agreement possible, such knowledge may have to be withheld. And this suggests, as a third possible reason for placing all conceptions of the good behind the veil of ignorance, that otherwise "we would not be able to work out any definite theory of justice at all."[18]

If we had to choose between Rawls's own version of hypothetical contractarianism and a version that allowed each party to know his own conception of the good, then this argument might have considerable force. However, in fact, we have many other options. Even if we remain within the Rawlsian framework, nothing yet said rules out augmenting the knowledge that Rawls himself allows the parties in the original position to have – knowledge of political affairs, economics, human psychology, and other general facts – with knowledge of one or a small number of well-supported views about the human good. Also, of course, nothing yet said shows why we should not altogether dispense with the contractarian trappings and simply derive our principles *directly* from premises about the good life. If we adopted either strategy, our conclusions would presumably be no less determinate than Rawls's own. Thus, whatever else Rawls says, he cannot justify concealing all conceptions of the good simply by invoking the need to achieve determinate results.

IV

Because *A Theory of Justice* is a long and complicated book, no cursory survey can conclusively demonstrate the failure of its arguments for neutralism. Still, the arguments just discussed are clearly important, and so their inadequacy does not bode well. Bearing this in mind, let us now turn to Rawls's later, more pragmatic work.

Rawls's later work is related to neutrality in two distinct ways. First, as we saw, he now presents his earlier theory as the favored realization of certain basic ideas of society and the person that he takes to be implicit in our public political culture. To whatever extent these shared ideas support his earlier theory, they also support its version of the original position. Hence, by extension, they support the neutrality that the original position imposes on the derivation of the principles of justice. But, second, when Rawls appeals to the shared ideas, he does so precisely on the grounds that any alternative defense of his theory must appeal to some "comprehensive religious,

18. Ibid., p. 140.

philosophical, or moral doctrine"[19] that cannot command general assent. Although what he calls comprehensive doctrines are not quite the same as what I have called conceptions of the good,[20] they are recognizably close relatives. Thus, when Rawls seeks to exclude appeals to all such doctrines, he is in effect espousing neutrality at a new and even more basic level.

The key move in all of this is clearly the exclusion of all comprehensive doctrines, so in what follows, I shall concentrate on the reasoning behind that move. Why does Rawls now think it important that a conception of justice be "as far as possible, independent of the opposing and conflicting philosophical and religious doctrines that citizens affirm . . . a freestanding view . . . a module, an essential constituent part, that fits into and can be supported by various reasonable comprehensive doctrines that endure in the society regulated by it?"[21] Why does he now want to "[apply] the principle of toleration to philosophy itself?"[22]

One possible answer is suggested by Joseph Raz. In an article published before *Political Liberalism* but after many of the essays it incorporates, Raz argued that despite his expressed intentions, Rawls is indeed committed to affirming at least one normative truth. He must do this because

> while the goal of political philosophy is purely practical – while it is not concerned to establish any evaluative truths – it accepts some such truths as the presuppositions which make its enterprise intelligible. It recognizes that social unity and stability based on a consensus – that is, achieved without excessive resort to force – are valuable goals of sufficient importance to make them and them alone the foundations of a theory of justice for our societies.[23]

In the second sentence of this passage, Raz interprets Rawls as arguing that if a (pluralistic) society is *not* organized around principles whose basis can be seen to be widely shared, it must be either unsta-

19. Rawls, *Political Liberalism,* p. 175.
20. On the one hand, they are broader than the views I have called conceptions of the good because these do not include religious or (all) philosophical doctrines. On the other hand, they are narrower because I have not previously required that a conception of the good "[cover] all recognized values and virtues within one rather precisely articulated scheme of thought" (ibid.).
21. Ibid., pp. 9, 12.
22. Ibid., p. 10.
23. Joseph Raz, "Facing Diversity: The Case of Epistemic Abstinence," *Philosophy and Public Affairs* 19, 1 (Winter 1990), p. 14.

ble or else oppressively coercive. Thus, as Raz reconstructs it, Rawls's argument rests on the single dominant value of uncoerced stability.

In the next chapter, I will contest the claim that a pluralistic society cannot be both stable and noncoercive unless its organizing principles are justifiable through an appeal to shared premises. Here, however, I want to make two different points. First, and most obviously, the central normative premise of the argument that Raz attributes to Rawls – the claim that uncoerced stability is the preeminent political value – is itself not universally accepted. While most of us do attach some value to stability, many would accept a degree of turbulence in return for a vital, dynamic society. Also, many would tolerate a fair amount of coercion in exchange for various other goods. Thus, on Raz's interpretation, Rawls's claim that no adequate theory of justice can be based on any controversial moral or philosophical doctrines is itself based on a controversial moral or philosophical doctrine. His argument thus violates at least the spirit, and perhaps also the letter, of its own conclusion.[24]

It also seems vulnerable to a further objection. As we saw, the great advantage of the respect-for-autonomy approach is that it treats autonomy not as a value to be pursued but rather as a constraint on the pursuit of value. This is significant because it eliminates the possibility of trade-offs between autonomy and other values. But if our autonomy-based constraint is rooted in an idea of the person whose importance lies in its common acceptance, and if the point of appealing exclusively to such ideas is simply to promote uncoerced stability, then the trade-off problem will only reappear at a new level. For even if uncoerced stability is more important than anything else – and that itself is by no means obvious – it will still be unclear why we should never regard some sacrifices in stability, or some amounts of coercion, as reasonable prices to pay for suitably large amounts of other goods.

Can Rawls provide a more convincing reason for excluding all comprehensive doctrines? To get a better sense of the possibilities, let

---

24. Compare Raz: "What about us, Rawls's readers? How are we to treat his arguments? Are we to accept his theory of justice as an autonomous political doctrine for the reasons he explains, or should each of us accept it as part of his or her comprehensive conception of the good? How does Rawls himself view his theory? Is it, in his eyes, part of an autonomous political theory with shallow foundations? Or is it part of his comprehensive conception of the good? One cannot have it both ways" (ibid., p. 22).

us look more closely at what he says. Rawls raises a version of our question when he asks

How can it be either reasonable or rational, when basic matters are at stake, for citizens to appeal only to a public conception of justice and not to the whole truth as they see it? Surely, the most fundamental questions should be settled by appealing to the most important truths, yet these may far transcend public reason![25]

To answer this question, Rawls invokes a principle that is rooted in two basic facts: first, that the political relationship is not something we choose but something into which we are born; and, second, that all government actions are backed by the state's overwhelming power.[26] These facts, he says, support a "principle of liberal legitimacy," which asserts that

our exercise of political power is proper and hence justifiable only when it is exercised in accordance with a constitution the essentials of which all citizens may reasonably be expected to endorse in the light of principles and ideals acceptable to them as reasonable and rational.[27]

Although Rawls does not take this principle to require the exclusion of comprehensive doctrines from all levels of political reasoning,[28] he does take it to require their exclusion from all reasoning about "questions arising in the legislature that concern or border on constitutional essentials, or basic questions of justice."[29]

This, however, does not follow from the principle as stated; for in its current form, that principle does not tell us *which* constitutional arrangements "all citizens may reasonably be expected to endorse." More specifically, nothing yet said shows that for each comprehensive doctrine, there are some citizens who cannot reasonably be expected to endorse any arrangements whose (only or actual) justification presupposes it. Thus, before we can evaluate Rawls's argument, we must get clearer about which arrangements a person *can* reasonably be expected to endorse.

---

25. Rawls, *Political Liberalism*, p. 216.
26. Ibid., pp. 216, 135–36.
27. Ibid., p. 217.
28. He says, for example, that "[c]itizens and legislators may properly vote their more comprehensive views when constitutional essentials and basic justice are not at stake" (ibid., p. 235).
29. Ibid., p. 137.

Because Rawls often appeals to the fact of pluralism – because he often stresses that, in any modern democratic society, each comprehensive doctrine is bound to be unacceptable to adherents of many *other* comprehensive doctrines – his benchmark for what someone can reasonably be expected to endorse may at first seem to be that person's own comprehensive doctrine. But on inspection, this cannot be Rawls's view; for many moral and religious doctrines imply that it is unreasonable, not merely to ground basic political arrangements in *other* doctrines, but also to exclude *them* from deliberation about basic political matters. The doctrines that claim authority over matters of basic justice and constitutional essentials include not only various views about salvation, but also such familiar secular views as act-utilitarianism.[30] Thus, if our actual comprehensive doctrines did determine what we can reasonably be expected to endorse, then Rawls's liberal principle of legitimacy could not support the exclusion of all comprehensive doctrines.

Rawls himself is well aware of this. He acknowledges the difficulty when he writes that

[i]f it is said that outside the church there is no salvation, and therefore a constitutional regime cannot be accepted unless it is unavoidable . . . we say that such a doctrine is unreasonable: it proposes to use the public's political power – a power in which citizens have an equal share – to enforce a view bearing on constitutional essentials about which citizens as reasonable persons are bound to differ uncompromisingly.[31]

In this passage, Rawls explicitly denies that a person's actual comprehensive doctrine is what determines what he may reasonably be expected to endorse. Instead, Rawls suggests that this at best depends on a person's comprehensive doctrine *if that doctrine is itself reasonable.*

This qualification, however, only shifts the problem; for now we cannot apply the principle of liberal legitimacy until we know when a comprehensive doctrine *is* reasonable. Rawls's own view is clearly that a comprehensive doctrine is unreasonable whenever it requires its own imposition on unwilling others; but by itself, this only restates what needs to be shown. Thus, to be convincing, the view needs some independent support. Moreover, that need is all the

30. For discussion of the relations between Rawls's theory (old and new versions) and utilitarianism, see Samuel Scheffler, "The Appeal of Political Liberalism," *Ethics* 105 (October 1994), pp. 9–11.
31. Rawls, *Political Liberalism*, p. 138.

more pressing because there are other, very different views of when a comprehensive doctrine is unreasonable. To cite just one alternative, we might combine the principle of liberal legitimacy with the view that an unreasonable comprehensive doctrine (or a comprehensive doctrine a political appeal to which cannot be reasonably endorsed) is simply one for which no adequate justification exists. On this alternative view, what determines whether a comprehensive doctrine is reasonable is simply the strength of the considerations that have been marshaled – or, perhaps, that can be marshaled – in its favor.

Before he can invoke the principle of liberal legitimacy, Rawls must defend his own view of what makes a comprehensive doctrine (un)reasonable. But how, exactly, could such a defense proceed? Ideally, it would appeal to the same facts that Rawls uses to justify the principle of liberal legitimacy itself. It would explain why, given the unavoidability and inherent coerciveness of the political relationship, we *must* regard as unreasonable any comprehensive doctrine that demands its own imposition on unwilling others. But, at least offhand, it is not obvious how this defense would run. Despite the cited features of the political relationship, it is unclear why a strong enough case for a given comprehensive doctrine could *not* vindicate its inclusion in deliberation about political essentials. Hence, at this crucial juncture, Rawls's argument remains badly incomplete.

V

He may, however, have the resources to complete it; for much of *Political Liberalism* deals precisely with what is reasonable. As Rawls himself says,

political constructivism specifies an idea of the reasonable and applies this idea to various subjects: conceptions and principles, judgments and grounds, persons and institutions. In each case, it must, of course, also specify criteria to judge whether the subject in question is reasonable.[32]

Although the specified criteria are tailored to the different subjects, the guiding thought is always that "we are to appeal only to presently accepted general beliefs and forms of reasoning found in common sense, and the methods and conclusions of science when these

32. Ibid., p. 94.

are not controversial."[33] Thus, before we end our discussion, we must consider the prospects for augmenting Rawls's argument with elements of his rich discussion of "public reason."

Unfortunately, those prospects are less promising than they initially appear; for much of what Rawls says about the reasonable is itself rooted in ideas from the public political culture – indeed, the very ideas of society and the person that he advances to support his substantive principles. As Rawls himself puts it, the notion of free public reason is an "essential companion conception"[34] to his political conception of justice; its "nature and content is . . . given by the ideals and principles expressed by society's conception of political justice."[35] This linkage is potentially damaging because our guiding question is precisely whether all reasoning about political essentials should be *restricted* to those shared ideas. Because this is our question, any answer that itself appeals exclusively to the shared ideas will immediately invite the charge of circularity.

However, in one section of *Political Liberalism*, Rawls suggests a line of argument that may seem to offer a way out of the circle; and to conclude the current discussion I want to examine it. This argument appeals to what Rawls calls the "burdens of judgment": certain aspects of the human condition whose collective implication is that "it is not to be expected that conscientious persons with full powers of reason, even after free discussion, will all arrive at the same conclusion."[36] The burdens of judgment include the complexity of the empirical facts upon which many disputes turn, the difficulty of assigning weight to radically different kinds of considerations, and the vagueness and indeterminacy of both our moral and our nonmoral concepts. They include, as well, the differences in perspective that are inevitable among people of different backgrounds, the different kinds of normative considerations that often bear on a single question, and the impossibility of simultaneously realizing all competing values.[37] Taken together, these six factors are said to insure that even the most conscientious and well meaning of inquirers will often reach radically divergent conclusions.

From our perspective, what is most important about the burdens of judgment is their (comparatively) straightforward factual status.

33. Ibid., p. 224.
34. Rawls, "The Idea of an Overlapping Consensus," p. 8.
35. Rawls, *Political Liberalism*, p. 213.
36. Ibid., p. 58.
37. Ibid., pp. 56–57.

Whatever else is true, they are real phenomena and not just ideas implicit in the public political culture. And because the burdens do have this independent status, an argument that uses them to show that our reasoning about political essentials should be restricted to uncontroversial premises and methods of reasoning will not immediately beg the question.

Still, when we ask *how* the burdens of judgment might support this conclusion, we quickly encounter difficulties. There are, in fact, two distinct questions here. First, if someone were to make such an argument, would his fundamental point be epistemological or moral? Would he be saying that those who rely on controversial methods or premises are attaching more weight to their own conclusions than they reasonably should, given the likelihood that other, equally reasonable persons will reach different conclusions? Or would he be saying, instead, that when citizens base their reasoning about political essentials on methods or premises that they cannot expect others to share, they are being *morally* unreasonable because they fail to respect those others as independent rational agents? Moreover, second, whichever claim was being made, would it assert that those who rely on controversial methods or premises are being unreasonable in relation to their own further beliefs and standards, or by some more objective criterion? By combining these two pairs of alternatives, we get a total of four permutations, which I shall examine in order.

1. Suppose first that those whose political decisions rest on controversial methods or premises are said to be *epistemologically* unreasonable because they fail to attach due weight to their own fallibility; and suppose, further, that their grounds for regarding the burdens of judgment as strong evidence of their fallibility are said to be supplied by their own background beliefs. If so, the obvious question is why the case for regarding the burdens of judgment as strong evidence of one's own fallibility should be thought to be equally strong no matter what one's other background beliefs *are*. To cite just one type of counterexample, many fundamentalists regard the Bible as the revealed word of God: according to them, a literal interpretation of Scripture definitively settles all questions. If someone allows this view to structure the rest of his beliefs, then he will *not* believe that any important questions turn on complex or indeterminate empirical or normative issues. Hence, relative to his background beliefs, Rawls's burdens of judgment will provide little support for the suspicion that he may be wrong and others right.

2. This, of course, does not mean that the true believer is immune to criticism. Even if he is in no position to realize his errors, the rest of us may be. Hence, the more promising version of the appeal to fallibility is one that criticizes those who base political decisions on controversial methods or premises from a perspective external to their own. Yet while this version of the argument does avoid our initial objection, it remains vulnerable to others.

For, first, even if the burdens of judgment did provide strong objective evidence that arguments based on controversial premises and methods of reasoning are especially unreliable, they would not show that those arguments are any *more* unreliable when their conclusions concern political essentials than when they concern other matters. Hence, if the burdens of judgment did make it unreasonable to use controversial methods and premises in our deliberations about basic political matters, they would make it no less unreasonable to use them in our deliberations about all other political and private matters. This, however, is absurd: whatever else is true, it must *sometimes* be reasonable to think and act against the conventional wisdom. Nor, second, *do* the burdens of judgment provide strong objective evidence that controversial premises and methods of reasoning are any less reliable than noncontroversial ones; for all the uncertainties that are introduced by empirical complexity, vague concepts, value-pluralism, and the rest would persist if we entirely *avoided* all controversy. Indeed, in some contexts, excluding all reasoning that relied on controversial scientific results would actually *decrease* the reliability of our conclusions. This would happen, for example, if the controversial scientific claims that were excluded were those that affirm or presuppose the theory of evolution.

3. Thus, if it is unreasonable to base decisions about basic justice or constitutional essentials on controversial methods or premises, this cannot be because those methods or premises are too unreliable to be trusted. Instead, the worry must be that it is *morally* unreasonable to base decisions about how to use "the public's political power" on premises that some of the affected parties cannot be expected to accept. By thus bypassing these people's rational capacities, the claim must be, we fail to treat them as fellow rational agents.

But failing to treat another as a fellow rational agent is, again, not something that is unreasonable in relation to any and all background (moral) beliefs. Indeed, to find a background moral belief in relation to which this is *not* always unreasonable, we need look no further than act-utilitarianism. Because act-utilitarians believe it is morally reasonable to do whatever maximizes utility, and because preempting another's decisions sometimes *can* be expected to maximize utility, act-utilitarians must believe that it sometimes *is* morally reasonable to bypass another's rational agency. Hence, even if Rawls's conception of reasonableness is a moral one, he cannot plausibly accuse all who invoke their comprehensive doctrines in connection with basic political matters of being unreasonable by their own lights. If he is to show that they are morally unreasonable, he must again adopt a perspective external to their own.

4. This brings us to the final version of the proposed argument: that it is morally unreasonable to deliberate about political essentials on the basis of controversial premises or methods of reasoning because respect for others' rational agency objectively *ought to* take precedence over all other moral, religious, and philosophical commitments. Of the four reconstructions of the proposed argument, this one is the most Rawlsian in spirit. Unfortunately, the reason the argument seems so Rawlsian is that its key normative premise – that respect for others' rational autonomy trumps all other moral, religious, and philosophical commitments – is itself a version of the respect-for-autonomy constraint. This is damaging because our aim has been precisely to assess the prospects for *justifying* that constraint. That was why we canvassed such notions as the shared ideas of society and the person, the liberal principle of legitimacy, and, most recently, the burdens of judgment. Thus, if in the end our reconstruction must presuppose a version of the constraint itself, we will have traveled a great distance only to gain no ground.

VI

Despite its richness and complexity, Rawls's theory has not yielded a convincing respect-for-autonomy argument. But what, next, of the alternative theory proposed by Ronald Dworkin? Unlike Rawls, Dworkin takes as his point of departure not any special ideal of the person, but rather a fundamental right to what he calls equal concern and respect. In his view, "the liberal's emphasis on neutrality in moral personality is not the source but rather one consequence of a prior and more general commitment to equality."[38] Thus, to under-

38. Dworkin, "Neutrality, Equality, and Liberalism," p. 2.

stand Dworkin's argument for neutrality, we must begin with his views about equality.

He develops those views at two distinct levels. At the deeper level, Dworkin defends a principle of equality that is extremely abstract. Although he takes that principle to rule out ethical egoism and nihilism,[39] he regards it as compatible with a variety of other ethical views, including utilitarianism and libertarianism as well as liberal neutrality. Each of these views, he suggests, reflects a particular interpretation of what equality demands. More to the present point, so does the view that governments should act on specific conceptions of the good. That view, he writes, combines the principle of equality with "the opinion that treating a person with respect requires treating him as the good man would wish to be treated"[40] – that is, bringing him to acquire the sorts of virtues, and to live the sort of life, that are genuinely valuable.

Because Dworkin takes the abstract principle of equality to underlie both neutralism and its denial, no argument that he makes for it is likely to favor neutralism *over* its denial. But precisely because his principle of equality is so abstract, Dworkin must also defend the neutralist interpretation that he favors. His attempt to do this constitutes the second level of his discussion. At that level, he argues, first, that the basic item that should be equalized is neither welfare nor economic freedom, but rather access to society's resources: each person must "be permitted to use, for the projects to which he devotes his life, no more than an equal share of the resources available to all."[41] He argues, in addition, that if the principle of equality *is* interpreted as requiring equality of resources, then something like the requirement of neutrality will indeed follow.[42]

39. For arguments to this effect, see Dworkin, "Comment on Narveson: In Defense of Equality," *Social Philosophy and Policy* 1, 1 (1983), pp. 31–35.
40. Ronald Dworkin, "Liberalism," in *A Matter of Principle* (Cambridge, Mass.: Harvard University Press, 1985), p. 198.
41. Dworkin, "Neutrality, Equality, and Liberalism," p. 4. For Dworkin's defense of the equality-of-resources interpretation, see "What Is Equality? Part 1: Equality of Welfare," *Philosophy and Public Affairs* 10, 3 (Summer 1981), pp. 185–246, and "What Is Equality? Part 2: Equality of Resources," *Philosophy and Public Affairs* 10, 4 (Fall 1981), pp. 283–345.
42. Dworkin's reasons for saying this are too complex to summarize here. However, in a nutshell, his position is that equality of resources is defined by the outcome of an imaginary auction in which all of society's resources are to be apportioned, and that the optimal baseline of liberties and constraints for the auction's participants turns out to be "innocent of any constraints justified on grounds of religious truth or moral virtue." For details, see Ronald Dworkin, "What Is Equality? Part 3: The Place of Liberty," *Iowa Law Review* 73, 1 (1987), p. 31.

Because Dworkin's theory has this overall structure, the pivotal element of his defense of neutrality may appear to be his argument for the "equality of resources" interpretation of equality. Unfortunately, whereas Dworkin argues at length that resources are more plausible candidates for equalization than welfare, he does *not* directly address the question of why the "equality of resources" interpretation is preferable to what we may call the *perfectionist* interpretation – that is, the view that treating persons as equals involves "treating [each one] as the good man would wish to be treated." For this reason, instead of discussing Dworkin's defense of equality of resources, I shall focus on two arguments that seek to ground neutrality in equality *without* mentioning resources.[43] Of these two arguments, one asserts that when a government bases its decisions on some people's preferences about how other people should live, it violates equality by counting some people's preferences twice. The other asserts that when a government forces its citizens to live what it regards as good lives, it violates equality by subjecting them to constraints that they "could not accept without abandoning [their] sense of [their] equal worth."[44]

Let us begin with the double-counting argument. Its central premise, that allowing policy decisions to be influenced by preferences about how others should live counts some people's preferences twice, first surfaced in an essay on preferential treatment. There Dworkin sought to make a utilitarian case for favoring black applicants to medical schools while avoiding the concession that, under other circumstances, the balance of utility might support a policy of *excluding* blacks. To accomplish this feat, he argued that any utilitarian case for excluding blacks would have to rely on preferences of a sort that he called "external" – preferences "for the assignment of goods and opportunities to others."[45] More specifically, any such utilitarian argument would have to rely on such facts as that "a white student prefers the company of other whites because he has racist, social, and political convictions, or because he has contempt for blacks as a group."[46] By contrast, Dworkin argued that a utilitarian

43. Because Dworkin believes that the "resources" interpretation of equality commits one to neutralism, it is possible to regard these equality-based arguments for neutralism as part of his reason for *accepting* the "resources" interpretation. However, nothing I say turns on this suggestion.
44. Dworkin, "Neutrality, Equality, and Liberalism," p. 3.
45. Ronald Dworkin, *Taking Rights Seriously* (Cambridge, Mass.: Harvard University Press, 1977), p. 234.
46. Ibid., p. 236.

argument for *favoring* blacks need *not* mention anyone's external preferences. Instead, it can appeal to such facts as that admitting more blacks will produce more physicians who are likely to practice in black areas, and thus will increase the satisfaction of black citizens' personal preferences for adequate health care.

Why, exactly, does this difference matter? According to Dworkin, it matters because counting external preferences gives some people more influence than others over the final result, and in that way violates the principle of equality in its utilitarian version. For example, if a community decides to build a swimming pool rather than a theater because "many citizens, who themselves do not swim, prefer the pool to the theater because they approve of sports and admire athletes,"[47] then "the result will be a form of double counting: each swimmer will have the benefit not only of his own preference, but also of the preference of someone else who takes pleasure in his success."[48] Similarly, counting the preferences of those who despise blacks would mean that "[b]lacks would be denied their right to be treated as equals because the chances that their preferences would prevail in the design of admissions policy would be crippled by the low esteem in which others hold them."[49] In both cases, the problem is solved by considering only the degree to which each action would satisfy purely personal preferences.

If successful, this line of reasoning will clearly support far more than the exclusion of racist preferences. In addition, it will tell against counting preferences directed against homosexuality, pornography, and various other unpopular forms of behavior. Recognizing this, Dworkin later tried to enlist the reasoning in a general defense of neutralism. He argued that even utilitarians should acknowledge that all persons have a general right

not to suffer disadvantage in the distribution of social goods and opportunities, including disadvantage in the liberties permitted to them by the criminal law, just on the ground that their officials or fellow-citizens think that their opinions about the right way for them to lead their own lives are ignoble or wrong.[50]

47. Ibid., p. 235.
48. Ibid.
49. Ibid., p. 236.
50. Dworkin, "Do We Have a Right to Pornography?" in *A Matter of Principle* (Cambridge, Mass.: Harvard University Press, 1985), p. 353.

This right, which Dworkin calls the "right to moral independence," is "one very practical way to achieve this restriction [of the preferences that utilitarian arguments may count]."[51] Hence, utilitarians must acknowledge the right "[i]f utilitarianism is to figure as part of an attractive working political theory."[52] Not to acknowledge it would "implicitly contradict" what must be "the neutral utilitarian's *case* for trying to achieve a political structure in which the average fulfillment of preferences is as high as possible."[53] But once it *is* acknowledged that all citizens have a right to moral independence, we have a powerful new weapon against nonneutral political arguments. We can, for example, use it to show that the law may not prohibit pornography merely because "the desires and preferences of publishers and consumers are outweighed by the desires and preferences of the majority, including their preferences about how others should live their lives."[54]

At first glance, this may look like exactly the sort of defense that neutralism requires. But on closer inspection, the defense is badly incomplete. It shows at most that all *utilitarian* reasoning must be constrained by a right to moral independence if that reasoning is not implicitly to contradict the very conception of equality *that underlies utilitarianism*. But the reasoning whose legitimacy is of most concern to us (and that arguably poses the greatest threat to Dworkin's neutralism) is not utilitarian but perfectionist. It asserts that governments should suppress pornography, not (merely) because enough people consider it disvaluable to tip the utilitarian balance, but (also) because it *is in fact* disvaluable. When someone advocates suppressing pornography on the latter grounds, he treats its disvalue not as the object or basis of any preference, but as an independent, freestanding normative consideration. In so doing, he makes no appeal to the principle of utility. Thus, he can accept with equanimity his argument's failure to satisfy the conception of equality that underlies utility. So if the policy he advocates nonetheless violates some right to which he is committed, this must be shown through some further argument.[55]

---

51. Ibid., p. 364.
52. Ibid., pp. 363–64.
53. Ibid., p. 362 (emphasis in original).
54. Ibid., p. 360.
55. For a related argument, see H. L. A. Hart, "Utility and Rights," *Columbia Law Review* 79 (1979), p. 840.

Can such an argument be produced? At one point, Dworkin hints that it can; for he writes in his pornography essay that his discussion of the link between utility and rights is meant only to be illustrative. Just as the utilitarian interpretation of the abstract principle of equality commits its proponents to certain rights, so, too, do at least some *non*utilitarian interpretations.[56] And since we know that Dworkin takes the available nonutilitarian interpretations to include the view that "treating a person with respect requires treating him as the good man would wish to be treated," we may suspect that he takes perfectionists, too, to be committed to something like the right to moral independence.

But, in fact, Dworkin cannot consistently say this; for that right is flatly inconsistent with his own reconstruction of the perfectionist interpretation of equality. As he reconstructs it, the perfectionist interpretation says that governments treat citizens as equals precisely *by* trying to induce them to live genuinely good lives. Thus, if anything, the perfectionist conception of equality will be violated when a government does *not* try to induce its citizens to live good lives. In any event, it will certainly *not* be violated when a government *does* try to induce its citizens to live good lives. But governmental efforts to induce citizens to live good lives are just what the right to moral independence prohibits. Thus, whatever the perfectionist interpretation of equality does imply, it cannot commit its adherents to a right to moral independence.

VII

Even by themselves, these objections would block any attempt to parlay the double-counting argument into a general defense of neutralism. But that argument is also deficient in its own terms, and it is worth pausing briefly to see why.

Consider first an objection that was raised by H. L. A. Hart. In a well-known critical discussion, Hart asked exactly *which* preferences are counted twice when utilitarians count external as well as personal preferences – when, for example, they count X's external preference that Y swim as well as Y's personal preference *to* swim. The answer, Hart suggested, is "none": "it is only the case that the proposal for the allocation of some good to the swimmers is supported

56. Dworkin, "Do We Have a Right to Pornography?" pp. 369–72.

by the preferences both of the swimmer and (say) his disinterested non-swimmer neighbour."[57] Indeed, *"not* to count the neighbour's disinterested preference on this issue would be to fail to treat the two as equals. It would be 'undercounting' and presumably as bad as double counting."[58] Since this reasoning obviously can be generalized, Hart concluded that even utilitarians need not discount external preferences.

But Hart's objection, though natural, is not decisive. Dworkin's rejoinder is instructive:

There would be something in [Hart's] point if votes rather than preferences were in issue, because if someone wished to vote for Sarah's success rather than his own, his role in the calculation would be exhausted by this gift. . . . But preferences, as these figure in utilitarian calculations, are not like votes in that way. Someone who reports more preferences to the utilitarian computer does not (except trivially) diminish the impact of other preferences he also reports; he rather increases the role of his preferences overall, compared with the role of other people's preferences, in the giant calculation.[59]

This rejoinder clarifies Dworkin's position. It shows that his real worry is not that counting external preferences will count any *given* preference twice, but rather that if someone has both external and personal preferences, counting them all will give that person *more preferences that count* than someone with only personal preferences. What will be excessive, in other words, is not the weight attached to any one of the person's preferences, but rather the sheer number of his preferences to which weight is attached.

By thus shifting the argument's focus, Dworkin provides a clear answer to Hart's question of what is made unequal when utilitarians count external preferences. But, in so doing, he makes several further assumptions that themselves require defense. Let us not contest Dworkin's assumption that the principle of utility requires that we count the same number of preferences for each person. For the moment, let us also concede that different people have different numbers of external preferences. Even so, discounting all external preferences will only allow us to count the same number of preferences for each person if all persons *do* have the same number of *personal* preferences. But do they? Some people seem to care about their work or

57. Hart, "Utility and Rights," p. 842.
58. Ibid.
59. Dworkin, "Do We Have a Right to Pornography?" pp. 365–66.

their families but little else, whereas others seem to care about these things plus much else. There are persons who want close family lives and satisfying jobs, but to whom it is also important to participate in athletic or aesthetic activities, to sustain deep religious involvements, or to have rich networks of friends. At least offhand, these persons seem to have many *more* personal preferences than the others. But if so, then even discounting all external preferences will not mean counting the same number of preferences for each.[60]

Could Dworkin describe the situation differently? Could he say that when someone is indifferent toward engaging in a certain activity, his indifference can itself be located on a continuum that runs from intense desire to intense aversion, and hence is itself a kind of personal preference? And, having said this, could Dworkin go on to argue that, despite the differences in how many activities people care about engaging in, all people still *do* have the same number of personal preferences?

The answer, I think, is that there is no harm in saying this, but that if Dworkin does say it about personal preferences, he must, to be consistent, also say it about external preferences. Yet if Dworkin *did* extend the maneuver to external preferences – if he did rank as an external preference Z's indifference to Y's swimming or not swimming, or Z's indifference to Y's reading pornography or not reading it – then the same strategy that shows that each person has the same number of *personal* preferences would also show that each person has the same number of *external* preferences. In that case, a utilitarian would not *have* to discount all external preferences in order to count the same number of preferences for each person.

Thus, whether or not we take indifference to be a kind of preference, Dworkin's clarified double-counting argument rests on a false assumption. But suppose, finally, that it did not. Suppose Dworkin were right to imply both that different people have different numbers of external preferences and that all people have the same number of personal preferences. Even *this* would not establish that utilitarians must discount all external preferences in order to count the

60. Indeed, if persons can differ in their numbers of both external *and* personal preferences, then discounting all external preferences while counting all personal preferences may actually bring less equality than counting all preferences of both sorts. Suppose, for example, that X has one external preference and two personal preferences, while Y has no external preferences but four personal preferences. Then counting all preferences of both sorts will mean counting three of X's preferences and four of Y's, while excluding all external preferences will mean counting only *two* preferences of X's but all four of Y's.

same number of preferences for each person; for while discounting all external preferences is indeed one way of achieving this goal, it is hardly the only way. Another, equally good strategy would be to discount some of the *personal* preferences of those with more (personal plus external) preferences than others. Hence, to rule out the latter option, Dworkin would need yet a further reason for excluding external preferences – a reason which, if he had it, would vitiate the need to advance the double-counting argument. Thus, in the end, that argument is either inconclusive or superfluous.

VIII

What, next, of Dworkin's other attempt to ground neutralism in the principle of equality? As we saw, in addition to maintaining that nonneutral arguments count some people's preferences twice, he also maintains that policies with nonneutral justifications impose constraints that some people "could not accept without abandoning [their] sense of [their] equal worth." Can this second defense of neutralism succeed where the double-counting argument fails?

One hopeful sign is that the new defense clearly is directed at policies adopted for *perfectionist* reasons. Indeed, in his only extended treatment of it, Dworkin develops it precisely in opposition to (what he sees as) the strongest case for the perfectionist interpretation of equality.[61] That case, he suggests, turns on a certain (plausible) conception of a person's most basic interest. It turns, in particular, on the idea that each person has a highest-order interest in living

as good a life as possible, a life that has in it as much of what a life should have. . . . The claim does not mean that it matters fundamentally to each person that he have a life he thinks good. But rather that it matters to him that he have a life that is in fact good. We might . . . say that he has a "transparent" interest in leading a good life rather than an "opaque" interest.[62]

61. Although Dworkin alludes to the argument at a number of places, the only essay of which I know in which he even begins to elaborate it is "In Defense of Equality." In the relevant portion of that essay, he represents his target as the view that "government should aim that [people] have (what government believes to be) genuinely good lives however much the objects of this attention might, at least initially, despise the lives they are made to lead" (p. 28).

62. Ibid., 26–27.

If each person does have a highest-order interest in living the best possible life, then any government that is concerned about its citizens' highest-order interests must also be concerned with the goodness of their lives. Hence, it may seem to follow immediately that a government can best treat its citizens as equals by bringing them – by force if necessary – to live whatever sorts of lives it knows (or has strong reason to believe) are good.

But, according to Dworkin, this really does not follow; for when an agent tries to benefit someone by taking over his life – "by creating, for himself, a clone of that other person's highest-order interest, and acting towards that person as he would act towards himself if that cloned interest were his own most important interest"[63] – the effort is bound to fail. The reason, Dworkin suggests, is that it is only from a person's own perspective that his transparent interest in living the best life and his opaque interest in living the life that seems best to him can coincide. When others try to advance his interests,

the transparent and the opaque interests not only can but inevitably will come apart. This means that Y, who is somehow put in charge of X's life, must stipulate a project for X [that] X could not possibly endorse or accept for himself, but must on the contrary disown, which is the project of coming to believe some particular proposition about what gives value to life.[64]

And this, Dworkin writes, "indicates at least one reason we have for rejecting the idea, if not the possibility, that politics might show the mode of concern just described for the interests of its individual members."[65]

Although Dworkin's argument is very compressed – I have, indeed, already quoted all the passages that seem relevant – it clearly consists of two main steps. The first is an inference from the premise that

(1) X has a transparent highest-order interest in living a good life

to the intermediate conclusion that

(2) X must disown the project of coming to accept Y's conception of the good.

63. Ibid., p. 28.
64. Ibid.
65. Ibid., pp. 28–29.

The second is a further inference from (2) to

(3) Y must never force X to live by Y's conception of the good.

In what follows, I shall mainly be concerned to contest the inference from (2) to (3). However, before I do, I want briefly to examine the earlier move from (1) to (2).[66]

Although Dworkin does not explain how he gets from "X has a transparent highest-order interest in living a good life" to "X must disown the project of coming to accept Y's conception of the good," he might unpack his reasoning as follows. Suppose – as is inevitable over the long run – that X's conception of the good life does not match Y's; and suppose, further, that X and Y both know this. Suppose, as well, that X has no special reason to believe that Y is in a better position to know the good than he himself is. In that case, X must believe that Y's conception of the good is, on the whole, less likely to be true than his own. Believing this, X must also believe that coming to live in accordance with Y's conception – and, by extension, coming to accept it – would actually reduce his chances of living a good life. But if X believes this while also believing that living a good life is in his highest-order interest, then he must indeed disown the project of coming to accept Y's conception. Given all that he believes, X cannot regard undertaking this project as furthering his own highest-order interest.

Although this reasoning may require additional refinement,[67] something like it may well be correct. But the same cannot be said of Dworkin's further inference from (2) to (3). Here the basic question is why anything beside X's actual highest-order interest should affect the way in which Y ought to treat X. More specifically, if Y would

66. A further question about this argument, which I shall not pursue, is whether it fairly represents the case for the perfectionist interpretation of the principle of equality. As Dworkin reconstructs it, the basic reason for accepting that interpretation is that each person has a highest-order interest in living the best possible life. But if this interest is capable of satisfaction, then some lives must *in fact be* better than others; and if they are, then quite apart from any reasons provided by people's interests, a government might be justified in promoting the best ways of life – and, by extension, in compelling citizens to adopt them – simply because these *are* the best.

67. One problem with the reasoning is that one of the beliefs attributed to X – namely, that coming to accept Y's conception of the good would decrease his chances of living a good life – appears to commit him to resisting not only Y's forcible efforts to alter his conception of the good, but also Y's efforts at rational persuasion. A more plausible rendering of X's belief would equip him to make this distinction; but I shall not attempt the necessary formulation.

really further X's highest-order interest by imposing his own conception of the good on X, then why should X's attitude toward that
conception justify his not imposing it? Even if X's other beliefs commit him to the view that living by Y's conception is *not* in his highest-
order interest, shouldn't X's actual interests, and not his mistaken
beliefs about those interests, determine how he should be treated?

To answer this question, Dworkin could take one of three tacks. He
could argue, first, that Y's forcing X to live the best sort of life cannot
serve X's highest-order interest because it cannot bring X to live such
a life for the right reasons; or, second, that Y's forcing X cannot serve
X's highest-order interest because it must override resistance that is
called for by that very interest; or, third, that although Y's forcing X
can further X's highest-order interest, it would do so at the cost of
violating some powerful independent constraint. To end my discussion of Dworkin's argument, I shall contend that none of these responses can succeed.

The first response – that Y's use of force cannot serve X's highest-
order interest because it cannot bring him to live a good life for the
right reasons – has already been dealt with. As we saw in the preceding chapter, many do believe that no way of life has value (or, by
extension, that no way of life can serve a person's highest-order
interest) unless it is adopted for the right reasons. However, as we
also saw, persons often initially adopt ways of life because they are
forced to, but later persist in living in those ways because they have
come to appreciate their value "from the inside." When a person
undergoes this kind of change, the use of force does indirectly lead
him to see the point of accepting the very conception of the good
whose acceptance he was originally committed to resisting. Hence,
the premise upon which the first response rests – that using force can
never lead anyone to live a (potentially) good life for the right
reasons – seems simply to be false.

The second response – that Y's use of force cannot advance X's
highest-order interest because it must override resistance that is
made reasonable by that very interest – is no more plausible. To bear
the argument's weight, this suggestion would have to construe the
success of X's resistance as a necessary condition for the realization
of X's highest-order interest. But if X's highest-order interest is
transparent – if it requires that X live a life that is in fact good – then
X's success in resisting the acquisition of Y's conception of the good
will only be in X's highest-order interest if Y's conception is false. If
instead Y's conception is true, then the success of X's resistance will

mean that X's highest-order interest has not been realized. In that case, Y will best advance X's highest-order interest precisely by overcoming his resistance.

This leaves only the third rejoinder: that even if Y's using force to bring X to live by his conception *would* advance X's highest-order interest, Y still should not force X because his doing so would violate some strong independent constraint. Since what is at issue is Y's advancing X's interests in a way that X's own rationality commits him to resisting, the relevant constraint would pretty clearly be one that forbids treating others in ways that ignore or override their own autonomous decisions. Hence, it would in effect assert that respect for rational autonomy always takes priority over the demands of other values. But whether respect for autonomy always takes priority – and, if so, why – is of course just the question that Dworkin's argument is supposed to answer. Hence, if Dworkin took this third tack, his argument would succeed through the simple expedient of begging the question.

IX

This concludes my examination of the two theories that seemed most likely to yield a viable respect-for-autonomy constraint. Upon inspection, neither does. Thus, though many other possibilities remain, the prospects at this point do not seem bright.

This conclusion should not be overstated. As I stressed at the end of the preceding chapter, there are many reasons to acknowledge a strong presumption for allowing citizens to make their own decisions and exercise control over their own lives. This presumption is especially weighty when force or threats are involved, and it should loom large in the decisions of any government. However, no such presumption can justify ignoring, or taking entirely out of play, the weighty reasons that considerations of goodness can provide; and as long as these reasons remain in play, they can be expected sometimes to be decisive.

Still, even if neutralism cannot be grounded in either the value of autonomy or respect for autonomy, its overall status is not yet settled. Two further lines of defense, one less and one perhaps even more rarified than the appeals to autonomy, remain to be considered. The less rarified defense extends the pragmatic and political themes that we have already encountered in Rawls's recent work. It allows that it might in principle be desirable for governments to induce their citizens to live good lives, but insists that this is either practically impossible or else unacceptably destabilizing. For this reason, it endorses neutralism as an unavoidable accommodation – a necessary modus vivendi – in any complex and pluralistic society. By contrast, the second defense denies that nonneutral policies are desirable even in principle. It asserts that judgments about the goodness of different ways of life – judgments that, for simplicity, I have so far simply assumed are sometimes defensible – are either altogether without a rational basis or else hopelessly problematical. In either case, they are said to be inappropriate guides to public policy. To complete my critical discussion of neutralism, and to begin to flesh out a view of what should replace it, I shall take up each defense in turn.

Chapter 5

Prophylactic neutrality

So far, I have considered and rejected several autonomy-based defenses of neutralism. But what, next, of the argument that the modern state's power is so vast, and those who wield it so flawed, that no government can be *trusted* to promote its citizens' good? Unlike arguments that defend neutrality on elevated moral grounds, this one defends it simply as a way of protecting citizens against certain dangers. Neutrality, on this account, is merely a prophylactic device. Yet while the cited dangers clearly are real, and clearly call for protective measures, it is far less obvious that neutrality is the best protection against them. In this chapter, I shall argue that it is not. By relying on other sorts of protection, we can approach nonneutral policies as we do all others, evaluating each one strictly on its merits.

I

Broadly speaking, the dangers posed by government fall in three main categories.

OPPRESSION

First, any modern state needs vast power. To keep order, to protect citizens from external threats and from each other, and to provide essential services and public goods, a government must have both a (near-)monopoly on force and access to great wealth. But, quite obviously, these resources can also be used in less salutary ways: to suppress dissent, to consolidate and maintain personal power, and to create and sustain unjust patterns of advantage and privilege. And, unfortunately, these dangers are not just hypothetical. As we all know, bureaucracies can be insensitive, arrogant, and self-perpetuating; the police, the courts, and the prisons are easily transformed into instruments of oppression; and efforts to suppress the bad can lead to the suppression of the merely unpopular. As we all know, too, the habits of dominating and submitting to domination are all too readily acquired.

Because all governments have great power, many of these dangers would exist even in a neutral state. Nevertheless, by limiting government to its most essential functions, we may at least minimize the dangers of abuse. And, hence, a first practical reason to favor a neutral state is simply to prevent government from misusing its power.

INSTABILITY

Because power is always subject to abuse, this danger is not restricted to heterogeneous societies. But a second danger is raised precisely by heterogeneity. When a society is composed of different religious, cultural, or social groups, some are bound to want to impose their conceptions of the good on others, while many of the others are bound to resist. In this way, any pluralistic society contains the seeds of destabilizing conflict. To avoid such conflict, we are urged to place all efforts to promote the good strictly off limits. On this account, neutrality is put forth as a "modus vivendi, a means of accommodation among individuals having divergent conceptions of the good life."[1]

ERROR

And there is also a third reason to favor neutrality – namely, that what the state or its agents take to be good may not be good at all. This danger exists because there is no guarantee that any official conception of the good will be any better grounded than – or even as well grounded as – the conception of any individual. If the state's conception is not well grounded, then its successful promotion may

1. Charles Larmore, *Patterns of Moral Complexity* (Cambridge: Cambridge University Press, 1987), p. 91.

only make people's lives worse. To avoid this danger, we are again urged to take all conceptions of the good off the political agenda.

It is important to emphasize that this is not a skeptical argument. Although skeptical defenses of neutrality have indeed been advanced – their merits will be discussed in the next chapter – the point here is *not* that the good cannot be known, but only that how well one knows it bears no relation to one's political power or influence. Those with the deepest insight may be unable to affect public policy because they have little money or power, because they lack the rhetorical skill to influence those who do have power, or because their potential audience is biased, preoccupied, or inattentive. And, conversely, those who do wield power and authority may hold views about the good that are shallow, incomplete, or simply wrong. Because knowledge and politics run on separate tracks – because there are no philosopher-kings – a government's conception of the good can be expected often to be mistaken. If this probability is high enough, we are all better off if the state remains neutral.

Thus, any nonneutral state will pose three distinct dangers. Its policies may lead to oppression; they may elicit destabilizing conflict; or they may simply be in error. There are, of course, also other dangers – for example, that nonneutral policies will have unexpected economic, environmental, or behavioral costs – but these are less central. Hence, to assess the prophylactic argument's main variants, we need ask only whether neutrality is the most promising way of preventing oppression, instability, or error.

II

The idea that the sheer magnitude of the state's power is itself a threat, and that this threat must somehow be tamed, has long been prominent in liberal thought. Here are two statements of that idea, the first from Benjamin Constant's *Principles of Politics*, written in 1815, and the second from Judith Shklar's contemporary work, *Ordinary Vices:*

When you establish that the sovereignty of the people is unlimited, you create and toss at random into human society a degree of power which is too large in itself, and which is bound to constitute an evil, in whatever hands it is placed. Entrust it to one man, to several, to all, you will still find that it is equally an evil. . . . it is in fact the degree of force, not its holders, which must be denounced.[2]

Justice itself is only the web of legal arrangements required to keep cruelty in check, especially by those who have most of the instruments of intimidation closely at hand. That is why the liberalism of fear concentrates so single-mindedly on limited and predictable government. The prevention of physical excess and arbitrariness is to be achieved by a series of legal and institutional measures designed to supply the restraints that neither reason nor tradition can be expected to provide.[3]

Though different in tone and emphasis, both quotations display the characteristically liberal fear of concentrated government power.

That fear is sometimes invoked in defense of neutralism. Bruce Ackerman, for example, regards "realism about the corrosiveness of power" as one of several "main highways to the liberal [i.e., neutral] state."[4] His arguments for neutralism include the observation that "Good government, always precarious, can readily degenerate into an awful parody of itself – with hypocrites using the awesome powers of the bureaucratic state to spy, torture, and kill, merely to aggrandize themselves without any attention to the goods they profess to value."[5] Of course, even in a neutral state, the danger of oppression would hardly disappear: a government that does not oppress in the name of virtue or true religion may still do so in the name of prosperity or state security (or, for that matter, under no justificatory cover at all). Still, by removing virtue, religion, and like topics from the public agenda, we would at least eliminate one important class of occasions for abuse.

But while a protective retreat to neutrality is clearly one way of avoiding oppression, it is neither the only way nor, arguably, the most important historically. Indeed, until recently, few liberals have spoken of neutrality at all.[6] Instead, their preferred solutions have

2. Benjamin Constant, *Principles of Politics Applicable to All Representative Governments,* in *Benjamin Constant: Political Writings,* trans. and ed. Biancamaria Fontana (Cambridge: Cambridge University Press, 1988), p. 176.
3. Judith Shklar, *Ordinary Vices* (Cambridge, Mass.: Harvard University Press, 1984), p. 237.
4. Bruce Ackerman, *Social Justice in the Liberal State* (New Haven: Yale University Press, 1980), p. 369.
5. Ibid., p. 363.
6. Thus, Jeremy Waldron quotes T. S. Eliot as opposing "the ideal of a neutral society" in a book that Eliot published just before the Second World War; but Waldron adds that "I have managed to find no evidence that any liberal view that Eliot was

involved the separation of government powers, the independence of the judiciary, and, above all, the legal codification of rights that guarantee each person a protected sphere of security and liberty. Judith Shklar speaks for many when she writes:

Enforceable rights are the legal powers that individual citizens in a liberal society can bring to bear individually and collectively in order to defend themselves against threats backed by force. This is not the liberalism of natural rights, but it underwrites rights as the politically indispensable dispersion of power, which alone can check the reign of fear and cruelty.[7]

As Shklar here suggests, liberals themselves disagree about whether rights can usefully be said to exist prior to their embodiment in law. But rights cannot protect anyone from oppression unless they are *backed by* the force of law, so for our purposes, the relevant rights are plainly legal ones.

How do the protections afforded by rights affect the prospects for grafting a defense of neutralism onto the earlier "liberalism of fear?" Given the impressive security that Western rights holders have long enjoyed, one obvious answer – and, I think, ultimately the correct answer – is that given a suitably potent array of legal rights, citizens have no need for any further protection. Because their rights *already* block the most dangerous abuses of power, they stand to gain little from the additional security of a neutral state. Thus, as long as governments recognize and enforce a suitable complement of rights, they can try to promote the good without raising the specter of oppression.

As I have said, I think this answer is ultimately correct. But before we can accept it, we must consider an important rejoinder. Instead of regarding rights and neutrality as rival protective strategies, we might see rights as mechanisms for *implementing* the neutralist strategy. On this account, when rights protect citizens from oppression, they do so precisely by *making* the state neutral. The suggestion that rights play this role – that they exist to prevent the state from acting on particular conceptions of the good – is advanced in Ronald Dworkin's important article "Liberalism."

opposing was ever actually formulated in these terms" (Waldron, "Legislation and Moral Neutrality," in Robert E. Goodin and Andrew Reeve, eds., *Liberal Neutrality* [London: Routledge, 1989], p. 62).
7. Shklar, *Ordinary Vices*, pp. 237–38.

Dworkin, to be sure, does not regard neutrality as a mere protective device. Rather, as we saw in the preceding chapter, he regards the principle of neutrality as the most favored interpretation of the more fundamental principle that the state should treat each citizen with equal respect. But although Dworkin does not try to ground neutrality in the danger of oppression, he does see rights as necessary ways of *implementing* neutrality. They accomplish this goal, he says, by ruling out in advance the sorts of laws and policies whose justifications are most apt to be *non*neutral. Thus, substantive civil rights, such as those which protect religious freedom and freedom of thought and expression, "determine those political decisions that are antecedently likely to reflect strong external preferences and . . . remove those decisions from majoritarian political institutions altogether."[8] And procedural civil rights serve the same end by "interven[ing] in the process, even at the cost of inaccuracy, to compensate in a rough way for the antecedent risk that a criminal process, especially if it is largely administered by one class against another, will be corrupted by the impact of external preferences that cannot be eliminated directly."[9] Taken together, these two classes of civil rights secure the neutrality that Dworkin regards as the core, or "nerve," of liberalism.[10]

Dworkin's remarks flesh out the suggestion that rights are mechanisms for making the state neutral. In so doing, they give definite content to the rejoinder that far from eliminating the need for a neutral state, rights may protect us from oppression precisely by *securing* it. Still, it is one thing to give content to this rejoinder, and quite another to establish its truth. To that issue, I now turn.

III

Do liberal rights make the state neutral? At least when applied to the contemporary United States, this claim seems dubious; for despite the protections afforded by our celebrated Bill of Rights and our vigorous judiciary, we remain subject to many laws whose justifications seem largely perfectionist.

8. Ronald Dworkin, "Liberalism," in *A Matter of Principle* (Cambridge, Mass.: Harvard University Press, 1985), p. 197.
9. Ibid., p. 198.
10. Ibid., p. 183.

Thus, for example, when the National Endowment for the Arts subsidizes artistic projects, its official justification asserts that art "nourishes the human spirit" and that "it is through art that we can understand ourselves and our potential."[11] When the Environmental Protection Agency preserves wilderness and protects endangered species, it treats the continued existence of species and habitat as intrinsic goods. When federal regulators prohibit the use of obscene language on television and radio, and when the state criminalizes public nudity, public sexual activity, and public defecation, their usual rationale is just that these modes of behavior are indecent. And, at least before AIDS became a threat, the standard justification of laws against "victimless crimes" – prostitution, pornography, sodomy, bestiality, and the like – was precisely that they are unseemly, degraded, or in some other way unworthy of human beings. Moreover, despite the current overlay of concern about health (and, in the case of pornography, of causal claims about harm to women), such justifications still often lurk just below the surface.

There is, of course, much room for disagreement about these claims. I have not yet defended any version of perfectionism, much less one that would support all of the cited judgments. But for present purposes, this does not matter; for the present point is simply that many familiar laws and policies have a clear perfectionist rationale. That is important because if enough nonneutral laws and policies *do* coexist with our current rights, then we obviously can have adequate protection without having a neutral state.

Or, at least, this will be obvious if our current rights do protect us adequately. But do they? Dworkin, for one, seems to have his doubts. In the same essay in which he suggests that rights are devices for making the state neutral, he cites with approval the common liberal claim that "the protection of the individual in certain important areas, including sexual publication and practice, are [sic] much too weak."[12] Although some of the laws against pornography and homosexuality to which he alludes have since been repealed or weakened – his essay originally appeared in 1978 – many others remain on the books. They are, moreover, still among the clearest examples of nonneutral laws. Hence, one way to contest my claim

11. These phrases are from the mission statement of the National Endowment for the Arts. David T. Schwartz points out their perfectionist implications in "Can Intrinsic-Value Theorists Justify Subsidies for Contemporary Art?" *Public Affairs Quarterly* 9, 4 (October 1995), pp. 331–43.
12. Dworkin, "Liberalism," p. 197.

that our current rights prevent oppression without making the state neutral is simply to argue that the nonneutral laws that those rights permit are themselves oppressive.

But, whatever else is true, these laws do not involve the kind of oppression that has historically worried liberals. On the whole, the legal prohibitions against pornography, homosexuality, and prostitution have not been administered especially cruelly or arbitrarily; and neither have they been used to swell the wealth, influence, or power of those who currently hold office, or to institute or perpetuate unjust patterns of privilege. Moreover, if even these uses of the criminal sanction have not been oppressive in the standard sense, then neither, a fortiori, have the government's noncoercive efforts to promote culture or preserve the environment.

Of course, even if laws against homosexuality, prostitution, and pornography, are not oppressive in the standard sense, they may still have *other* bad effects from which only a neutral state can protect us. But which other effects could those be? One possible answer is that these laws oppress homosexuals, prostitutes and their clients, and producers and consumers of pornography precisely by compelling them to live in accordance with conceptions of the good they do not share. But if oppression is understood to involve just this, then any nonneutral law will *by definition* be oppressive. Hence, if someone were to argue that we need a neutral state to *block* this kind of oppression, he would merely replace the question of why the state should be neutral with the equivalent question of why oppression, understood as compelling citizens to conform to conceptions of the good that they do not share, is in itself an evil. This move, clearly, would gain the neutralist no ground.

Is there any better reason to suppose that our current rights do not adequately protect us from oppression? One other possibility, perhaps, is worth exploring. It could be argued that even if today's nonneutral laws are not oppressive, they increase the risk of *future* oppression by setting a damaging precedent. When we allow the state to promote what it considers virtuous or excellent, and when we allow it to suppress what it regards as base or corrupt, we may be said to initiate a dynamic of intrusion that is hard to control. By allowing neutrality to be breached at all, we take the first fateful steps toward an officious, omnipresent Big Brother.

Such slippery-slope arguments are, of course, instantly familiar. Indeed, a fondness for them is probably the main point of contact between the American Civil Liberties Union and the National Rifle

Association. But however compelling the arguments of these organizations are – and in both cases, J think the answer is usually "not very" – the current argument is less convincing still. For while the ACLU and NRA claim only that the state is likely to become oppressive if certain rights that we (allegedly) now possess are *abridged*, the current argument makes the stronger claim that oppression is likely to result if long-standing practice is simply *continued*. Unlike the ACLU and the NRA, the neutralist who mounts this argument must hold that our government is likely to abuse its power if it merely continues to act on specific views about the good. To defend that prediction, he must claim either that continued nonneutral legislation will somehow lead to oppression *without* eroding our long-standing rights, or else that it will do so precisely *by* eroding those rights. However, of these two claims, the first verges on the unintelligible, while we have had enough experience to test the second.

The results, it must be said, are not impressive. Despite two centuries of nonneutral laws and policies, the long slide into authoritarianism simply has not occurred. Indeed, the long-range tendency seems, if anything, to be in the other direction. Our civil rights were significantly expanded by the Miranda decision, the exclusionary rule, and the series of court decisions that drastically extended the sphere of privacy. Of course, the movement has not all been one way: it has been argued that during the same period, our economic liberties have undergone some contraction.[13] Still, all things considered, the sphere of protected activities seems significantly larger now than fifty or a hundred years ago.

IV

There is, then, considerable commonsense evidence that the standard liberal rights can provide adequate protection without making the state neutral. But the decisive objection to the idea that a scheme of rights might make the state neutral is not that this is unnecessary but that it is impossible. For to rule out all government efforts to promote the good, a scheme of rights would have to be so extensive as to prevent the state from functioning at all.

To see why, we must recall a distinction that was made earlier. As

13. For arguments to this effect, see Stephen Macedo, *Liberal Virtues* (Oxford: Oxford University Press, 1990), ch. 5.

we saw, a common challenge to neutrality is that every law and policy conforms to many conceptions of the good while conflicting with many others. Because neutrality of results is therefore impossible, I have interpreted neutrality exclusively in justificatory terms. On this familiar account, what must be neutral are only the *justifications* of political arrangements, and not those arrangements themselves. But, we may now add, legal rights have a very different structure. Instead of ruling out only certain modes of justification, they standardly rule out certain ways in which governments or individuals might *treat* (other) people. For example, if someone owns a farm or a factory, his property rights do not merely prohibit his government (or his fellow citizens) from seizing it for nonneutral reasons. Instead, and more reassuringly, they prohibit its seizure for *any* reason unless certain conditions are met.

Because neutralism prohibits only acts performed for certain reasons while legal rights prohibit certain acts themselves, the two notions are logically at cross purposes. They do not mesh cleanly because any sort of reason can be advanced to justify many sorts of actions and any sort of action can be supported by many sorts of reasons. This does not mean that no system of rights can prevent a government from acting for a particular sort of reason; but it does mean that if any system of rights is to do this, it must block *all the different* laws and policies that the government might enact for that sort of reason. Thus, in particular, to prevent a government from acting for any *nonneutral* reasons, a scheme of rights must block all the laws and policies that it might enact on nonneutral grounds.

I can now advance a preliminary version of my argument that no scheme of rights can make a government neutral without paralyzing it. Its central premise is simply that every law and policy does conform to, and hence also can be enacted on the basis of, a variety of different conceptions of the good. Combined with the observation that no scheme of rights can prevent a government from acting for reason R without ruling out all government actions that could be based on R, this immediately implies that if a scheme of rights is to prevent a government from acting for any nonneutral reason, it must rule out any law and policy that the government could enact at all. However, needless to say, any scheme of rights that provided this much "protection" would indeed paralyze the state.

How convincing is this argument? Before we can accept it, we must consider the commonsense objection that although any law or policy could *conceivably* be adopted because the activities it requires

115

are considered intrinsically valuable,[14] this is often extremely im-probable. Many important laws – for example, the tax and traffic codes – require activities that no one *in fact* considers intrinsically valuable. No one really believes that living a good life requires pay-ing taxes or signaling before making left turns. Moreover, although some do believe that the suffering of rapists and murderers has intrinsic value, the laws that attach harsh penalties to rape and mur-der seem unlikely to have been adopted mainly for this reason. And, given these facts, can't a scheme of rights still make a government *effectively* neutral *without* paralyzing it? To do so, can't that scheme simply rule out only those laws and policies that can *reasonably be expected* to be adopted on the grounds that the required activities are intrinsically valuable?

The problem with this rejoinder is that even if no one regards an activity as intrinsically valuable or disvaluable, the neutrality of a law requiring or forbidding it is not yet settled. In particular, such a law may still qualify as nonneutral if it has been adopted in order to promote some *other* outcome that *in turn* is considered intrinsically valuable or disvaluable. Thus, to continue the tax example, even if no one attaches intrinsic value to the payment of taxes, the justification of a given tax or exemption will remain nonneutral as long as its aim is to encourage religion, to strengthen the traditional family, or to foster the arts. Similarly, even if a legislator does not attach intrinsic value to the suffering of rapists or murderers, his support of harsh punitive laws may remain nonneutral if his aim is (e.g.) to improve the character of rapists and murderers by *making* them suffer.

The full force of the difficulty should now be clear. To show that rights can bring neutrality without paralysis, one would have to isolate a class of activities that few persons could be expected to regard *either* as intrinsically valuable or disvaluable *or* as likely to have intrinsically valuable or disvaluable effects. But given the end-less variety of effects that any activity can have, and given the equally endless variety of *beliefs* that people can hold about what causes what, isolating such a class of activities is plainly impossible. Because future causal predictions are themselves unpredictable, we cannot partition activities into those that will and will not be believed to have intrinsically valuable or disvaluable effects. Hence, we also

14. Here and in the remainder of this chapter, I shall, for brevity, ignore the distinction between intrinsic and inherent value.

cannot partition laws and policies into those that will and will not be adopted for nonneutral reasons. Thus, even if a scheme of rights sought only to exclude laws and policies that had a real chance of being adopted for nonneutral reasons, it *still* would be so extensive as to paralyze the state.

Or, at least, it still would be so extensive as long as each right required or forbade only certain types of action or ways of treating people. But must all legal rights really take this form? Instead, can't we envision a single omnibus right not to be subjected to any law or policy that has been adopted for nonneutral reasons? If such a right were recognized and scrupulously enforced, then wouldn't it indeed prevent the state from legislating for any nonneutral reasons while at the same time permitting it to legislate for all purely neutral reasons?

The problem, though, is that such a right could never *be* enforced. The great virtue of rights not to be subjected to specific modes of treatment is that the courts can (comparatively) easily discover when they are violated. By contrast, rights not to be subjected to laws adopted for specific types of reasons raise much harder discovery problems. Because policy makers and legislators are not always candid, because individuals often lack insight into their own reasons, and because different persons can support the same laws or policies on very different grounds, there is often no way to discover whether, or to what degree, a proscribed sort of justification has been operative.

This objection might not be decisive if the proscribed reasons were more narrowly focused. Our legal system contains various mechanisms for discovering racially or sexually discriminatory intent, and these might be adapted to the discovery of other well-defined justifications. But such mechanisms seem grossly inadequate to the open-ended task of discovering whether a law or policy is grounded in *any* particular conception of the good. It was, indeed, precisely the fact that "it is sometimes impossible to distinguish, even by introspection, the external and personal components of a political position"[15] that led Dworkin to propose encoding neutrality in rights in the first place.[16] Thus, any recasting of rights as regulating forms of justification rather than modes of treatment would entirely defeat the point of Dworkin's proposal.

15. Dworkin, "Liberalism," p. 197.
16. That this is Dworkin's motivation emerges clearly in "Liberalism," p. 197.

V

So far, I have discussed only the worry that government power may be used cruelly or oppressively. But what, next, of the concern about discord and social strife? The members of any pluralistic society are bound to disagree radically about how it is best to live, and some are bound to think themselves justified in imposing their conceptions upon the rest. Others in turn are bound to think themselves justified in resisting. Despite good intentions all around, the situation may spiral into destabilizing conflict. To prevent this, we are urged to embrace neutrality as a device of accommodation that all can accept.

Although this argument has a Hobbesian flavor, the most significant danger is not violent conflict. Any system of laws will prevent such conflict as long as it effectively forbids the private use of force. Without doing that, no government can maintain order. Thus, even a nonneutral state can prevent the endless "rapines and slaughters" that Locke saw as consequent upon religious intolerance.[17]

But precisely because it has a near monopoly on force, any government can, if it wishes, base its own decisions on the very conceptions of the good that it prevents individuals from forcibly imposing on others. If a government does this, many whom it deters from forcing their own conceptions on others will try to achieve the same end by enlisting its coercive apparatus. Knowing this, many others will enter the fray to stop them; and still others will enter to block the second group. In this way, the Hobbesian dialectic will be at least partially replicated. Carried to its extreme, the resulting struggle may spill over into extralegal activity, and so may weaken the rule of law. In less extreme cases, it may issue in endless unproductive litigation, divisive media campaigns, or costly economic boycotts. Moreover, quite apart from its specific effects, any no-holds-barred contest to control the state's coercive apparatus is sure to engender animosity and bitterness. In this way, if in no other, such a contest will impoverish our social relations.

If these effects were severe enough, they might indeed justify taking all competing conceptions of the good "off the political agenda." But *are* they really this severe? Here again, experience shows the worry to be grossly exaggerated. As we saw in the preceding sections, our own government has long been nonneutral; yet we man-

17. John Locke, *A Letter concerning Toleration,* in *John Locke on Politics and Education* (Roslyn, N.Y.: Walter J. Black, 1947), p. 34.

age to live in comparative harmony. Completely to explain why, one would have to tell a detailed story of a kind that I have neither the training nor the inclination to attempt. Still, even from the philosopher's armchair – the same armchair from which others argue the contrary thesis – we can discern a number of important stabilizing factors.

The most obvious is simply fear of punishment. As was just noted, even the least neutral of governments must attach severe penalties to many methods of getting one's way. The danger of punishment (and the attendant unpleasantness of legal entanglement) gives each person a strong motive for self-restraint. As a result, others are made more secure and so become more able to restrict *their* activities. Moreover, these nested incentives for restraint also have extralegal analogues: obnoxious and obsessively zealous behavior elicits well-known informal sanctions which, with time and maturity, we learn to disregard only at our peril.

The comparative harmony of nonneutral liberal societies also has other causes. For one thing, every form of government elicits a characteristic mind-set; and, as Stephen Macedo has pointed out, the mind-set associated with liberalism includes "a reflective, self-critical attitude, tolerance, openness to change, self-control, a willingness to engage in dialogue with others, and a willingness to revise and shape projects in order to respect the rights of others or in response to fresh insight into one's own character and ideals."[18] If this summary is correct – and in its essentials, I am confident it is – then citizens of liberal states will by temperament be disinclined to press their claims to the limit. Hence, far from needing a modus vivendi *more* than others, they may, ironically, actually need one less.

The irony would, of course, vanish if these "liberal virtues" were themselves rooted in neutrality. Their stabilizing tendencies would help rather than hurt the modus vivendi argument if they either expressed the liberal citizen's own commitment to neutrality or were sustained by his society's commitment to it. It is therefore worth noting that neither connection holds.

For, first, it is one thing always to be open to *new* arguments, and quite another to refuse to base one's political decisions on what, after reflection and on balance, one takes to be the *best* arguments. Hence, even persons who are reflective, tolerant, and the rest need feel no qualms about enlisting the state's power to promote the good. Sim-

18. Macedo, *Liberal Virtues*, p. 129.

ilarly, it is one thing to respect the rights of others and quite another to take any particular position about what those rights are. Hence, even those who are most solicitous of rights need not see them as violated by all (or indeed any) nonneutral laws. And, in general, *no* characteristic liberal virtues appear to have close conceptual links to a personal commitment to neutrality.

Nor, second, are any of those virtues best explained by any broader *societal* commitment to neutralism. My reason for saying this is not merely that each virtue has demonstrably thrived in many nonneutral states. It is, in addition, that each virtue can be convincingly explained as an effect of one or more liberal institutions which themselves do not require or presuppose neutrality. Thus, to quote Macedo again, "[l]iberal justice requires that we respect the rights of people with whom we disagree strongly";[19] "[c]ommerce . . . requires and facilitates the peaceful mixing of peoples from disparate cultural and religious backgrounds";[20] and liberal politics involves a "commitment to public justification and the constitutional citizen's engagement in critical interpretation."[21] Because impartial justice, commerce, and public justification can all flourish even in nonneutral political environments, any traits to which they give rise must also be independent of a society's commitment to neutrality.

In the preceding paragraphs, I attributed our society's comparative stability to certain psychological tendencies that are characteristic of liberalism. But other, more cognitive factors may also play a role. One is the attitude, currently shared even by most perfectionists, that the good is fragmented and plural. Instead of ordering values along any single dimension, or in any neat hierarchy, most seem to attach value to an unstructured hodge-podge of states, activities, excellences, and virtues. In addition, most appear to believe that autonomy, desire-satisfaction, and happiness are also important goods. As a result, even most perfectionists would agree that while many things are worth having, few are worth paying any price to get. Hence, most can also agree that if a policy generates enough disharmony, any expected gains will be outweighed by what is lost. Whatever their exact beliefs about what *is* good, most can easily see the point of moderating their efforts to *promote* the good.

19. Ibid., p. 266.
20. Ibid., p. 256.
21. Ibid., p. 255.

Also, many can be expected to moderate those efforts for more narrowly moral reasons. Many if not most regard each person as a rational agent with a perspective that is worth taking seriously. Hence, many must regard each person's considered views – even views with which they strongly disagree – as worthy of respect. This attitude is reinforced by our awareness of our own intellectual short-comings and of the complexity and difficulty of many disputed topics. Although I argued earlier that the "burdens of judgment" do not make it reasonable to accept neutralism, they may well support some more moderate principle of moral compromise.[22] Moreover, and more to the present point, they may well lead many to *accept* some such principle. If enough do, this will further explain why our nonneutral politics does not degenerate into bitter conflict.[23]

One additional stabilizing factor warrants brief mention. The government acts that are most likely to engender discord are heavy-handed applications of the criminal law. It is only natural to resent being forced to do things for reasons one cannot accept. But instead of punishing those who engage in a disvaluable activity, a government can punish those who make it possible – prostitutes, drug dealers, pornographers, and the like. Also, as I have repeatedly urged, governments can promote what they regard as good by manipulating rewards, prices, and incentives; by nonrationally influencing citizens' attitudes and preferences; and by creating valuable new opportunities and social forms. Because these methods are relatively unprovocative, their destabilizing effects are often minor.

If the stability of nonneutral societies is so easily explained, why is the modus vivendi argument even taken seriously? Its prominence, I think, reflects the salience of a few atypical paradigms. If someone believes the price of wickedness is an eternity in hell, he will quite properly take worldly harmony to be of little moment. By his lights, saving souls – his own and those of others – will indeed be the only

22. For cogent discussion of moral compromise, see Arthur Kuflik, "Morality and Compromise," in *Nomos XXI: Compromise in Ethics, Law, and Politics* (New York: New York University Press, 1979), pp. 38–65. The other essays in that volume are also helpful. For discussion of this issue as it relates to abortion, see George Sher, "Subsidized Abortion: Moral Rights and Moral Compromise," *Philosophy and Public Affairs* 10, 4 (Fall 1981), pp. 361–72.
23. According to Larmore, the case for equal respect lends essential support to the modus vivendi defense of neutralism (see *Patterns of Moral Complexity*, pp. 55–66). By contrast, my own suggestion is that the wide recognition of that case is part of what makes a neutral modus vivendi unnecessary.

thing worth doing.[24] But not all religious doctrines do have such extreme implications, and many conceptions of the good are not religious at all. Thus, very few in our (or any other Western) society have this sort of reason to pull out all the stops. Similarly, although opposition to abortion is not always religious, it, too, has unusually extreme implications. In much the more usual case, even the most passionate adherent of a particular conception of the good is well able to moderate his demands.

And that, for present purposes, is all that matters; for as long as it is true, we can nicely explain why our nonneutral politics does not degenerate into animosity and conflict. The explanation, we can say, lies somewhere in the cumulative effects of fear of punishment, the character of the modern citizen, his value-pluralism, the pull of moral compromise, and the availability of nonprovocative ways of influencing behavior. Of course, because many of these factors are contingent, the proposed explanation is contingent too. If conditions were to change drastically enough, that explanation would no longer apply. But the relevant factors seem no more likely to change than our society's pluralism itself; and because it is just that pluralism that gives rise to the problem, we may quite properly respond by invoking other contingent yet fixed features of contemporary Western life. Here, if not elsewhere, we can agree with Rawls that an adequate solution need not apply to every conceivable social world, but only to our own.

VI

But is this the whole story even about our social world? To explain why our nonneutral laws and policies are not destabilizing, I cited fear of punishment, the liberal temperament, and various other factors. But even if each factor is a force for stability, each may play this role only when certain background conditions prevail. Moreover, the requisite background conditions may include a broader political framework whose justification is itself neutral. Thus, to complete our discussion of stability, we must consider the suggestion that what

24. The idea that some religious doctrines imply that one value infinitely outweighs all others is nicely brought out by David Lewis in "Mill and Milquetoast," *Australasian Journal of Philosophy* 67, 2 (June 1989), pp. 152–71.

requires neutral justification is not a society's laws or policies, but only what Rawls calls its "basic structure" – the constitution, the fundamental legal, social, and economic institutions, and the ground rules of the political process.[25]

As we saw in Chapter 2, anyone who speaks of *the* justification of a set of political arrangements needs to explain which justification he has in mind. As we also saw, the best answer is usually that neutralism is a practical principle, and so constrains all the reasons for which agents may seek to influence their government. But that answer is unsatisfactory where stability is in question, for no one's reasons can affect another's behavior unless the other knows *what those reasons are.* Thus, because most people's political reasoning is *not* known to many others, most can act for blatantly nonneutral reasons without eliciting significant destabilizing behavior.

To give the proposed argument a fighting chance, we therefore must specify the relevant reasons differently. Instead of concentrating on the reasoning of agents, we must focus on reasons that are somehow *in the public domain.* The most promising way to do this is suggested by the work of the later Rawls. As we saw, Rawls now stresses the connections between social stability and ideas implicit in "the political institutions of a constitutional regime and the public traditions of their interpretation (including those of the judiciary), as well as historic texts and documents that are common knowledge."[26] Because these ideas pervade what Rawls calls "the public political culture," any reasons they provide will indeed be accessible to many people.

Cast in these terms, the current proposal asserts that a society is unlikely to be stable unless its basic structure conforms to principles whose neutral justification is implicit in its political culture. But should we take this proposal to specify a necessary condition for the stability of *all* societies or only those whose public political culture *already supports* a neutral justification of a set of principles? On the first reading, the proposal asserts that *no* society can be stable unless

25. Along these lines, Peter De Marneffe has argued *for* a neutrality constraint on the justification of the basic structure, but *against* such a constraint on the justifications for specific laws and policies, in "Liberalism, Liberty, and Neutrality," *Philosophy and Public Affairs* 19, 3 (Summer 1990), pp. 253–74. De Marneffe, however, does not base his position on the requirements of social stability.
26. John Rawls, *Political Liberalism* (New York: Columbia University Press, 1993), pp. 13–14.

its public political culture supports a neutral justification of a set of principles of justice to which its basic structure conforms; on the second, it asserts only that because our own public political culture *does* support a neutral justification of a set of principles of justice, *our own society* is unlikely to be stable unless its basic structure conforms to those very principles. Of the proposal's two variants, it is obviously the second that comes closer to Rawls's own view.

At least prima facie, the proposal's two variants raise very different issues. The first seems incautiously sweeping, whereas the second is far more cautious but rests on a debatable interpretation of our public political culture. Still, despite these differences, neither variant will provide even a partial explanation of our own (American) society's evident stability unless (1) the ideas implicit in our public political culture do support a neutral justification of certain principles of justice; and (2) our own basic political framework conforms to those neutrally justified principles; and (3) our society's members – ordinary Americans, you and I – are widely (though no doubt inchoately) aware of (1) and (2). Thus, to rebut both variants, it seems sufficient to discredit one of these three claims.

At first glance, this may seem hard to do, since (1)–(3) can each be fleshed out in many different ways. That is, because (1) does not mention any particular principles or neutral justification of them, it, and so also (2) and (3), can be made true by many *different* principles and neutral justifications. Still, for reasons that will become apparent, each way of giving content to (1)–(3) raises essentially the same difficulties. Hence, for convenience, we may couch our discussion exclusively in Rawlsian terms.

This is convenient because the content of a Rawlsian version of (1) has already been specified. As we saw in the preceding chapter, the neutrality of the arguments for Rawls's two principles is guaranteed by the fact that the parties in the original position are ignorant of their own (and all other) conceptions of the good. As we also saw, Rawls's larger theory, which encompasses his various arguments for the design of the original position, is now put forth precisely as embodying the main ideas implicit in our public political culture. As Rawls himself puts it, justice as fairness tries to

organiz[e] familiar ideas and principles into a conception of political justice that expresses those ideas and principles in a somewhat different way than before . . . by using a fundamental organizing idea within which all ideas and principles can be systematically connected and related. This organizing idea is that of society as a fair system of social cooperation between free and equal persons viewed as fully cooperating members of society over a complete life.[27]

Thus, taken together, the different components of Rawls's theory yield precisely the claim that our public political culture supports a neutral justification of his principles of justice – that is, a version of (1).

They also arguably support a version of (2) – the claim that our society's basic framework *conforms* to (1)'s neutrally justified principles. This is somewhat less obvious because Rawls was not trying to establish the justice of any actual institutions in *A Theory of Justice*. His aim there was simply to tell us what a just society would be like. Still, his discussion remains relevant to the justice of our own society because his principles appear to permit, if not require, a basic framework much like ours. His principle of maximal equal liberty calls for a constitutional democracy that secures for each citizen the various political liberties and a full complement of familiar procedural and civil rights; and his difference principle is at least compatible with a free-market economy adjusted by welfare transfers. Hence, Rawls's defense of his principles can be viewed as an indirect defense of the justice of (something like) our own framework.[28]

We can, then, easily enough construct Rawlsian versions of both (1) and (2). Moreover, because we can, we can also formulate a Rawlsian version of (3). At a minimum, this Rawlsian (3) will assert that most people in our society are inchoately aware that its basic structure conforms to Rawls's two principles. But such inchoate awareness is unlikely to affect anyone's behavior unless he also *accepts* Rawls's principles; and few are likely to do that without understanding the principles' rationale. Thus, to have any explanatory impact, (3) must also postulate an inchoate acceptance of the *case* for Rawls's principles. And since that case encompasses both Rawls's arguments

27. Ibid., p. 9.
28. Rawls himself is not willing to accept this conclusion without substantial qualification. He writes, for example, that "as [our] institutions presently exist they are riddled with grave injustices" (*A Theory of Justice* [Cambridge, Mass.: Harvard University Press, 1971], p. 87). Still, there is considerable weight to Raz's observation that "[i]t would seem that Rawls, as many suspected, thinks that the United States and other modern Western democracies are basically just societies. This . . . is a necessary, indeed a crucial, assumption if his theory is to be applicable to the contemporary societies it is meant for" (Joseph Raz, "Facing Diversity: The Case of Epistemic Abstinence," *Philosophy and Public Affairs* 19, 1 [Winter 1990], p. 6, n. 6).

for the design and authority of the original position and his arguments that the two principles would emerge from it, the augmented Rawlsian (3) must in effect assert that we inchoately accept Rawls's theory itself.

But do we? Do most Americans accept, even in an inchoate and inarticulate way, either Rawls's basic premises or the conclusions that he derives from them? In *A Theory of Justice*, Rawls described his initial assumptions as "generally shared and . . . weak";[29] but he made no similar claims about either the reasoning from his initial assumptions to the design or moral authority of the original position, or the further reasoning from the design of the original position to the conclusion that his two principles would emerge from it. Indeed, if anything, his aim in that book appeared to be precisely to *convince* us to accept each of these inferences. Hence, at least in *A Theory of Justice*, Rawls did not attribute the stability of our society to our prior acceptance of his (or any other) arguments.

And given the nature of his arguments, this reticence was surely wise. Because Rawls's arguments are many-sided, complex, and extremely controversial, it would strain credulity to suppose that most ordinary citizens have from the beginning inchoately accepted them. A fortiori, it would strain credulity to suppose that a widespread inchoate awareness that our basic structure conforms to the principles they yield plays any significant role in preventing us from engaging in destabilizing behavior. One might argue with as much cogency (i.e., none) that most Americans are prevented from making gross statistical errors by their deep inchoate awareness of the details of the probability calculus. And, of course, a parallel objection will block the claim that our society owes its stability to our inchoate awareness that its basic structure conforms to any *other* neutrally derivable set of principles.

Perhaps, however, this objection misses the point. Perhaps we should take (3) to claim that we inchoately believe, not that our society's basic structure conforms to Rawls's (or any other) neutrally derivable principles, but only that it conforms to the broader ideas from which Rawls (now) claims his principles can be "worked up." Perhaps, in other words, the crucial stabilizing belief is simply that

29. Rawls, *A Theory of Justice*, p. 20. They include, among others, the assumptions that any adequate justification of a set of social arrangements must be able to withstand public scrutiny and that "no one deserves his place in the distribution of native endowments" (p. 104).

our society *is* a fair scheme of cooperation for the allocation of benefits and burdens among free and equal persons.

Because the idea of a fair scheme can be understood in many ways, the supposition that many of us hold some such belief, and that this leads many of us to moderate our demands, is not entirely implausible. But just because the idea of a fair scheme is so open-ended, the proposed stabilizing belief is too deracinated to preserve a link between stability and neutrality. For even if the best interpretation of fairness does involve neutrality – even if, for example, the best interpretation is Rawlsian – most citizens are unlikely to be aware of this fact. Hence, a fortiori, most are also unlikely to be influenced by it. Instead, most who refrain from destabilizing behavior because they regard their society as fair are apt to understand fairness very differently (if, indeed, they assign it any definite meaning at all). Some may believe that democracy is fair in the sense that it gives each citizen an equal voice in matters of common concern. Others may take our framework to be fair in the sense that its procedures for making, revising, and enforcing laws and policies are impersonal and the same for all. Still others may take those procedures to be fair because they are fixed prior to any of the controversies whose orderly resolution they make possible. And, of course, there are many further possibilities.[30]

Thus, even if some inchoate belief about our framework's fairness *did* contribute to our society's stability, we would have little reason to suppose that the operative notion of fairness had any connection to neutrality. But, further, we have so far encountered no positive reason to suppose that beliefs about our framework's fairness *do* contribute much to our society's stability. Although I have accepted this assumption for purposes of discussion, neither Rawls nor anyone else has offered any real argument for it. Thus, for all that anyone has said, our society may not owe its stability to any shared beliefs at all. Instead – to cite just one alternative – "affective and symbolic elements may well be the crucial cement of society."[31] So for this reason,

---

30. Raz makes a similar point when he writes that while the citizens of stable societies do share attachment to certain values, "these are normally expressed at a high level of abstraction (liberty, equality, fraternity) which is compatible with complete disagreement about constitutional principles (for example, between royalists and republicans, or between fascists, democrats, and revolutionary communists)" ("Facing Diversity," p. 31).

31. Ibid., p. 30.

too, the link between our society's stability and a neutral justification of its basic structure has not been established.

VII

That leaves only the third prophylactic argument, which focuses not on the dangers of oppression or instability, but rather on the risk of error. Its main premise is that when a government tries to improve its citizens' lives, its conception of the good may be distorted, misguided, or false. If a government is thus mistaken, its nonneutral policies may actually make people's lives worse. To avoid such counterproductive effects, the state is sometimes urged to remain neutral toward all questions about the good. Indeed, in John Stuart Mill's view, "[t]he strongest of all the arguments against the interference of the public with purely personal conduct is that, when it does interfere, the odds are that it interferes wrongly and in the wrong place."[32]

Despite its illustrious provenance, the argument as stated is radically incomplete. We certainly may concede that all judgments about the good are uncertain and prone to error. We may concede, as well, that those with the most political power are unlikely also to be wisest. But in return, a neutralist must concede that if the state does *not* try to promote the good, then other, equally unreliable determining factors will rush in to fill the void. The goodness of people's lives will then depend more heavily on *their own* fallible judgments, and on the unintended consequences of government decisions reached for quite different reasons. Because these factors, too, can worsen as well as improve lives, it is far from obvious that nonneutral policies are on the whole counterproductive.

Indeed, if anything, the presumption surely runs the other way; for conscientious, self-correcting efforts to improve a situation usually *do* make it better. That is why persons seek medical treatment despite the dangers of misdiagnosis and harmful side effects; and it is why governments try to stimulate economic growth despite the risk of worsening the economy by increasing inflation. In these and innumerable other contexts, the reasonable response to the possibility of making things worse is not to do nothing but to temper meliorism with thought and care.

32. John Stuart Mill, *On Liberty* (Indianapolis: Bobbs-Merrill, 1956), p. 102.

This in turn does not *defeat* the third prophylactic argument. It shows only that the argument's proponents must augment it with an account of why the state's efforts to promote the good are especially prone to error, and why this increased probability of error tips the balance against them. Not surprisingly, some of the most important attempts to show this are again to be found in *On Liberty*. I shall concentrate on three.

THE APPEAL TO EPISTEMIC AUTHORITY

In general, an agent's efforts to improve a situation are most likely to succeed when the agent is most fully informed. Hence, one obvious reason why government is apt to inferfere "wrongly and in the wrong place" is that it is too remote from its citizens to know their individual tastes, capacities, aspirations, strengths, and weaknesses. Such information is important because any reasonable theory of the good – even a reasonable perfectionist theory – must allow that how well a person lives depends partly on how enjoyable and fulfilling he finds his life. Thus, to have the best chance of improving its citizens' lives, a government would need not only a well-grounded theory of the good, but also a vast store of fine-grained information about individuals. But given the prohibitively high cost of gathering such information, the state's decisions must instead "be grounded on general presumptions which may be altogether wrong and, even if right, are as likely as not to be misapplied to individual cases, by persons no better acquainted with the circumstances of such cases than those are who look at them merely from without."[33] This reliance on aggregate data is entirely reasonable when the aim is (e.g.) to promote economic growth or to reduce infant mortality; but when the goal is to induce citizens to live well, it threatens to channel many into stifling, unfulfilling lives.

By contrast, each individual is in a much better position to know his own requirements. As Mill observed, "with respect to his own feelings and circumstances the most ordinary man or woman has means of knowledge immeasurably surpassing those that can be possessed by anyone else."[34] And because each person is so intimately acquainted with his own tastes, predilections, and capacities,

33. Ibid., p. 93.
34. Ibid.

the state is urged to leave all self-regarding decisions entirely up to him.

THE APPEAL TO MOTIVATION

Another factor that determines whether one's efforts are likely to make things better or worse is one's degree of commitment. We make the best decisions when we try hardest, and we try hardest when we have most at stake. Thus, a second reason to mistrust the state's efforts to improve citizens' lives is that those who initiate them have so *little* at stake.

The main point here is not that policy makers are often unaffected by their own decisions. This, though true, does not distinguish legislators who seek to promote the good from officials who set economic policy, or from physicians who minister to others. The more important difference is that whereas success in stimulating the economy or improving someone's health is comparatively easy to recognize, success at inducing persons to live well is far less clear-cut and is subject to no generally recognized test. Thus, whereas physicians and economic policy makers can expect eventually to be judged by their results, voters, legislators, and bureaucrats who act on their conceptions of the good have no comparable expectations. They are therefore under little pressure to think critically about those conceptions. This poses an obvious danger that when they try to promote the good, they will act on unexamined and ungrounded prejudices.

But that danger, too, recedes when the decision is left to the individual; for he "is the person most interested in his own well-being: the interest which any other person, except in cases of strong personal attachment, can have in it is trifling compared with that which he himself has; the interest which society has in him individually . . . is fractional and altogether indirect."[35] Because each person has only one life, each person has a strong motive to take the care to make his life as good as possible.

THE APPEAL TO FUTURE KNOWLEDGE

A final reason to be wary of the state's efforts to promote the good concerns their longer-term epistemic effects. Most governmental

35. Ibid.

decisions do not affect the information that will be available to us in the future. For example, when a government adopts a new economic policy, it does not impede the future flow of economic data. But if the state were to channel all citizens into a single way of life, it arguably *would* choke off a crucial source of future insight; for by suppressing diversity, it would eliminate a main laboratory for generating and testing new hypotheses about the good life. Quoting Mill yet again, "[t]here is always need of persons not only to discover new truths and point out when what were once truths are true no longer, but also to commence new practices and set the example of more enlightened conduct and better taste and sense in human life."[36] According to this final argument, the worry is not so much that the state's *present* judgments about the good may be wrong, but that an artificially induced uniformity may render its *future* judgments less reliable.

VIII

All three of Mill's subarguments clearly contain much truth. Taken together, they may well support some restriction on the use of state power to promote the good. But even if they do, it does not follow that the restriction they support is neutralism. Instead, what they show may be only that before we base a political action on any conception of the good, we must scrutinize that conception to make sure that it satisfies our normal standards of justification.

To make this alternative easier to compare with neutralism, let us put them both in the same form. Roughly speaking, what the principle of neutrality says is

(N) Do not support any law or policy on the basis of any particular conception of the good life.

By contrast, the proposed moderate alternative says only:

(M) Do not support any law or policy on the basis of any conception of the good that you have not scrutinized and found to satisfy your usual standards of justification.

36. Ibid., p. 78.

Like (N), (M) may be taken to constrain either governments themselves or individuals seeking to influence them; and, also like (N), (M) may be taken to apply at various political levels. In each case, our question is which principle represents a more reasonable response to Mill's worries.

Mill himself foresaw, but did not take seriously, a response along (M)'s general lines. He wrote at one point that it "is easy for anyone to imagine an ideal public which leaves the freedom and choice of individuals in all uncertain matters undisturbed and only requires them to abstain from modes of conduct which universal experience has condemned."[37] However, immediately afterward, Mill dismissed this possibility by asking, "But where has there been seen a public which set any such limit to its censorship? Or when does the public trouble itself about universal experience?"[38] These rhetorical questions suggest that Mill's reason for not taking (M) seriously is that we cannot realistically expect it to be widely followed.

But this rejoinder proves too much; for if it succeeds against (M), it is no less successful against (N). If Mill can plausibly say that no actual public has consistently refrained from acting on (what it should regard as) all *indefensible* conceptions of the good, then we can say, with no less plausibility, that no actual public has consistently refrained from acting on *any conceptions of the good at all.* Thus, if principles that were not followed consistently in the past are not acceptable now, then we must reject (N) as well as (M); while if such principles may still be acceptable – as, surely, they sometimes can – then we need not reject either.

Perhaps, however, this rejoinder misses Mill's point. Instead of maintaining only that no public *actually has* conformed to (M), perhaps he is making the more substantive point that no public can *reasonably be expected* to conform to (M). That is, because political agents pay no price for acting on indefensible conceptions of the good, perhaps Mill is objecting that they will also pay no price for ignoring (M)'s demand that they *not* act on indefensible conceptions

---

37. Ibid., p. 102. The restriction Mill envisions is not identical to (M), since the members of Mill's "ideal public" would ask not whether their conception of the good is justified, but only whether their judgment is supported by "universal experience." However, because both restrictions forbid us only to base political decisions on conceptions of the good that fail certain tests, they are obviously closely analogous.

38. Ibid.

of the good. On this interpretation, Mill's point will be not merely that historical experience shows (M) to be ineffective, but that (M) *must* be ineffective because it only reraises the difficulty it is introduced to solve.

Yet even on this interpretation, Mill's argument proves too much; for if introducing (M) would only reraise the original problem, then so, again, would introducing (N). This follows from the fact that anyone who conforms to (N) must at the same time conform to (M), and hence, by contraposition, that anyone who violates (M) must at the same time violate (N). Given this linkage, anyone who pays no penalty for basing a political decision on what he takes to be an indefensible conception of the good, and so violating (M), will also pay no penalty for basing his decision on a conception of the good *simpliciter,* and so violating (N). Thus, if the absence of penalties for disobedience undermines the effectiveness of (M), it will also and equally undermine the effectiveness of (N).

Even on its more substantive reading, Mill's argument does not distinguish (N) from (M). But what, exactly, should we make of this? Should we conclude that the argument succeeds and, hence, that *neither (M) nor (N)* can effectively constrain political behavior? Or should we conclude that the argument fails and, hence, that *both (M) and (N)* remain live options?

Although the first conclusion would make shorter work of neutralism, I am inclined to favor the second; for even if (M) and (N) are *not* backed by penalties, it hardly follows that neither can significantly influence behavior. To draw this inference, one would have to assume that *only* penalties (or other external incentives) can give persons new motives; and that assumption is surely false. Many people are motivated to refrain from lying and acting unfairly by their belief that these acts are wrong; and there is no reason why many could not be similarly motivated by their acceptance of (M) or (N). Moreover, someone might be led to accept (M) or (N), and thus to acquire such motivation, either through his own reflections on the danger that government may act "wrongly and in the wrong place," or else through a public political culture that affirms one or another principle as a basic ground rule of political debate. Also, of course, either principle may underwrite the creation of legal or political structures which *in their turn* channel political decisions in the desired directions. To do that, a legal or political structure may either make it more difficult to base political decisions on the proscribed reasons, or else filter out laws or policies whose main justifications are apt to involve such reasons.[39] Thus, all in all, it seems safe to set aside the worry about (M)'s and (N)'s potential effectiveness.

IX

But which principle, if either, do Mill's arguments support? Will people's lives go best if political agents always act on their conceptions of the good; if they act only on conceptions that on reflection seem justifiable to them; or if they act on no conceptions at all?

That depends, in part, on the relation between justification and truth. Let us say that a given standard of justification is *truth-conducive* if beliefs that satisfy it are more likely to be true than beliefs that do not. If our standards are not truth-conducive in this sense, then we will not increase our odds of improving people's lives by conforming to (M). Thus, to decide among the possibilities, we may seem forced to ask whether our standards of justification *are* truth-conducive, and thus to confront the difficult and perhaps unsolvable problem of skepticism.[40]

But, fortunately, we need not get bogged down in the skeptical morass; for our question is not whether to abandon our ordinary standards of justification – how else could we approach any practical decision? – but only which constraint on political decision making best satisfies them. That is, what we want to know is whether, given our ordinary standards, we are justified in believing that we should not base political decisions even on beliefs about the good whose own justifications *satisfy* those standards. Far from casting doubt on our ordinary standards of justification, this question actually presupposes them. Hence, when we raise the question as individual agents, we may simply assume that our individual standards are truth-

39. I argued earlier that rights cannot effectively filter out nonneutral reasons; but other ways of institutionalizing (N) or (M) may be more effective. To cite just one example, one effect of the difficulty of amending the United States Constitution is surely to compel those who urge amendments to defend them in detail. In so doing, they may well be compelled to scrutinize any perfectionist premises more carefully than they otherwise might.

40. By putting this point in terms of truth, I have of course used the language of moral realism. But this is not essential to my argument, since even antirealists must make some distinction between acceptable and unacceptable moral claims. Thus, everything I say in this paragraph can be recast in terms of acceptability, validity, or whatever other property the antirealist takes as his proxy for moral truth.

conducive; when we raise it as a collectivity, we may similarly assume this about our collective standards.

Assuming, then, that our ordinary standards are truth-conducive, what should we conclude about the competing principles? Should we accept (M), (N), or neither principle? One easy inference is that conforming to (M) is better than conforming to neither principle, since if our standards are truth-conducive, then any conception of the good that satisfies them will be more likely to be true than one that does not. Hence, basing political decisions only on conceptions of the good that satisfy our standards will indeed increase our odds of improving people's lives. But do we increase those odds most by following *only* (M) or the more demanding (N)? Is it more reasonable to base our political actions only on *justified* conceptions of the good, or on *no such conceptions at all?*

These alternatives are not necessarily distinct; for (M) will collapse into (N) if no conceptions of the good *are* justified. Thus, one way to argue for (N) would be to combine (M) with value-skepticism. But thus construed, the argument for neutralism would be skeptical rather than prophylactic. This sort of argument will be considered later. Thus, for now, let us assume that from each (individual and collective) agent's perspective, at least some beliefs about the good *can* be justified.

Granting this, do any of Mill's arguments support (N) over (M)? Do considerations of epistemic authority, motivation, or future knowledge make it unreasonable to base political decisions even on conceptions of the good that careful reflection endorses as justified?[41] To find out, let us begin with the appeal to epistemic authority. This argument, it will be recalled, rests on the premise that each person has exclusive and intimate knowledge of his own capacities, requirements, and limitations, and it concludes that basing political arrangements on any particular conception of the good is bound to condemn many to unhappy and unfulfilled, and therefore bad, lives.

When this argument is advanced to support (N) over (M), the main question about it is *whom it should convince.* To find it convinc-

---

41. This seems to be the sort of question that Mill himself was asking; for there are many places at which he implies that the inherent goodness or badness of a type of activity can sometimes be known. He writes, for example, that "[t]here is a degree of folly, and a degree of what may be called (though the phrase is not unobjectionable) lowness or deprivation of taste, which, though it cannot justify doing harm to the person who manifests it, renders him necessarily and properly a subject of distaste, or, in extreme cases, even of contempt" (*On Liberty*, p. 94).

ing, one must accept Mill's premise that unhappiness and lack of fulfillment make a person's life worse. But if someone accepts this premise, and so regards happiness or fulfillment as at least a partial determinant of a life's goodness, then he must also believe that to live good lives, individuals need enough options to accommodate their own tastes and abilities.[42] Moreover, if someone believes *this*, he must expect a conscientious application of his own standards to lead him to support policies that at most prune or shape, but do not radically reduce, the prevailing option range. He must expect (M) to lead him to support policies that will make intrinsically valuable activities easily available while making intrinsically *dis*valuable activities harder or impossible to pursue, but *not* to support policies that ignore the importance of individuality or impose the same regimen on everyone. And, hence, his acceptance of Mill's premise about the value of enjoyment and fulfillment will not give him reason to adopt (N) instead of (M); for precisely *because* he accepts that premise, he can expect (M) itself to prevent him from supporting overly restrictive policies.

But neither, of course, will someone who *rejects* Mill's premise have grounds for adopting (N) rather than (M). Because such a person will *not* regard happiness or fulfillment as an important contributor to a good life, he may well expect (M) to lead him to favor rigid, restrictive policies. However, this expectation, if he has it, will be based precisely on his belief that rigid, restrictive policies really are best. Thus, such a person will not regard these policies as *overly* restrictive at all. So from his perspective too, adopting (M) rather than (N) will increase his odds of improving rather than worsening lives. And because the two alternatives are exhaustive, there appears to be *no one* whom Mill's appeal to epistemic authority should convince to accept (N) rather than (M).

There may, however, still be some whom Mill's argument should convince to try to bring *others* to accept (N) rather than (M), or to want (N) rather than (M) to be widely promulgated or institutionally realized. In particular, someone might have reason to seek these goals if, on the one hand, he himself believed that a life's overall goodness *was* a complex function of both the intrinsic value of its

42. Compare Raz: "There are many possible options the provision of which can make the available options adequate. It is in deciding which options to encourage more than others that perfectionist considerations dominate" (*The Morality of Freedom* [Oxford: Oxford University Press, 1986], p. 418).

activities and the amount of satisfaction and fulfillment it contains, but, on the other hand, he believed that most *other* people believe that a life's overall goodness depends *only* on the intrinsic value of its activities. If someone expected most others to make (what he considers) this mistake, then he would expect (M)'s general acceptance to lead most people to favor policies that, if adopted, *would* lead to widespread frustration and unhappiness. And given this expectation, he might indeed have reason to conclude that (N)'s wide acceptance would on the whole bring better results than (M)'s.

But this reasoning is no stronger than the assumption that most others do entirely deny that unhappiness and frustration are disvaluable; and I have already suggested that that assumption is implausible. The occasional fanatic aside, most contemporary perfectionists – both philosophers and ordinary citizens – will gladly acknowledge that no single trait, activity, or relationship has a monopoly on intrinsic value. Most also will acknowledge that happiness and fulfillment are additional important determinants of well-being. And because most contemporary perfectionists are in both senses pluralists, there is little danger that (M) would lead many to favor the sorts of restrictive policies that, if adopted, would leave many unhappy or frustrated. These are, of course, empirical claims, but so too are their denials. I think there is little doubt about which empirical claims are more plausible.

Having come this far, we can deal more quickly with Mill's other two arguments. According to the argument from motivation, we should not base political decisions on even those conceptions of the good that we consider well grounded because we have independent reason to question our own motivation to give such issues careful enough thought. Because we are far less strongly motivated to think carefully about another's well-being than he himself is, we should simply quit the field and let him decide the matter for himself. To this argument, it seems sufficient to respond by simply repeating two of our earlier conclusions: first, that if we lacked the motivation carefully to apply (M), we would also lack the motivation carefully to apply (N); but, second, that there is no real reason to believe that we lack motivation carefully to apply *either* principle. To these conclusions, I shall add only that Mill appears not only to have underestimated the degree to which persons may care about others' well-being, but also to have overestimated the degree to which persons must care about themselves. Given the truly impressive array of social pathologies with which we are surrounded, Mill's assumption that most people are robustly self-protective seems, at the least, an overstatement.[43]

That leaves only the third, experiments-in-living argument for favoring (N) over (M). According to this final argument, even the best-grounded efforts to promote the good would stamp out originality and bring a stifling conformity. In so doing, they would deprive us of the many new insights about the good that a diverse array of activities and practices can yield. But here, again, it seems sufficient to point out that very few contemporary citizens believe either that only a single way of living has intrinsic value, or that happiness and fulfillment play no significant role in determining how well people live. Because most people reject both claims, most are no less committed than Mill to preserving both a wide range of options and a high degree of freedom to choose among them. And this means that even if we do opt for (M) rather than (N), the policies we end up favoring will still leave ample room for innumerable "experiments in living." Furthermore, even when certain "experiments" are ruled out, much of the insight they might yield will often be available in other ways. For example, even if the state bans the sale and use of narcotics, it may and should still allow both their study in the laboratory and a full and free debate over their decriminalization.

This last point requires special emphasis, for it brings out an implication that must not be overlooked. Precisely because (M) permits us to base political decisions only on conceptions of the good that we have critically scrutinized, it must require that every person have every chance to engage in such scrutiny. This means that far from justifying restrictions on study or debate, (M) positively requires that all modes of inquiry be protected and encouraged. It requires that everyone have the freest access both to everything that might be said for and against any conception of the good and to all empirical information that might be relevant to such debates. Like Mill himself, any proponent of (M) must place an extremely high premium on open discussion and unfettered scientific investigation. Precisely *because* it leaves all questions about the good on the public agenda, (M) requires an especially uncompromising commitment to freedom of thought and expression.

43. This point is well made by Gerald Dworkin in his essay "Paternalism," *Monist* 56 (1972), pp. 64–84.

X

This concludes my discussion of the prophylactic arguments for neutralism. Against them, I have argued that neutrality is not warranted by the risks of oppression, instability, or error. Although I readily concede that each danger is real, I have argued that the best defense against each is an array of protections that leave ample room for a nonneutral politics. Because those protections include many familiar procedural and civil rights, my argument turns out to reaffirm much of what liberals have always believed.

This I take to be a strength rather than a weakness; for my quarrel is not with the whole liberal tradition, but only with the interpretation or strand that demands that governments take no position about the good life. By insisting on such neutrality, we would needlessly relinquish important benefits. Few would find it reasonable to respond to the risks of oppression, instability, or error by refusing to marshal the state's resources to strengthen the national defense or improve economic productivity. It is, I have argued, no more reasonable to refuse to marshal those resources in support of excellence, virtue, or the good.

Chapter 6

Knowing about the good

So far, I have criticized a number of attempts to ground neutralism in the demands of autonomy, and a number of others to ground it in the dangers posed by nonneutral states. But what, finally, of the third main class of arguments, which seek to ground neutralism in the impossibility (or the inordinate difficulty) of *knowing* the good? In the current chapter, I shall conclude my critique of neutralism by arguing that these arguments also fail. However, because the question of how we can know the good leads naturally to the question of what *is* good, the chapter also marks the transition to a more positive discussion of the values that governments *should* promote.

I

Historically and conceptually, the epistemological defense of neutralism is less important than the others. The majority of neutralists either say nothing about whether we can know the good or else say or imply that we sometimes can. Rawls, for example, has written that "it would be fatal to the idea of a political conception to see it as skeptical about, or indifferent to, truth, much less as in conflict with it."[1] Similarly, Ronald Dworkin has observed that "skepticism seems exactly the wrong answer to make, because if . . . each person should be free to choose personal ideals for himself, then this is surely because the choice of one life over another is a matter of supreme

1. John Rawls, *Political Liberalism* (New York: Columbia University Press, 1993), p. 150.

importance, not because it is of no importance at all."[2] Still, despite these disavowals, I think skepticism about the good has been a significant though often unacknowledged source of neutralism's appeal. Also, even when neutralists are not skeptics, their arguments often contain a substantial epistemological component. For both reasons, we must now consider the prospects for an epistemological defense.

Perhaps the most ambitious such defense, and certainly the baldest, is Bruce Ackerman's appeal to "skepticism concerning the reality of transcendent meaning." This is another of Ackerman's "four main highways to the liberal [i.e., neutral] state."[3] Ackerman bases his argument on the "hard truth" that there is "no moral meaning hidden in the bowels of the universe. All there is is you and I struggling in a world that neither we, nor any other thing, created."[4] From this nihilistic premise, Ackerman infers that we all must "impress our own meanings on the world."[5] That in turn is said to show that no one may compel another to live in a way that he, but not the other, considers meaningful.

As just presented, Ackerman's skeptical argument raises many questions. Without hearing more, many will be reluctant to accept his strong moral antirealism. Moreover, whatever "impressing meanings on the world" involves, even many antirealists may wonder why this must be a solitary endeavor. A natural alternative is that the construction of value is a *social* enterprise: moral meanings are often said to be generated by the practices, understandings, or conventions of the entire community. However, if values are a common product, then why can't a government that expresses a community's will base its decisions upon them?

Because these questions are raised by gaps in Ackerman's argument, a neutralist might answer them by filling in the gaps. Alternatively, he might simply develop the argument differently. But even if one of these strategies worked, any broadly skeptical argument would remain vulnerable to the further and less easily answered objection that it *proves too much.*

2. Ronald Dworkin, "Neutrality, Equality, and Liberalism," in Douglas MacLean and Claudia Mills, eds., *Liberalism Reconsidered* (Totawa, N.J.: Rowman and Allanheld, 1983), p. 2. See also Will Kymlicka, *Liberalism, Community, and Culture* (Oxford: Oxford University Press, 1989), pp. 17–20.
3. Bruce Ackerman, *Social Justice in the Liberal State* (New Haven: Yale University Press, 1980), p. 369.
4. Ibid., p. 368.
5. Ibid., p. 369.

For if a neutralist does appeal to skepticism about all normative beliefs (and, a fortiori, if he appeals to skepticism about *all* beliefs), then his skeptical premise will imply not only that we cannot know that (say) excellence is better than mediocrity or virtue than vice, but also that we cannot know what justice demands, what rights any individual has, or what any person is obligated to do or refrain from doing. But, needless to say, this is a price that few neutralists would wish to pay. Nor, more important, can they *afford* to pay it; for in doing so, they would undermine their ability to affirm one of the very premises that their own argument requires.

To see this, we need only state the argument a bit more precisely. So far, I have represented it as moving from the single premise that no one can know any normative proposition to the conclusion that the state should not base its decisions on any propositions about the good. But in this form, this argument is an enthymeme. To link its premise to its conclusion, we need a bridging premise: roughly, that the state *should not* base its decisions on any proposition whose truth cannot be known. But because this bridging premise is itself normative, it asserts just the sort of proposition that, according to the argument's skeptical premise, can never be known. Thus, in mounting his skeptical argument, the neutralist must be claiming to know what his bridging premise asserts – since otherwise he cannot claim to know anything he infers from it – while at the same time claiming to know something that implies that he *cannot* know it. He must, in effect, be advancing two premises, one of which commits him to just the sort of knowledge-claim whose possibility the other denies. And, hence, his argument must be pragmatically inconsistent.[6]

II

This objection tells against any defense of neutralism whose antirealism or skepticism extends to its own normative premises. It thus undermines both attempts to ground neutralism in antirealism or skepticism about *all* beliefs and attempts to ground neutralism in antirealism or skepticism about all *normative* beliefs. The objection also tells against any attempt to ground neutralism in a noncognitive

6. In the text, I focus only on the relations between the skeptical argument's premises. However, the same reasoning that shows them to be pragmatically inconsistent could of course be used to show that the argument's skeptical premise is pragmatically inconsistent with its conclusion.

analysis that applies to all normative discourse.[7] However, the objection does *not* discredit attempts to ground neutralism in forms of antirealism, skepticism, or noncognitivism that apply only to particular *conceptions of the good*. For as long as the neutralist doubts only our ability to know the good, he may consistently claim to know a bridging premise whose central normative notion is obligation and not value.

To be charitable, we should perhaps read Ackerman only as gesturing extravagantly in the direction of some kind of selective skepticism. Moreover, whatever Ackerman believes, a number of other neutralists do seem to regard the good as harder to know than the right. For example, D. A. Lloyd-Thomas not only implies that we can know what is just or right – his own argument rests squarely on a right of self-ownership – but also comes close to saying that we know various things about the good. He says, for instance, that "some of our [present] beliefs about what is of intrinsic value are very probably true.[8] However, Lloyd-Thomas also says that "it is not the case that we already know (everything) that is of intrinsic value,"[9] and that some common beliefs about the good – for instance, that pleasure is intrinsically valuable – are probably false.[10] And because Lloyd-Thomas believes that "[w]e are not certain, beyond reasonable doubt, what things are of intrinsic value,"[11] he concludes that we need the freedom to experiment that a neutral state would provide.

Because Lloyd-Thomas does not say that any aspects of the good *cannot* be known – the point of experimentation, after all, is precisely to *extend* our knowledge – his defense of neutralism is in no way skeptical. However, because he assumes that we are *currently* ignorant of many aspects of the good, his basic premise does remain epistemological. Moreover, because Lloyd-Thomas advocates experimentation to improve our knowledge of the good, but not our knowledge of justice, rights, or obligation (or, for that matter, of the value of health, safety, or freedom from suffering), he evidently sees the epistemic situation as somehow asymmetrical. Thus, whatever

---

7. For a version of the objection that specifically mentions efforts to ground neutralism in noncognitivism, see Jeremy Waldron, "Legislation and Moral Neutrality," in Robert E. Goodin and Andrew Reeve, eds., *Liberal Neutrality* (London: Routledge, 1989), p. 73.
8. D. A. Lloyd-Thomas, *In Defence of Liberalism* (Oxford: Basil Blackwell, 1988), p. 120.
9. Ibid., p. 121.
10. Ibid., pp. 113–21.
11. Ibid., p. 92.

his exact reasoning, he evidently takes some aspects of the good to pose some special epistemological problem.

And so too, perhaps, does Charles Larmore. We saw earlier that Larmore defends neutralism on the grounds that "even where we do believe that we have discerned the superiority of some ways of life to others, reasonable people may often not share our view."[12] But, as we also saw, there is just as much disagreement about what is right or just: think, for example, of the lack of consensus about the legitimacy of economic inequalities, or about the scope, or even the existence, of positive duties. Because Larmore does *not* urge that we refrain from basing political actions on all disputed beliefs about *these* topics, he evidently takes the two classes of beliefs to be importantly different. And although he nowhere explains the difference, one natural suggestion is that he takes disputes about what is right or just to be somehow less reasonable, or somehow less inevitable in light of the subject matter, than disputes about the good. However, if Larmore does hold any such view, then he too will take the good to pose some special epistemological problem.

But exactly why *should* the good be any harder to know than the right or just? Here one possibility is that judgments about the good are more emotionally loaded. As Rawls (among others) has observed, many who advance ostensibly perfectionist claims – for example, claims that "certain kinds of sexual relationships are degrading and shameful, and should be prohibited on this basis"[13] – are really only expressing their own visceral prejudices. Their judgments are "likely to be influenced by subtle aesthetic preferences and personal feelings of propriety."[14] Because judgments about the right are far less likely to be subject to these distorting influences, aren't they indeed more trustworthy than judgments about the good?

In fact, they are not; for even if judgments about the good are more vulnerable to distortion by prejudice and aesthetic preference, they are correspondingly *less* vulnerable to *other* sorts of distortion. In particular, because questions of right and justice are generally raised by conflicts of interest, our answers to them seem far more likely to reflect our own stake in the outcome. More specifically, those answers seem more likely to be swayed both by emotions such as envy,

12. Charles Larmore, *Patterns of Moral Complexity* (Cambridge: Cambridge University Press, 1987), p. 43.
13. John Rawls, *A Theory of Justice* (Cambridge, Mass.: Harvard University Press, 1971), p. 331.
14. Ibid.

resentment, and fear, and by motives such as selfishness, solidarity with favored economic classes or social or ethnic groups, and partiality toward known individuals. I am not sure which class of distorting factors is worse, but, either way, susceptibility to distortion is no basis for discounting judgments about the good but not the right.

Is there any deeper reason to single out judgments about the good? This question is hard to answer because the way we approach it will depend – no doubt among other things – on our theories of knowledge and justification. Because these topics are themselves disputed, I cannot explore all the possibilities. However, I can at least argue that according to one particularly influential theory – not coincidentally, the one I favor – the prospects for justifying claims about the good and the right are exactly on a par. Other theories, I believe, would lead to the same conclusion by somewhat different routes.

III

The theory whose implications I want to trace is broadly coherentist. It asserts that there are no epistemologically privileged beliefs and, hence, that a belief's justification cannot reside either in the fact that it is self-evident or in its relations to *other* self-evident beliefs. Instead, to be justified, a belief need only hang together, in a certain hard-to-specify but recognizable manner, with as much else as possible of what the subject believes. As Rawls puts (what I take to be) the same point, a belief is justified when, and because, it would survive if the subject were to bring all of his beliefs into "reflective equilibrium."[15]

This broadly coherentist approach is very widely accepted.[16] It is shared both by many internalists, who maintain that a belief's justifi-

---

15. Ibid., especially sec. 9. See also John Rawls, "Outline of a Decision Procedure for Ethics," *Philosophical Review* 60 (1951), pp. 177–97, and "The Independence of Moral Theory," *Proceedings and Addresses of the American Philosophical Association* 47 (1974–75), pp. 5–22.
16. Indeed, although it is hard to measure these things, it seems to me that coherentism may have replaced foundationalism as the dominant view. This judgment is shared by Bernard Williams, who writes that "the foundationalist enterprise, of resting the structure of knowledge on some favored class of statements, has now generally been displaced in favor of a holistic type of model, in which some beliefs can be questioned, justified, or adjusted while others are kept constant, but there is no process by which they can all be questioned at once, or all justified in terms of (almost) nothing" (*Ethics and the Limits of Philosophy* [Cambridge, Mass.: Harvard University Press, 1985], p. 113).

cation must be accessible to the person who holds it, and by many who reject internalism. It is also common both to many naturalists, who see no discontinuity between philosophy and the natural and social sciences, and to many others who are more aprioristically inclined.[17] Moreover, the view's popularity is no accident: it has much to recommend it, including both its evident fit with the un-avoidable fact that all inquiries must be initiated, pursued, and checked against a background of already formed beliefs and its abil-ity to avoid the many technical difficulties that beset the idea of a self-justifying belief.[18] But this is not a book about epistemology, and I cannot elaborate these arguments here. They have been ably developed by others. Thus, having registered my confidence in them, I shall proceed directly to those aspects of coherentism that have the greatest bearing on the good.

As I just said, the basic coherentist insight is that no belief is epis-temically privileged. Whatever a belief's content, it is justified when and only when it would survive (or, on some versions of the theory, it actually has survived) a process in which the believer evaluates each of his convictions in light of all the others, and makes whatever additions and deletions are needed to render the whole set as coherent as possible. In this context, coherence involves considerably more than simple logical consistency. In addition, it encompasses a belief-set's scope, simplicity, and explanatory power.[19] Thus, other things being equal, a more comprehensive belief-set is more coherent than a less comprehensive one. Moreover, a belief-set's coherence will be further increased if it contains general beliefs that unify and explain disparate particular ones, and if it incorporates causal princi-ples that license second-order beliefs that various first-order beliefs

17. Compare, for example, the versions of coherentism advanced by W. V. O. Quine and by Lawrence BonJour. Quine develops his naturalistic version in many places, among them "Two Dogmas of Empiricism," in *From a Logical Point of View* (New York: Harper and Row, 1953), pp. 20–46. BonJour's version appears in *The Struc-ture of Empirical Knowledge* (Cambridge, Mass.: Harvard University Press, 1985).
18. What one regards as the crucial problems will depend on one's views about other matters. To an internalist, for example, one very important problem is that even if a belief is infallible or highly reliable, a person is not justified in holding it unless he has good reason to regard it *as* infallible or highly reliable. This means that the person must rely on some further belief about what *makes* the first belief infallible or highly reliable. But if the original belief's justification does thus depend on a further belief, then it is not self-justifying after all.
19. For discussion, see BonJour, *The Structure of Empirical Knowledge*, pp. 93–101, and W. V. O. Quine and J. S. Ullian, *The Web of Beliefs* (New York: Random House, 1970), ch. 5.

are (likely to be) true.[20] Because each of us is constantly acquiring new beliefs, each belief's justificatory status is always subject to revision in light of new information. Hence, even beliefs whose rejection is unimaginable now may later have to be abandoned if they fail to cohere with (enough) others.

How, exactly, does this model apply to normative claims? Because so much ethical argumentation consists mainly of attempts to square moral principles with moral intuitions, we may be tempted to suppose that justifying a normative belief consists exclusively of showing it to cohere with other normative beliefs. However, on inspection, this cannot be right. The problem is not merely that without appealing to nonnormative premises, we could not know which actions satisfy whatever criteria of rightness or goodness we accept. It is, more deeply, that without appealing to the facts of psychology (including both the truisms of "folk psychology" and the results of experimental research), we would have no basis for discounting moral beliefs that were formed under conditions unconducive to rational thought; that without appealing to the full range of political, economic, and scientific theories, we could not know which social and political arrangements are feasible; and that without marshaling philosophical arguments, we could not decide which sorts of evidence are relevant to normative claims. Because we obviously must invoke these and various other considerations, it seems best to set no a priori limits on the kinds of beliefs that can contribute to the justification of a normative claim. Reverting again to Rawls's terminology, it seems best to opt for wide rather than narrow reflective equilibrium.[21]

Although this approach to justification avoids many difficulties, it is no panacea against either general or moral skepticism. The general skeptic asks what reason we have to accept *any* beliefs. Instead of supposing that our beliefs correspond to reality, why not suppose that they were produced en masse by a Cartesian demon, or by a mad scientist stimulating a brain floating in a vat? Confronted by

20. See, for example, W. V. O. Quine, "The Nature of Natural Knowledge," in Samuel Guttenplan, ed., *Mind and Language: Wolfson College Lectures* (Oxford: Oxford University Press, 1975), pp. 67–81, and BonJour, *The Structure of Empirical Knowledge,* part 2. The role of second-order beliefs is stressed by Michael Williams, "Coherence, Justification, and Truth," *Review of Metaphysics* 34 (December 1980), pp. 243–72.

21. See Rawls, "The Independence of Moral Theory," and Norman Daniels, "Wide Reflective Equilibrium and Theory Acceptance in Ethics," *Journal of Philosophy* 76, 5 (May 1979), pp. 256–82.

these questions, coherentists often appeal to background theories that imply that our having various beliefs is best explained by the very facts that would make those beliefs true.[22] However, because the background theories are themselves part of what the skeptic doubts, it is unclear whether this maneuver can avoid begging the question.

Even if it can, the answer that works against *general* skepticism will not necessarily also succeed against *moral* skepticism. Here the problem is to provide a theoretical account of how our moral beliefs could be shaped by moral facts or, alternatively, of why it does not matter if they are not. Despite the strenuous efforts of naturalists to show that the moral supervenes on the nonmoral in the same way that (say) the psychological supervenes on the physical, it is far from clear that moral facts are part of the best explanation of the existence of our moral beliefs in the same way that nonmoral facts are part of the best explanation of the existence of our nonmoral beliefs.[23] Nor, despite the equally strenuous efforts of constructivists to explain how moral beliefs can have objective content without aspiring to truth, is it clear that any nonrealist notion of moral objectivity can be both intelligible and intellectually satisfying.[24] Of course, a plausible account along one or both lines may still emerge. There may also be room for a nonvacuous Platonism that combines the naturalist's aspiration to moral truth with the constructivist's insistence that ethics, unlike

22. Thus, for example, they cite physiological theories that allow us to infer, from the fact that we believe we are confronted by an object with characteristic C, that our sense organs are probably being stimulated by an object with C; psychological theories that give us reason to regard our inferential practices as, within limits, reliable; and biological theories that suggest mechanisms through which reliable inference patterns might have developed in creatures like us. If a belief's truth is suggested by a combination of such considerations, then – so these theorists argue – our background theories provide evidence that it probably *is* true.
23. The supervenience of the moral upon the nonmoral is defended in Richard Boyd, "How to Be a Moral Realist," in Geoffrey Sayre-McCord, ed., *Essays on Moral Realism* (Ithaca: Cornell University Press, 1988), pp. 181–228. See also Nicholas Sturgeon, "Moral Explanations," in David Copp and David Zimmerman, eds., *Morality, Reason, and Truth* (Totowa, N.J.: Rowman and Allanheld, 1985), pp. 49–78; Peter Railton, "Moral Realism," *Philosophical Review* 95, 2 (April 1986), pp. 163–209; and David O. Brink, *Moral Realism and the Foundations of Ethics* (Cambridge: Cambridge University Press, 1989). For criticism of the view that postulating moral facts helps us explain the existence of moral beliefs, see Gilbert Harman, *The Nature of Morality*, ch. 1.
24. The constructivist approach is defended by John Rawls in "Kantian Constructivism in Moral Theory: The Dewey Lectures 1980," *Journal of Philosophy* 77, 9 (September 1980), especially pp. 554–72. Rawls's constructivism is criticized by Brink in *Moral Realism and the Foundations of Ethics*, appendix 4.

science, is not in the business of providing causal explanations of anything including moral beliefs.[25] However, at present, the only certainty is that the metaphysics of morals is very much in flux.

IV

But for our purposes, this does not matter; for we have already seen that neither general nor moral skepticism can adequately support neutralism. The only form of skepticism that might possibly do this is skepticism exclusively about the good. Hence, for us, the question is only whether, from a broadly coherentist perspective, there is reason to accept such selective moral skepticism.

If so, the reason is unlikely to lie in the metaphysics of value; for none of the broadly metaphysical arguments for moral skepticism makes any distinction between the good and the right. One such argument is J. L. Mackie's contention that "objective values . . . would be entities or qualities or relations of a very strange sort"[26] since, unlike any other entity, "[a]n objective good would be sought by anyone who was acquainted with it . . . just because the end has to-be-pursuedness somehow built into it."[27] Another is Gilbert Harman's claim that we need not postulate moral facts because we can adequately explain all (moral and nonmoral) beliefs and actions without doing so.[28] Yet a third is the argument that even if moral facts existed, they would lack the causal efficacy to influence our beliefs and, hence, could not be known.[29] Cast in the coherentist mode, each argument appeals to certain background beliefs (about the criteria for successful explanations, the causal structure of the world, etc.) that are said to cast doubt on moral facts; and each

25. Platonism is often thought to be refuted by its inability to explain how Platonic forms, or nonnatural moral facts, could causally influence our beliefs, or how, if they cannot causally influence our beliefs, we could possibly come to know them. However, on a coherentist view of justification, the claim that all entities or facts are part of a single causal network is itself something that must be accepted or rejected on the basis of its coherence with our other beliefs. Hence, our independent commitment to moral objectivity, and the inadequacy of other theories of such objectivity, itself exerts pressure against that claim.

26. J. L. Mackie, *Ethics: Inventing Right and Wrong* (Harmondsworth: Penguin, 1977), p. 38.

27. Ibid., p. 40.

28. See Gilbert Harman, *The Nature of Morality*, ch. 1.

29. This is a natural extension of Paul Benacerraf's argument against Platonism in mathematics in "Mathematical Truth," *Journal of Philosophy* 70, 19 (November 8, 1973), pp. 661–79.

concludes that we can increase our belief-scheme's coherence by excluding such facts from our ontology.

But whatever force these arguments have, they clearly have no *more* force against facts about the good than against facts about the right. As their proponents well realize, facts about obligation, or about how we should act, seem every bit as strange, every bit as explanatorily redundant, every bit as causally inefficacious as facts about goodness or value. Hence, if any of the metaphysical arguments did succeed, it would establish not only that we cannot know the good, but also that we cannot know the right. And, though I shall not develop the point, I think precisely the same is true of such *non*metaphysical defenses of moral skepticism as Mackie's "argument from relativity." Indeed, of all the skeptical arguments of which I am aware, each proves either too much or too little to help the neutralist.

Perhaps, however, the difficulty is not that we are less able to know *that* some ways of living are better than others than *that* some acts are right and others wrong, but only that we are less able to know *which* things are good than *which* are right. Although it is hard to be sure, I suspect that many people's sympathy for selective moral skepticism is pitched at just this level. I suspect, as well, that their doubts are usually rooted not in any arcane metaphysical considerations, but simply in their inability to imagine how a specific conception of the good could convincingly be defended. For while it is not hard to envision an argument that (e.g.) theft or murder is wrong – indeed, if anything, what is hard is choosing among the competing arguments – it seems considerably harder to envision an argument that one kind of state or event is, just in itself, better than another.

But even if such arguments are hard to envision, it hardly follows that they are in principle unavailable. Indeed, far from implying that no specific conception of the good can be defended, coherentism sets no principled limits on our ability to defend one. For because coherence is a holistic relation – because it obtains among all a person's beliefs if it obtains at all – coherentism implies that anyone who seeks to justify a given belief has virtually unlimited resources on which to draw. In particular, if someone wishes to defend a particular conception of the good, he can appeal to its deductive, explanatory, probabilistic, or analogical relations to any of his other beliefs. His justificatory premises may thus include any further normative intuitions or principles (about either the good *or* the right); any his-

torical, political, or other factual claims; any of the findings of economics, psychology, or the other social sciences; and any of the principles or discoveries of the natural sciences. Indeed, from a coherentist perspective, there is no premise that *cannot* support a specific
conception of the good if it is backed by suitable bridging premises.
This of course does not mean that all such conceptions are equally
defensible or that a convincing argument for any particular one can
always be found. But even where all efforts at justification fail, the
problem is never that no argument is even potentially relevant, or
that the quest for suitable premises could never get started. From a
coherentist perspective, we are never in danger of running out of
things to say.

If anything, we face the opposite danger; for just *because* more can
always be said, there is a clear sense in which no defense of any
conception of the good is ever decisive. However compelling any
argument is, its premises are never more than a tiny fraction of what
any person believes. Thus, each person's further beliefs may always
contain the seeds of a convincing rejoinder to his reasoning about the
good. They may also support a convincing general argument against
the possibility of knowing what is good or, for that matter, against
the possibility of knowing *that* anything is. But this perpetual vul-
nerability to refutation does not especially threaten arguments for
conceptions of the good because all other arguments are perpetually
vulnerable too. Moreover, while arguments for conceptions of the
good *would* be singled out if our background beliefs licensed a convincing higher-order argument that they are especially likely to fail,
the same again is true of all other types of argument. Thus, pending
some more substantive challenge, we may safely regard conceptions
of the good as epistemically on a par with all other beliefs.

V

But it is one thing to say that such conceptions can in theory be
defended and quite another actually to defend one. Until we take
this further step, the bare claim that it is possible will ring somewhat
hollow. Thus, before the neutralist abandons his position, he may
reasonably challenge his opponents to specify which ways of living
are best and why.

I think it is fair to say that most critics of neutralism have not met
this challenge. When the critics have themselves been liberals, they

have often been fairly explicit about which sorts of lives the state should promote. These, predictably, are usually said to be marked by autonomy, rationality, and various related virtues.[30] But liberal critics have been far less forthcoming about *why* such lives are most worth promoting. Instead of defending their value-claims, they are often content to remind us that theirs *are* the values of liberalism, and that most neutralists themselves accept those values. However, these reminders, though not without dialectical force, are obviously no substitute for a full positive argument.[31]

By contrast, the communitarians who reject neutralism have taken questions of justification more seriously. Although their arguments are often sketchy – some of these will be examined shortly – they clearly seek to trace the superiority of certain ways of life either directly to the relevant society's history, culture, traditions, and narratives, or else to the connections between these social factors and the identities of individuals. However, these communitarian critics have had much less to say about *what* our traditions, narratives, and the like require of us. Hence, on their account, it is the *content* of the relevant values that has remained obscure.

In the next three chapters, I shall respond to the neutralist's challenge in a way that is neither communitarian nor (purely) liberal. Like the liberal critics but unlike those who are communitarians, I shall try to be quite specific about which traits, activities, and forms of relationship the state should promote (although, unlike the liberal critics, I shall not take these to be exhausted by autonomy- and rationality-related goods and virtues). Conversely, like the communitarian critics but unlike those who are liberals, I shall also try to explain *why* these traits, activities, and the like are more worthy of promotion than others (although, unlike the communitarians, I shall not base my argument on facts about culture, society, or tradition).

30. Three liberal critics of neutralism who take roughly this line are William Galston in *Liberal Purposes* (Cambridge: Cambridge University Press, 1991), Stephen Macedo in *Liberal Virtues* (Oxford: Oxford University Press, 1990), and Joseph Raz in *The Morality of Freedom* (Oxford: Oxford University Press, 1986). Galston nicely summarizes the view when he writes that "[b]ecause, as members of the liberal community, we share a conception of the good (limited and partial, but still significant), the liberal polity as a whole pursues certain ends defined by that good, and individual contributions to those ends can be assessed" (*Liberal Purposes*, p. 186).

31. For further criticism of Galston on this point, see my review of *Liberal Purposes* in *Journal of Philosophy* 90, 1 (January 1993), pp. 49–52.

Questions about the good life are central to ethics, and their importance needs no defense. However, what may require some attention is how the discussion that is to follow is related to what came before. Because questions about value raise so many new issues, the impending axiological turn may seem to mark a radical break. However, the earlier and later chapters are continuous at two levels.

For, first, the chapters to follow will extend and complete this chapter's critique of the epistemological arguments for neutralism. That is, one reason to defend a specific conception of the good is precisely to show (as opposed to merely asserting) just how much can be said in defense of at least one such conception. By actually doing what I have said can be done, I shall try to back up my claim that conceptions of the good pose no special epistemological problems. Because neutralism and its denial are both metaviews – because they are both second-order views about the proper political role of first-order views about the good – my argument will succeed at this level as long as it shows that the resources available for justifying conceptions of the good are no less diverse, and no less promising, than those available for justifying any other views.

But few who oppose neutralism will be content with this; for much of their position's urgency reflects a clash of substantive views. It is no accident that neutralism has become popular when long-cherished values are being eroded by powerful social forces, and when many of those same values are under attack by resourceful critics. This unsettled cultural situation has led some to try to enlist the state's resources to shore up the traditional values; others to try to enlist the state's resources to hasten their decline; and still others to urge that government remain above the fray. Having rejected the third alternative, we are bound to wonder what can be said for the others, and, at a second level, the chapters to come are my attempt to find out. By defending a specific list of values and virtues (and, by extension, any laws or policies that they themselves justify), I shall try to make a positive contribution to the very debate whose legitimacy I defended in the book's first part.

VI

My discussion will be structured around the distinction between subjectivism and perfectionism. Although these terms were defined in Chapter 1, the discussion there was brief and much has transpired in the interim. Thus, before we proceed, it may be helpful to review what was said and to clarify some related issues.

As defined, the subjectivist–perfectionist distinction marks a point on a continuum of increasingly objective (or, in the other direction, increasingly subjective) theories of value. Subjectivist theories trace the noninstrumental value of any individual's activities, traits, and relationships entirely to his own actual or possible mental states. They identify the good life exclusively with the life that the agent would want, choose, or enjoy under actual or (more) ideal conditions. By contrast, all perfectionist theories take at least some activities, traits, or forms of relationship to be noninstrumentally valuable for reasons *independent* of the agent's actual or potential mental states. Some perfectionist theories do this by tracing noninstrumental value to certain facts about society, others by grounding it in certain fundamental capacities that all (or almost all) humans possess, and still others simply by construing it as intrinsic. Although perfectionist and subjectivist theories can both be viewed either as accounts of what is good *for persons* or of what is good *simpliciter*, I shall argue in Chapter 8 that only claims that things are good *simpliciter* imply that they are objectively worth advancing and pursuing. Still, it would be strange if a person's having what is good for him were not *itself* good *simpliciter*, so this implication is less important than it first appears.

Why structure a discussion of the good life around the distinction between subjectivism and perfectionism? In part, the reason is simply that perfectionism is so often associated with opposition to neutralism. But a deeper reason is that the distinction tracks what is arguably the most fundamental question of value theory: namely, are things valuable only because individuals seek them, or do individuals sometimes seek things because they are independently valuable? For despite their obvious differences, all the theories I have labeled "subjectivist" represent variants of the first answer. Even when they appeal to merely hypothetical desires or choices, these theories retain the implication that individuals are the ultimate sources of value because each hypothetical desire or choice is (presumably) a complex function of the relevant individual's actual psychological makeup. Conversely, all the theories I have labeled "perfectionist" represent variants of the second answer. Even when they appeal to fundamental *goal-seeking* capacities, they retain the implication that value originates outside the individual because they construe the relevant goals as species-specific rather than peculiar to individuals.

A full perfectionist theory would discuss every type of thing whose intrinsic or inherent value might be advanced to justify state action. But although I shall end up defending a form of perfectionism, my discussion will not be this wide-ranging. I will, for example, say nothing about the value of natural objects such as unspoiled wilderness areas, beautiful lakes and impressive mountains, and rare species of animals; and neither will I say much about the value of outstanding *products* of human activity such as great works of art, literature, and architecture. However central these topics are to a perfectionist account of the *good*, they are peripheral to a perfectionist account of the good (human) *life*, and producing such an account is my main concern.

Even within this limited sphere, I shall not discuss every relevant topic. In particular, I shall not consider what virtually everyone takes to be the minimal prerequisites for a *decent* human life: health, freedom from suffering, the satisfaction of biological needs, an adequate range of opportunities, and, of course, life itself. My reason for ignoring these goods is not that they are unimportant – they are obviously fundamental – but is, rather, that their importance is undisputed. Because of this, I shall move directly to more controversial questions about the intrinsic or inherent superiority of certain kinds of activities (e.g., poetry over pushpin), certain character traits (e.g., middle-class bourgeois virtues), and certain modes of interaction or association (e.g., monogamy, the traditional family). In short, I shall mainly be concerned with the question of which *activities, traits, and relationships* are best, and why. And here I shall begin by confronting – finally – the views of the communitarians.

Chapter 7

Three grades of social involvement

Communitarianism is, among other things, a form of perfectionism. Unlike subjectivists, who identify good lives exclusively with lives that agents would want, choose, or enjoy under actual or ideal conditions, many communitarians maintain that each self is hopelessly compromised by the broader society's culture, traditions, and shared understandings. Because they believe that individuals are not the fundamental moral units, these communitarians contend that what constitutes a good life depends not on any agent's actual or possible desires, choices, or enjoyments, but rather on the culture, traditions, and shared understandings that have shaped these or that provide them with content. However, in the current chapter, I shall contest both the negative and the positive components of this position. Although I share the communitarians' opposition to subjectivism, I shall argue that society's involvement in the self has no clear implications about the good.

I

The claim that individuals are indissolubly bound up with their society is very familiar. It is easily locatable in the writings of Marx,[1] and is echoed by many on both the political left and the right. The following passages are representative:

1. Thus, for example: "What is to be avoided above all is the re-establishing of 'Society' as an abstraction vis-à-vis the individual. The individual *is the social being*. His life, even if it may not appear in the direct form of a *communal* life carried out together with others – is therefore an expression and confirmation of *social life*." Karl Marx, *Economic and Philosophical Manuscripts of 1844*, trans. Martin Milligan, in Robert C. Tucker, ed., *The Marx-Engels Reader* (New York: Norton, 1972), p. 72 (emphases in the original).

In contrast to the individualistic picture of individuals as like onions which, once their outer, culturally-relative skins are peeled off, are "much the same in all times and places," the sociological apperception reveals society as irreducibly constitutive of or built into the individual in crucial and profound ways. His distinctly human qualities, even his very capacity (and of course opportunities) to achieve autonomy and self-development are in large measure socially determined.[2]

Why should we start with such an unhistorical, abstract, and ultimately inexplicable idea as an independent individual? It is now well known that our ancestors were social beings long before they were human beings, and could not have become human beings, with the abilities and capacities of human beings, had they not been social beings first.[3]

The individual possesses a self only in relation to the selves of the other members of his social group. . . . The process out of which the self arises is a social process which . . . implies the pre-existence of the group.[4]

Some who assert that selves are socially constituted may intend only to advance a claim of metaphysics, or only to propose a thesis of social scientific methodology. However, many others who say this clearly mean something normative. For example, one contemporary communitarian, Charles Taylor, inveighs against both "a normative position in which rights are the ultimate standard"[5] and "views of the properly human which give absolutely central importance to the freedom to choose one's own mode of life."[6] A second, Michael J. Sandel, objects to the inference that "[s]ociety is best arranged when it is governed by principles that do not presuppose any particular conception of the good, for any other arrangement would fail to respect persons as beings capable of choice."[7] Yet a third, Alasdair MacIntyre, complains that philosophers as different as Rawls and Nozick share a "view which envisages entry into social life as – at least ideally – the voluntary act of at least potentially rational indi-

2. Steven Lukes, *Individualism* (New York: Harper and Row, 1973), p. 151.
3. Peter Singer, "Rights and the Market," in John Arthur and William H. Shaw, eds., *Justice and Economic Distribution* (Englewood Cliffs, N.J.: Prentice-Hall, 1978), p. 210.
4. George Herbert Mead, *Mind, Self, and Society* (Chicago: University of Chicago Press, 1934), p. 164.
5. Charles Taylor, "Atomism," in *Philosophy and the Human Sciences: Philosophical Papers 2* (Cambridge: Cambridge University Press, 1985), p. 190.
6. Ibid., p. 196.
7. Michael J. Sandel, *Liberalism and the Limits of Justice* (Cambridge: Cambridge University Press, 1982), p. 9.

viduals with prior interests who have to ask the question 'What kind of social contract with others is it reasonable for me to enter into?' "[8]

Although these complaints have political as well as moral overtones, each can be read as denying that all value flows from, or attaches to the objects of, the preferences, choices, or enjoyments of individuals. And in what follows, I shall interpret the appeal to society's involvement in the self in just this way. In so doing, I shall take no position about what any particular writer has actually or most centrally meant: my aim is not to explicate any text, but only to assess the argument that society's involvement in the self undermines subjectivism about value.[9]

However, before we can evaluate that argument, we must make it more precise; for because individuals stand in various relations to society, there are several theses from which the denial of subjectivism might be thought to follow. First and most obviously, this may be said to follow from certain well-known *causal* claims. It is clear that our social environment shapes many of our traits and preferences (including, significantly, traits like the willingness to question our aims, and to seek alternatives to them, that many take to be prerequisites for autonomy). Also, our society profoundly influences our opportunities and the alternatives among which we may choose. Given these causal facts, many find it obvious that the line between the individual and his society is hopelessly blurred.

But, second, the argument might also (or in addition) appeal to the social nature of *what* we prefer or choose. As several philosophers

---

8. Alasdair MacIntyre, *After Virtue,* 2d ed. (Notre Dame, Ind.: University of Notre Dame Pres, 1984), p. 251.
9. This interpretation of the communitarian argument differs from the one I advanced in a previously published version of this chapter ("Three Grades of Social Involvement," *Philosophy and Public Affairs* 18, 2 [Spring 1989], pp. 133–57). There I took the communitarians to be arguing against a version of moral individualism which asserts that "when we are warranted in concluding that an action is right or ought to be performed, or that a state of affairs is good or valuable, the ultimate basis for this conclusion is always some normative premise about autonomous individuals or their preferences or choices" (p. 136). On the earlier interpretation, the argument's conclusion was a thesis about the structure of (all) moral justification, while on the current interpretation, it is a substantive thesis about what has value (and, perhaps, also a metaphysical thesis about the source(s) of value). In addition to meshing better with both the arguments of this chapter and the wider argument within which they are embedded, the new interpretation avoids the objection, advanced by Joseph Raz and Avishai Margalit, that no justification can rest exclusively on one kind of normative proposition if all justification is holistic ("National Self-Determination," *Journal of Philosophy* 87, 9 [September 1990], pp. 456–57, n.).

have recently emphasized, even an autonomous person's aims and attitudes presuppose, and are conceptually impossible in the absence of, a highly specific cultural, legal, social, and historical context. Even so simple an act as buying groceries presupposes the conventions of our economic and legal systems as well as the less formal conventions that define the role of food in our society.[10] Hence, to discredit the distinctness or independence of the individual, one might appeal to society's conceptual involvement in, as well as its causal contribution to, his attitudes, preferences, or choices.

And there is yet a third possibility. If society's causal and conceptual relations to the individual's choices, attitudes, and traits have seemed compatible with his independence, the reason may be that the individual is viewed as *distinct from* his choices, attitudes, and traits. According to this view, the core self is an entity of a different and deeper sort – an entity that resists society's incursions and thus can adjudicate among the (sometimes conflicting) preferences that his society inculcates. But this idea of a deeper self is itself problematical; for if we strip away all of a person's particular beliefs, attitudes, and traits, we are left with an abstract, featureless center of volition. The idea that such featureless entities could make reasoned, authoritative decisions is not obviously intelligible. Hence, a third argument against subjectivism is that it presupposes a separation between selves and their ends and attributes that is ultimately incoherent.

II

Let us designate these three ways of attacking subjectivism the *causal, conceptual,* and *ontological* arguments. Although these arguments are not always clearly distinguished, they construe the relations between self and society in very different ways. According to the first argument, society causally influences a person's preferences, traits, and options, but otherwise fails to penetrate the self. According to the second, society enters more intimately into one aspect of the person – the content of his attitudes, abilities, and options – but

10. Again, "[b]ird watching seems to be what any sighted person in the vicinity of birds can do. And so he can, except that that would not make him into a bird watcher. He can be that only in a society where this, or at least some other animal tracking activities, are recognized as leisure activities, and which furthermore shares certain attitudes to natural life generally" (Joseph Raz, *The Morality of Freedom* [Oxford: Oxford University Press, 1986], p. 311).

does not reach the deeper self who *has* these attitudes, abilities, and options. According to the third, there is no deeper self, and society thus does penetrate to the only core the person has. The arguments appeal, we might say, to three distinct grades of social involvement. Because each grade of involvement raises different issues, we must discuss each argument separately.

Let us begin with the causal argument. There is no denying that our attitudes, traits, abilities, and options are profoundly influenced by our social background and environment. The question we need to answer, though, is whether, and if so how, this sociological commonplace supports any particular view about value. Given the metaphysical tone of much communitarian writing, one possibility is that the argument works by denying the metaphysical distinctness of individuals. That is, the fact that society shapes each individual's preferences and traits may be held to show that the divisions between the individual and his society are not metaphysically deep. This in turn may be said to show that there are no truly independent selves from whose desires, choices, and the like any value could stem.[11] Although I know of no philosopher who has explicitly advanced this argument, it is one obvious route to (and, I suspect, a main unacknowledged source of) the view that individuals are not morally basic.

Yet whatever the argument's appeal, its first step – from causal to metaphysical dependency – is surely invalid. Even if A is caused to exist or have its characteristic nature by B, it simply does not follow that there is no deep or significant distinction between A and B. Neither does it follow that B is any part of A's essence. Thus, a virus sometimes causes the symptoms of pneumonia, but the resulting lung fluid is in every sense distinct from the virus, and can have other causes altogether. Again, parents cause their children to come into existence and influence many of their later traits, but a person's metaphysical (and moral) independence from his parents remains unproblematic. Indeed, if we accept Hume's strictures against self-causation, then whenever A causes B there *must* be a (numerical) difference between A and B. And, hence, the facts of social causation do not themselves eradicate – indeed, do not even blur – the metaphysical distinction between self and society.

11. The idea that a distinction's metaphysical depth can affect its ability to support moral conclusions is developed in Derek Parfit, *Reasons and Persons* (Oxford: Oxford University Press, 1984), ch. 15. However, Parfit does not endorse the argument we are discussing.

Might a nonmetaphysical version of the argument do better? Although I cannot canvass all the possibilities, one in particular seems worth examining. In several interesting articles,[12] Charles Taylor has argued that because the sorts of individuals whose desires and choices matter cannot thrive outside a society that promotes the traits and attitudes characteristic of autonomy, and because many types of society do *not* promote these, it is anomalous to protect particular choices without also protecting the social forms that produce autonomous individuals. Thus, the same considerations that call for rights to property and noninterference with choice must also demand a certain kind of society – a society that is willing to constrain rights in order to perpetuate the capacities whose exercise they protect. As Taylor summarizes this argument,

since the free individual can only maintain his identity within a society/ culture of a certain kind, he has to be concerned about the shape of this society/culture as a whole. He cannot . . . be concerned purely with his individual choices and the associations formed from such choices to the neglect of the matrix in which such choices can be open or closed, rich or meagre. It is important to him that certain activities and institutions flourish in society. It is even of importance to him what the moral tone of the whole society is . . . because freedom and individual diversity can only flourish in a society where there is a general recognition of their worth.[13]

On this account, the facts of social causation do not undermine either the reality or the significance of the divisions between selves. However, because autonomous selves can only flourish in a certain kind of society, we are forced to consider those selves and that kind of society as a single package.

As stated, Taylor's argument takes as its point of departure the view that autonomy or its exercise is itself valuable. That, clearly, is not something that every subjectivist believes. Thus, at best, Taylor's argument tells only against some versions of subjectivism. But even those who do hold such beliefs need not fear his fundamental message; for however close the ties between particular social forms and the production of autonomous individuals, it is still the value of autonomy that provides the rationale for actualizing the whole package. If autonomy could thrive in other sorts of societies, or in the state of nature, the present argument – unlike others Taylor advances –

12. See, for example, "Atomism" and "The Nature and Scope of Distributive Justice," both in Taylor, *Philosophy and the Human Sciences*, pp. 187–210 and 289–317.
13. Taylor, "Atomism," p. 207.

would provide no support for the type of society he favors. And because Taylor's defense of that type of society does rest solely on its capacity to produce autonomous individuals, the defense does not undermine, but if anything supports, the view that such individuals are morally basic.

There are, of course, still other ways of invoking facts about social causation to discredit subjectivism. In particular, one might still argue that because all choices stem from desires that were shaped by society, no individual is the real author of any of his choices. This may be said to show that no choice has the authority that a genuine source of value would need. But this argument, too, is not relevant to all versions of subjectivism. Even if sound, it would fail against those versions that attribute value not to what people choose, but simply to what they want (or, even more simply, to what they enjoy). Also, of course, it is far from clear that the argument *is* sound. Its central premise – that social causation precludes meaningful agency – is a variant of the familiar claim that people who are caused to act do not act freely. But while some ways of causing people to act (e.g., brainwashing them) clearly do make them unfree, the claim that *all* causation does so is subject to well-known objections. Because these objections are beyond our scope, I shall simply register my confidence that some succeed. If they do, then this version of the causal argument will be no more successful than the others.

III

Let us turn next to the conceptual argument. In addition to causally influencing our preferences, choices, and other subjective states, society is often said to invest these with meaning:

We cannot . . . characterize behavior independently of intentions, and we cannot characterize intentions independently of the settings which make those intentions intelligible both to agents themselves and to others.[14]

I am never able to seek for the good or exercise the virtues only *qua* individual. . . . the story of my life is always embedded in the story of those communities from which I derive my identity.[15]

14. MacIntyre, *After Virtue*, p. 206.
15. Ibid., pp. 220–21.

The crucial questions about this line of reasoning are, first, exactly how the social background is supposed to lend significance to our ends and, second, how any such contribution might undermine subjectivism.

There is, I think, no single conceptual link between the social background and the contents of our ends to which all communitarians have appealed. Rather, in different places, the social background has been said to supply or make possible both (1) the linguistic and conceptual categories in terms of which individuals speak and think, and (2) the nonlinguistic conventions that give meaning to acts such as repaying a debt or getting married. In addition, shared social practices are sometimes said to (3) generate goods internal to themselves (as, for instance, the goods internal to chess include "the achievement of a certain highly particular kind of analytical skill, strategic imagination and competitive intensity").[16] Finally, because we understand our past in terms of interlocking narrative histories, it is claimed that (4) a given narrative may call for completion by, and thus supply the goal of performing, some actions rather than others. Thus, to quote MacIntyre again, "I can only answer the question 'What am I to do?' if I can answer the prior question 'Of what story or stories do I find myself a part?'"[17]

Because the links between society and the preferences, choices, and ends of its members are so diverse,[18] they also can threaten subjectivism in more than one way. There are, indeed, at least four ways of filling in the argument (which do not correlate one-to-one with the four conceptual links). To show that the conceptual links discredit subjectivism, one might argue either that (a) an individual's society is a source of value *distinct from* his choices and preferences; that (b) an individual's choices and preferences can only create value *in concert with* the social practices that give them their meanings; that (c) to evaluate society's contribution, we must acknowledge some values that depend neither on an individual's choices and preferences *nor* on his society's history and practices; or that (d) the indi-

---

16. Ibid, p. 188. MacIntyre's book also contains useful discussion of the other links just cited.
17. Ibid., p. 216. MacIntyre's point is not the commonplace that promises and isolated past acts can affect one's moral situation, but that that moral situation is a function of a whole larger history of which one's entire past life is only one small part.
18. For related discussion that centers on society's contribution to the content of beliefs, see Tyler Burge, "Individualism and the Mental," *Midwest Studies in Philosophy* 6 (1979), pp. 73–121.

vidual's choices and preferences do not confer value at all. I shall examine each suggestion in turn.

The first suggestion – that society is a source of value distinct from preference or choice – is most naturally grounded in links (3) and (4). That is, if society is to be an independent source of value, the reason is apt to be either that the excellences internal to its practices are goods with independent moral standing or else that such standing attaches to the proper continuation of its ongoing narratives. But although we *can* interpret the goods internal to practices or the satisfactory completion of narratives as having moral significance, we can also interpret them differently. We might, for example, take their demands to be merely aesthetic, or to be mere projections of our psychological tendencies. Also, of course, even if the goods internal to a practice do have real moral standing, this may itself be grounded exclusively in the desires or choices of the individuals who engage in the practice. Similarly, even if the proper completion of a narrative has real moral standing, this may be a (complex) function of the desires or choices of those who have initiated and perpetuated the narrative's trajectory. Of all the discussion of these issues that I have read, none motivates a decision among these alternatives. Thus, pending further elaboration, the first version of the argument is at best incomplete.

What, next, of the suggestion that individuals can only create value *in concert with* society? The reasoning behind this suggestion is that if one's desires and choices do derive their meaning from some aspect of the social background – if, for example, they depend on either the society's linguistic or nonlinguistic conventions or its characteristic narratives (links [1], [2], and [4]) – then no individual could have those desires or make those choices if the relevant aspect of the social background did not exist. Thus, we may be tempted to regard society as a kind of silent partner – an unnoticed but omnipresent coconspirator – in all of our most significant preferrings and choosings. And when we attribute value to what is preferred or chosen, we may therefore be tempted to regard that value as a joint product of society and the individual.

But this temptation should be resisted; for even if social conventions do constitute many of the actions that individuals prefer and choose, this no more establishes that society is an equal partner in the individual's production of value than the contribution of the rules of basketball establish that Michael Jordan cannot lay sole claim to his achievements. The rules of a sport provide only the framework within which an outstanding athlete can display his mettle; and, just so, the most that any society can contribute is a history and a set of conventions that make possible many different choices and ends. Since nothing acquires value merely from the fact that it *could* be wanted or chosen – otherwise, all the choices that our history and conventions make possible would be equally valuable – the individual's actual desires or choices remain decisive. If society abets these, it does so only by supplying one of their necessary conditions. Thus, if society's contribution has no further implications, subjectivism will remain unrefuted.

Does society's contribution have any further implications? In particular, might it undermine subjectivism in the third of the suggested ways – namely, by calling attention to values that stem neither from desire or choice *nor* from the social background that gives these meaning?

At least initially, this may seem possible; for as we just saw, an individual can only choose what he can conceive, and his categories of thought are supplied by his society's conventions, understandings, and narratives. In supplying those categories, the social background sets each person's basic choice-agenda. But some choice-agendas seem themselves to be better than others, and so at least one class of value-claims – namely, claims about the merits of alternative choice-agendas – appears to elude the subjectivist's grasp. For because choice-agendas are logically prior to preferences and choices, we cannot evaluate them by appealing to *what* individuals prefer or choose. Thus, any attempt to distinguish better from worse choice-agendas appears to presuppose some standards independent of preference or choice. But if such standards exist, then must not some values be independent both of preferences and choices *and* of the society that furnishes the choice-agenda?

As presented, this argument simply assumes that it is possible to evaluate choice-agendas. Hence, in rebuttal, the subjectivist may be tempted to reject that assumption. But this rejoinder would itself reduce the appeal of his position, so it is worth noting that subjectivists can make a better reply. The more promising way to challenge the third conceptual argument is to contest its inference from "the social background always sets the terms of choice" to "choice-agendas cannot themselves be chosen." For if choice-agendas are outgrowths of social practices and institutions, and if practices and institutions are affected by human actions, then choice-agendas must themselves be affected by human actions. Hence, there is no obvious reason why the social meanings that will determine the range of choices available at t_2 should not themselves be topics of deliberation and choice at an earlier t_1. Of course, whatever deliberations take place at t_1 will themselves be framed in terms of the concepts available at t_1; but this poses no greater threat to the choice of (later) choice-agendas than it does to any other choices directed at later moments. Like Quinean scientists revising their beliefs from within (or, to use one of Quine's favorite similes, like sailors trying to re-build their boat while remaining afloat), we can in theory reject any (and perhaps even all) elements of our current choice-agenda; but we can do so only through a progression of steps whose starting point is precisely that agenda itself.[19] Because future choice-agendas can themselves be objects of present preferences and choices, they need not be evaluated by any standard independent *of* those preferences and choices. So for this reason, too, the third argument fails to discredit subjectivism.

IV

I have now rejected several attempts to move from the conceptual links between an individual's ends and his society's history and practices to the conclusion that choice and preference are not the only sources of value. But in focusing on these arguments, I may be said to have missed the real point. For if society is conceptually implicated in each of a person's most significant choices and attitudes, then isn't the person himself social through and through? And, hence, doesn't the real threat to subjectivism lie not in the availability of alternative sources of value but rather in the self's own lack of ontological independence?

Let us simply grant that every significant preference, goal, and trait is infused with meaning by the social background. Even so, what this implies about the individual's ontological status is not immediately clear. On the surface, the most that seems to follow is that the *content* of his preferences, goals, and traits is ineliminably social. But a preference's content is one thing, the preference itself is another, and the person with the preference still another. Moreover, of the three, the person himself is the most plausible candidate for

19. Interestingly, MacIntyre himself appears to endorse a similarly dialectical view of moral progress; see his postscript to the second edition of *After Virtue*, especially pp. 266–71.

the role of source of value. Thus, what the current argument shows to be conceptually linked to society is not obviously the same as what a subjectivist must take to be distinct.[20]

This rejoinder rests squarely on a distinction between the self and all its (significant) preferences, goals, and traits. Hence, it will only succeed if that distinction itself is defensible. But is it? In segregating the "true" self from all its attitudes and traits, don't we make a hopeless mystery of its relations *to* those attitudes and traits? And, hence, doesn't the need for the rejoinder merely reveal the inadequacy of the subjectivist's metaphysics?

V

That it does is an implication of Michael J. Sandel's influential book *Liberalism and the Limits of Justice*. Although Sandel's main target is not subjectivism about value but the view that "principles of justice are justified in a way that does not depend on any particular vision of the good,"[21] he takes the latter view to imply precisely each self is ontologically prior to all its ends. However, against Rawls, Dworkin, and other "deontological liberals," Sandel argues that there are no such "unencumbered selves." In taking this position – in arguing that each self is constituted by some (sub)set of its ends – he is in effect defending the maximal third grade of social involvement.[22]

Why does Sandel deny that selves are distinct from their ends? Although he mounts more than one argument, the most important,

20. It is now generally agreed that the action theorists of the 1960s were wrong to argue that because the propositional object of a desire cannot be specified without mentioning an action, that desire is not distinct from, and so cannot cause, that action. (The definitive rejoinder to this argument remains Donald Davidson, "Actions, Reasons, and Causes," *Journal of Philosophy* 60, 23 [November 7, 1963], pp. 685–700.) Wouldn't the social theorists of the 1980s be similarly mistaken to argue that, because the propositional objects of desires presuppose a background supplied by society, the persons with those desires are not ontologically distinct from their society?
21. Sandel, *Liberalism and the Limits of Justice*, p. 2.
22. Because we have arrived at the third grade of involvement through a discussion of the two lesser grades, it is worth remarking that Sandel, too, is aware of these. He writes, for example, that "What marks . . . a community is not merely a spirit of benevolence, or the prevalence of communitarian values, or even certain 'shared final ends' alone, but a common vocabulary of discourse and a background of implicit practices and understandings" (ibid., pp. 172–73). However, as far as I can see, the connection between the social background and the content of the self's ends plays no role in Sandel's account of the relations between selves and their ends.

and the only one that need concern us, is that any entity that *was* detached from all its ends would lack any basis for rational choice.[23] Being entirely cut off from the empirical world, it would be a "radically disembodied subject" without any essential or "constitutive" ends. Thus, all its choices, including moral ones, would simply be arbitrary. As Sandel realizes, this argument invites the reply that even if selves do lack constitutive ends, they may still be related to their ends in some way that, though weaker, remains sufficiently strong to provide a basis for choice. Sandel, indeed, attributes this sort of response to Rawls: "Rawls' solution, implicit in the design of the original position, is to conceive the self as a subject of possession, for in possession the self is distanced from its ends without being detached altogether."[24] But such a rejoinder will only succeed if we can find a coherent interpretation of "possession"; and the burden of Sandel's argument is precisely that this cannot be done.

The reason, as he sees it, is that possession must itself be understood in terms of will. If a self has no essential desires that are capable of making inescapable demands, then which desires will enter its motivational structure becomes a question for it to decide: "Where the self is disempowered because detached from its ends, dispossession is repaired by the faculty of agency in its voluntarist sense, in which the self is related to its ends as a willing subject to the objects of choice."[25] In short, if the self is not initially constituted by any ends, it can only acquire these by choosing among its competing desires and urges.

But, as Sandel points out, this only defers the difficulty; for if prior to choosing its ends the self lacks a basis for action, it must also lack a basis for choosing among its desires. If it selects among these ar-

---

23. Sandel's other main argument against the view that selves are entities distinct from their ends and other attributes is that this view is inconsistent with an influential liberal approach to distributive justice. More specifically, Sandel argues that when Rawls, Dworkin, and other liberals deny that an individual's efforts and achievements affect what he deserves, they treat that individual's abilities and other traits as common assets to which others may lay claim. This, Sandel believes, commits these liberals to postulating an intersubjective self to which all the traits and abilities do in some strong sense belong. But at best this argument has polemical value; for even if the thesis that selves are distinct from their ends is *not* consistent with Rawls's treatment of the relation between persons and their abilities, we will need a further argument to tell us which of the inconsistent elements to reject.

24. Sandel, *Liberalism and the Limits of Justice*, p. 54.

25. Ibid., p. 58.

bitrarily, its choice will lack authority; while if its selection has a basis, then whichever ends provide that basis will, *contra* the original hypothesis, already be its own. In particular, if a choice of ends is grounded in preexisting desires, then "such a 'decision' decides nothing except how accurately the agent has perceived something already *there,* in this case the shape and intensity of his pre-existing desires. But if this is so, then the voluntarist aspect of agency would seem to fade altogether."[26] Moreover, the problem remains unchanged if the choice is grounded in a second-order desire to harmonize or select the more worthy among a set of preexisting desires.[27] Thus, a self without constitutive ends either could not choose among its desires and impulses, or else would have to do so in an arbitrary manner.

Given all this, Sandel concludes that each self must have some constitutive ends. But *which* of a self's ends does he take to be constitutive? Here one possible answer is simply "All of them." However, as Sandel notes, this answer implies that "just *any* change in my situation, however slight, would change the person I am. . . . this would mean that my identity would blur indistinguishably into 'my' situation."[28] To avoid these difficulties, Sandel argues that each self must be constituted by some but not all of its desires.

But what in that case *determines* which desires are constitutive? Here one possibility is that this is simply a brute fact to be discovered by introspection. But instead of exploring this answer, Sandel takes another tack. He proposes that each person *acquires* his constitutive ends through a complex reflective process that embodies elements of both cognition and will. Rather than either simply discovering our essential ends or arbitrarily choosing among our desires, we nonarbitrarily choose our ends in light of our best current understanding of ourselves and our surroundings. Such understandings are always provisional and fallible, but nonetheless provide the only possible starting point for self-definition:

26. Ibid., p. 162.
27. Thus, Sandel writes that a person motivated in this way "would still have only the psychological fact of his (now, second-order) preference to appeal to and only its relative intensity to assess. Neither the intrinsic worth of a desire nor its essential connection with the identity of the agent could provide a basis for affirming it, since on Rawls' account, the worth of a desire only appears in light of a person's good, and the identity of the agent is barren of constituent traits so that no aim or desire can be essential to it" (ibid., pp. 163–64).
28. Ibid., p. 20.

Unlike the capacity for choice, which enables the self to reach beyond itself, the capacity for reflection enables the self to turn its lights inward upon itself, to inquire into its constituent nature, to survey its various attachments and acknowledge their respective claims, to sort out the bounds – now expansive, now constrained – between the self and the other, to arrive at a self-understanding less opaque if never perfectly transparent, a subjectivity less fluid if never finally fixed, and so gradually, thoughout a lifetime, to participate in the constitution of its identity.[29]

In continually seeking a defensible answer to the question, Which ends are essential to me? we nonarbitrarily choose to be constituted by some ends rather than others.

Even by itself, the view that some ends are constitutive would, if defensible, undermine the claim that the true or "core" self is independent of all its (socially constituted) ends. But Sandel's attack on the self's independence also has another dimension: at some points, he seems concerned to deny not (just) the separateness of selves *from their ends*, but also the separateness of individuals *from each other*. He claims, for example, that his arguments tell against Rawls's assumption that "[t]he fundamental feature of the moral subject is its plurality, and . . . the number of its plurality corresponds to the number of empirically-individuated human beings in the world."[30] Because Sandel here denies that "empirically-individuated human beings" are the basic moral units, he also implies that the empirically individuated human's choices, preferences, or enjoyments cannot be the sole or ultimate sources of value.

Why, exactly, does Sandel hold that moral subjects are distinct from empirically individuated humans? On the surface, his point may seem to be simply that each person's constitutive ends are communal – that we generally do, and perhaps must, regard ourselves "as members of this family or community or nation or people, as bearers of this history, as sons and daughters of that revolution, as citizens of this republic."[31] But even if this view of our constitutive ends is correct – and Sandel offers no real evidence for it – it will not establish that the fundamental moral units are not "empirically-individuated human beings." To suppose that it did would be to conflate the claim that each person is constituted by the *aim* of standing in, or living up to the expectations of, certain relations to others,

29. Ibid., p. 153.
30. Ibid., p. 52.
31. Ibid., p. 179.

with the very different claim that each person is constituted *by those relations themselves.* Even if the *contents* of each person's constitutive ends are communal, it hardly follows that the moral subject *itself* is some kind of communal entity.

A more interesting argument for the view that the basic moral subjects are not empirically individuated humans can be extracted from the preceding discussion. As we saw, Sandel regards reflectively chosen ends as essential to, or constitutive of, the selves who adopt them. But if reflectively chosen ends *are* constitutive of selves, and if a single communal end is reflectively chosen by many empirically individuated human beings, then each of these individuals will be constituted by the very *same* communal end. Hence, though physically distinct, many individual humans will share a common essence. This means that the physical boundaries between humans will no longer determine how many selves there are. Rather, individual humans will sometimes encompass several selves, and – for Sandel, the more important possibility – single selves will sometimes span numerous individuals. As Sandel himself puts the latter point,

there is no reason to suppose that a "system of desires" in *this* sense corresponds in all cases to the empirically-individuated person. Communities of various sorts could count as distinct "systems of desires" in this sense, so long as they were identifiable in part by an order or structure of shared values partly constitutive of a common identity or form of life.[32]

As a result, the empirically individuated person will no longer be a plausible source of all values.

VI

As even this brief summary should make clear, Sandel's arguments for the maximal third grade of social involvement are ambitious and resourceful. But those arguments also face some serious objections. To bring these out, and thus complete my critique of the communitarian case against subjectivism, I now want to take a more critical look at Sandel's (implicit) argument for the existence of intersubjective selves, his account of how selves acquire their constitutive

32. Ibid., p. 167.

ends, and his reasons for holding that selves must *have* constitutive ends.

1. As we just saw, the argument for intersubjective selves turns on the premise that reflectively chosen ends are constitutive of, or essential to, selves. If such ends were not essential, then two individuals might reflectively adopt the same end without being elements of a single self. At the same time, Sandel must regard all reflectively chosen ends as merely provisional; for no conclusion reached through reflection is beyond further assessment and evaluation. But we must now ask whether these two features of reflectively chosen ends are really compatible. Can Sandel consistently say both that a given end is part of a self's essence – is part of what determines a self's very identity – and that further reflection might lead that self to abandon the end? As usually understood, the claim that X is essential to Y, or that X determines Y's identity, implies precisely that an entity that was otherwise similar to Y, but that lacked X, would not *be* Y. But if so, and if a self can continue to exist after abandoning an end, then that end is not essential to it after all.

This objection may seem unfair; for as Sandel employs it, the notion of an essential end is not all-or-nothing, but admits of degrees. He says, for example, that the members of a society may be "defined *to some extent* by the community of which they are a part."[33] Given this usage, Sandel could reply that someone who abandons an (erstwhile) essential end *does* remain substantially the same self as long as he retains enough of his *other* essential ends. Yet if he did make this reply, Sandel would raise a further and less tractable problem. For if no single "essential" end determines a self's identity, then neither does the fact that two individuals share a single essential end make them elements of a single self. Rather, two individuals who share a reflectively chosen end will remain substantially distinct if they do not share most if not all of their other reflectively chosen ends. And since each individual belongs to a variety of cross-cutting groups, it is very unlikely that any collection of individuals *will* hold most of their reflectively chosen ends in common. Hence, if essentiality is a matter of degree, there probably are no intersubjective selves.

2. Thus, Sandel's arguments do not warrant his conclusion that individuals are not distinct from one another. But what, next, of his contention that individuals must be constituted by, and hence cannot be ontologically distinct from, (some of) their *ends?* Sandel's argu-

33. Ibid., p. 150 (emphasis added).

ment here, we recall, is that only by regarding reflectively chosen ends as constitutive can we avoid both the unacceptable conclusion that the self's ends are simply discovered and the equally unacceptable conclusion that they are arbitrarily adopted. But how, exactly, does reflective choice combine cognition and will to take us between the horns of the dilemma? On what *basis* could a reflective self choose its ends?

One possibility is that its choice is *elicited* by the merits of the selected ends. On this account, the basis of a reflective choice is that the chosen desire is found to be more worthy of selection than its competitors. There are places at which Sandel's language hints at such a view. He says, for instance, that in reflecting on his ends, a person "feels the moral weight of what he knows."[34] But this suggestion will only do if the reflectively chosen end always *is* more worthy of selection than its competitors; and the diversity of the choices that Sandel considers legitimate appears to rule this out. On his account, a person may reflectively choose ends supplied by his family, friendships, or political community. Presumably, he may also choose ends supplied by his profession, religion, or preferred recreation. But it cannot be true both that the ends supplied by one's bowling league and church are superior to those supplied by one's trade union and political party and that the latter ends are superior to the former. Thus, if a person may legitimately choose to be constituted by either set of ends, at least some legitimate choices are not elicited by the chosen ends' intrinsic worth.

Yet if a reflective choice is not thus elicited, then on what basis *is* it made? At various points, Sandel implies that it is grounded in the self's *prior* constitutive ends. He writes, for example, that "[i]n consulting my preferences, I have not only to weigh their intensity but also to assess their suitability to the person I (already) am."[35] But this only shifts the question to how the agent *became* the person he (already) is. Since each self has existed for only a finite time, Sandel cannot say both that every reflective choice is grounded in some preexisting constitutive end and that all such ends were acquired through still earlier reflective choices. Yet if he admits that some constitutive ends were acquired in other ways, he faces a recurrence of his own dilemma. If at any stage an agent's constitutive ends were simply his (first- or second-order) desires, then any later decisions

34. Ibid., p. 179. See also the passage cited in note 29.
35. Ibid., p. 180.

173

that they justify will merely reflect this preexisting fact about him. This will invite Sandel's own complaint that "[s]uch a 'decision' decides nothing except how accurately the agent has perceived something already *there*." But if instead some initial end was chosen without a basis, then the primal decision will after all have been arbitrary. Finally, since the agent's lack of (the right kind of) initial constitutive ends prevents the reflective process from even getting started, there can be no question of its later stages repairing its initial flaws.

Thus, given the terms in which Sandel has framed the problem – every end is either constitutive or external, the self's only access to ends is through cognition or will – it seems clear that his dilemma is insoluble. As Sandel realizes, his way of posing the problem discredits the metaphysic that he associates with "deontological liberalism" (and that may also be associated with subjectivism about value). However, as Sandel does not appreciate, his way of posing the problem also defeats the possibility of any communitarian alternative.

3. Where, exactly, have things gone wrong? Although a number of moves arouse suspicion, one egregious suspect is the premise that nothing short of a constitutive end can provide a reason for acting. Although this premise is central to Sandel's argument – without it, he could not conclude that selves without constitutive ends would be "radically disembodied subjects" capable only of random, arbitrary choices – he defends it only by observing that a self without constitutive ends would be subject to many different, and often conflicting, desires and urges. But the multiplicity of the subject's desires would only be relevant if he were hopelessly without a basis for adjudicating among them; and since Sandel provides no separate argument for this, his view appears to be that only a constitutive end could provide such a basis. However, the view that only constitutive ends can provide reasons is precisely what needs to be *shown*, so Sandel's argument here seems to beg the question.

This problem might not be serious if the view that only constitutive ends provide reasons was independently plausible. But far from being plausible, it seems incompatible with most versions of the two most familiar approaches to practical reasoning. Of these approaches, one asserts that reasons are provided by desires themselves. On most versions of this view, many if not all nonconstitutive desires provide at least prima facie reasons to try to get what is desired. This means that many decisions to implement strong nonconstitutive desires are not arbitrary (though, of course, they may be ill-advised or defective in many other ways). And things do not improve when we turn to the alternative view that reasons for acting can be *independent* of desires. On most versions of this view, there are facts about the world that are not constitutive of us, yet which provide us with reasons for acting even when we do not want to act upon them. For example, the fact that someone else is in serious pain may give me a reason to relieve him whether or not I want to.[36] On this approach, too, many actions that are not grounded in constitutive desires turn out to be nonarbitrary. Although neither approach is free of difficulty, the burden of proof is surely on anyone who rejects both. Thus, Sandel's mistake may well lie in an inadequate theory of practical reasoning.

However that may be, Sandel's arguments for the maximal third grade of social involvement clearly fail. We may therefore conclude that no communitarian has yet shown either that the choices, preferences, or enjoyments of individuals cannot be the sole sources of value or that culture, tradition, or history is a plausible alternative. If subjectivism is to be rejected, it must be for reasons other than the self's lack of independence, and if a plausible version of perfectionism is to be defended, it must be on some basis other than society's involvement in the self. In the next two chapters, I shall take up each task in turn.

36. The example is Thomas Nagel's; see *The View from Nowhere* (New York: Oxford University Press, 1986), pp. 166–171.

Chapter 8

Against subjectivism

Subjectivism draws its appeal from the compelling thought that what counts as a good life for us is somehow rooted in our psychological makeup – that if our subjectivity were sufficiently different, the things we value would be valueless. But, as we will see, subjectivism is neither the only nor the best way of capturing this thought. In the current chapter, I shall argue that subjectivism has various unpalatable implications, both about what does and does not have value and about how value enters into practical deliberation. I shall argue, too, that certain apparently countervailing advantages – in particular, its ability to explain how value motivates, what makes value-claims true, and how value is created – are, in fact, no advantages at all. Then, in the next chapter, I will show how we can accommodate the central subjectivist insight within a recognizably perfectionist framework.

I

Intuitively, some kinds of activities, traits, and relationships seem far more worthwhile than others. For example, it has already been observed that autonomous lives are, all else being equal, far better than nonautonomous ones. To account for such intuitions, a subjectivist must show that each valuable type of activity, trait, and relationship stands in the right relation to whichever subjective state he takes to be the source of value. But in what follows, I shall argue that this often *cannot* be shown. This may not force the subjectivist to reject the intuitions in question; but it does force him to concede that each is unsupported by the only sort of evidence that, on his view, could possibly justify it.

176

Before I can mount my argument, I must be more specific about which intuitions I have in mind. Thus, to begin, I shall review a number of common (and, I think, extremely plausible) beliefs about which sorts of activities, traits, and relationships are most worth engaging in or having. Although I will eventually argue that most of these entries are *inherently* valuable, I cannot say that here without begging the question against subjectivism. Thus, for now, I shall take no position about the basis of any entry's value.

Because autonomy has already been mentioned, I shall begin with it. As we saw in Chapter 3, some thinkers affirm, while others deny, that no activity is valuable unless it is undertaken on the basis *of* its potential value. Here, however, I need not say anything so extreme. Instead, I need make only the more modest point that most of us take autonomy to be *among* the determinants of a good life. Other things being equal, it seems better to exercise control over one's own fate than to be governed by other people or external forces. This means, among other things, that it is better to make decisions after due reflection, and because one genuinely appreciates what is involved, than to decide or act (e.g.) on the basis of false beliefs, because one is afraid or exhausted, or simply through inertia.[1]

It also seems better to do things that are important, and to seek results that matter, than to while away one's life at pleasant but pointless diversions. Lives devoted exclusively to recreation and play seem wasteful and lost. By contrast, a sustained commitment to any serious project, from seeking a cure for cancer to being a good parent, can give one's life meaning and worth. Because agents can seriously pursue many kinds of goals – because their "ground projects"[2] can be (at least) intellectual, artistic, political, or personal – this good can be realized in indefinitely many ways. However, within each domain, a project's value seems proportional to its complexity and the challenge it presents.

So far, I have mentioned only the value of autonomously chosen and serious, challenging pursuits. But a further relevant factor is *how well* an agent does whatever he does. There is wide agreement that

1. Even if someone thinks that no one can live a good life without being embedded in a tradition, he may believe that it is better to remain embedded in one's tradition for the right reasons than for the wrong ones. As long as a traditionalist is willing to say this, he must attach some value to the proper appreciation of reasons.
2. This useful term is introduced by Bernard Williams in "Persons, Character, and Morality," in Amèlie Oksenberg Rorty, ed., *The Identities of Persons* (Berkeley: University of California Press, 1976), pp. 197–216.

excellence of any sort is worth striving for – "if it's worth doing, it's worth doing right" – and that outstanding intellectual, athletic, and aesthetic performances are always significant goods. Other things being equal, it always seems best to perform as well as possible. And, by extension, simply having the skill to perform at a high level seems itself to be a good.

Even together, these are only a few of our intuitions about how it is good to live. But because my argument does not require completeness, I shall mention only a few others. First, other things again being equal, it seems far better to have wide and deep knowledge of the world, and of one's place in it, than to lead a narrow, blinkered existence. Our lives are enriched by all forms of scientific, historical, and social insight (including, importantly, the insight into the human condition provided by art and literature). Moreover, second, they are enriched by suitable attachments to others. Even if a loner is quite contented, we take the absence of companionship, talk, shared goals, and mutual caring to impoverish his life. And, third, we also find it natural to distinguish better from worse character traits. Although some have stressed our inability to agree about which traits are virtues, I think most of the disagreement takes place only at the margins. In our society (and, I suspect, elsewhere) it is widely considered good to be – among other things – fair, courageous, wise, kind, patient, compassionate, generous, self-controlled, and persevering. There is also wide agreement about what each trait involves. And, toward the other end of the spectrum, I think most would agree that servile, cringing behavior is unseemly, that spite and malice are ugly, unworthy traits, and that indifference to filth in one's surroundings or person is degraded.

All this, of course, is very quick. Not every reader will feel the pull of every intuition, and even many who do will disagree about their provenance or force. Yet at least when we are not defending a philosophical or sociological theory, I think most of us are strongly attracted to many of these views; and for this reason, they are a suitable touchstone against which to test aspiring theories of the good.[3]

To elicit the intuitions as vividly as possible, I now want to invite the reader to examine his own reactions, and to speculate about the

3. Because I will argue that subjectivism cannot account for *any* of the cited intuitions, someone who does not accept them all may simply focus on any he does accept and disregard the rest. Alternatively, he may substitute any other value-intuitions of equal specificity and run a suitably altered version of the argument.

reactions of others, to a short passage from an article in the *New York Times*. In a discussion of the lives of female teen-aged crack cocaine users, the *Times* offered the following graphic description:

> At the crack houses, which are usually decrepit rooms in abandoned buildings, they go on binges that typically last for two or three days. . . . The girls often perform oral sex in exchange for a smoke. Between binges they sleep in alleyways or abandoned buildings.
>
> Adults at the crack houses become the only family the girls have. They often call the older women Ma and the older men Poppy.[4]

There are many reasons to find this passage appalling. Persons who live this way are at obvious grave risk of violence and disease. Many are surely also very unhappy. But to stop here would be grotesquely to distort what is so horrible about the case. A bland recital of dangers would entirely miss the sense of degradation that the passage conveys. It would fail to capture (what I take to be) the standard reaction that sleeping in alleyways and trading oral sex with strangers for intervals of drug-induced euphoria are simply not good ways for humans to live. In addition, it would fail to capture the sense that these are wasted lives, devoid of constructive activity or any meaningful prospects for it. Also overlooked would be the poignancy of the girls' misbegotten attachments to the older addicts – the sense that they are sad reminders of better, more innocent relationships. Moreover, it all becomes worse rather than better if the girls' lives are not merely an adaptation to their limited options and wretched circumstances but have been freely and willingly chosen. The most disturbing thought is that their activities accurately reflect the character of the persons whom they have become and who they now are.

II

There is, then, little doubt that we regard lives of autonomy, accomplishment, virtue, and knowledge as superior to lives of ignorance, idleness, and depravity. But *why* are lives of the first sort better? According to subjectivists, knowledge, excellence, virtue, and the rest are only valuable because:

4. *New York Times*, Friday, August 11, 1989, p. A13.

(1) They promote the happiness, satisfy the desires, or realize the choices of those who possess them; or

(2) They *would* promote the happiness, satisfy the desires, or realize the choices of their possessors if these persons were more fully informed or better situated in some other way; or

(3) They do or would promote the happiness, satisfy the desires, or realize the choices of persons in general.

But, as I shall now argue, each explanation rests on a factual claim that is neither supported by evidence nor independently plausible.

To see this, we need only look closely at each explanation's factual underpinnings. Explanation (1) attributes the value of knowledge, excellence, virtue, and the rest to their tendency to make their possessors happy or satisfy their desires. It thus assumes that knowledge, excellence, virtue, and the rest *do* tend to make their possessors happy or satisfy their desires. But what is the basis for this factual claim? We have no real evidence – not even the "evidence" of common sense – that serious and committed lives are on the whole more satisfying than superficial ones; that persons with broad knowledge or deep insight tend to get more of what they want than the complacently ignorant; or that high achievers are in general happier than persons of modest accomplishment.[5] We do not even have evidence that virtue is on the whole more satisfying than vice. Indeed, for all we know, precisely the opposite of each claim is true. On the whole, lives of striving and commitment may bring more disappointment than satisfaction; most high achievers may dwell more on their deficiencies than on their accomplishments; ignorance may usually be bliss; and selfish, insensitive people may tend to get more of what they want than those who are empathetic and kind. Thus, if the value of knowledge, excellence, virtue, and the rest did turn on their ability to make their possessors happy or satisfy their desires, we would have no reason to believe that knowledge, excellence, virtue, and the rest *are* particularly valuable.

We also would have no reason to believe this if their value turned on their ability to satisfy their possessors' *informed* desires. At first glance, this may seem harder to show because full information can itself be understood in various ways.[6] However, in fact, each version of the suggestion is vulnerable to very similar objections.

5. For doubts about this claim, see Vinit Haksar, *Equality, Liberty, and Perfectionism* (Oxford: Oxford University Press, 1977), ch. 11.
6. For three different accounts, see Henry Sidgwick, *Methods of Ethics*, 7th ed. (Lon-

Consider first Sidgwick's version. On his famous account, a person's good is what he "would now desire and seek on the whole if all the consequences of all the different lines of conduct open to him were accurately foreseen and adequately realized in imagination at the present point of time."[7] This means that to be adequately informed, a person must, at a minimum, have full imaginative awareness of what it would be like to live through all the lives that are now available to him. He may also need to know the effects of each available action on some or all other people. Thus, Sidgwick's view implies that if knowledge, excellence, virtue, and the rest are always to be valuable – or, to put the point in Sidgwick's own terms, if each is to be part of every person's good – then each must figure prominently in the life that every person would want if he knew all the relevant effects of everything he might do.

But, for several reasons, what any person would want under these conditions is hopelessly obscure. First, to compare the details of all the available lives, a person would have to hold them all in mind simultaneously; and to do that, he would need mental capacities that far outstrip those of any actual person. He also would have to make an unprecedented mental effort. Given these requirements, our experience offers little insight into what Sidgwick's fully informed person might want. And the issue is further clouded by the indeterminacy of what such a person is supposed to have wanted *prior* to deliberating. In general, what people want after they deliberate is some function of what they wanted beforehand, so Sidgwick's full information requirement, which imposes no constraints on a fully informed agent's antecedent desires, also seems compatible with a vast range of subsequent desires. Finally, whatever one antecedently wanted, one could not become fully informed in Sidgwick's sense without learning much that militates *against* an insightful, accomplished, and virtuous life. One might, for example, become vividly aware of the frustrations that would accompany one's quest for excellence; and one would surely acquire a keen sense of the unpleasantness of many truths and the (by all accounts extremely intense) pleasures of drugs

don: Macmillan, 1922); Richard Brandt, *A Theory of the Good and the Right* (Oxford: Oxford University Press, 1979); and Peter Railton, "Facts and Values," *Philosophical Topics* 14, 2 (Fall 1986), pp. 5–31.

7. Sidgwick, *Methods of Ethics*, pp. 111–12. See also John Rawls, *A Theory of Justice* (Cambridge, Mass.: Harvard University Press, 1971), ch. 7, and James Griffin, *Well-Being* (Oxford: Oxford University Press, 1986), part 1.

like crack cocaine. How these and innumerable other items of information would interact to shape desire is far beyond our ken.[8]

For all these reasons, we are hopelessly ignorant of what Sidgwick's fully informed agents would want. We therefore have no grounds for believing either that they would want lives of knowledge, excellence, or virtue, or that such lives would contain much of whatever else they wanted. But does this problem arise only if we accept *Sidgwick's* version of the informed-desire theory, or does it extend also to other versions? Is the difficulty peculiar to his definition of full information, or can it be generalized?

To find out, let us turn next to Richard Brandt's version of the theory.[9] For our purposes, its distinctive feature is Brandt's contention that "[a] piece of information is relevant if its presence to awareness would make a difference to the person's tendency to perform a certain act, or to the attractiveness of some prospective outcome to him. Hence [relevance] is essentially a causal notion."[10] Unlike Sidgwick, Brandt here professes to be agnostic about what information an agent must have. His strategy is simply to let this depend on what would causally influence each agent's desires. Thus, we can interpret Brandt as saying that an agent is *fully* informed whenever *no* further information would causally influence his desires.

Because Brandt's account is more naturalistic than Sidgwick's, it may come somewhat closer to allowing us to predict what a fully informed agent would want. But it still does not come very close. For one thing, because Brandt thinks that what matters about any item of information is its causal impact, his account implies that becoming fully informed may require repeated exposure to the *same* information.[11] In particular, further exposure will be required whenever it would have a further effect on what the agent wants. Thus, on Brandt's account, becoming fully informed may take a long time. It may, indeed, take far longer than humans actually live. This alone should make us reluctant to speculate about what Brandt's fully informed agent would want. But, further, to have any real basis for prediction, we would need to know not only all the factors that

8. For relevant discussion, see Don Loeb, "Full-Information Theories of Individual Good," *Social Theory and Practice* 21, 1 (Spring 1995), pp. 1–30.
9. Strictly speaking, what Brandt's theory is introduced to elucidate is not what is good for persons, but rather what it is rational for them to choose. However, for our purposes, the difference is irrelevant.
10. Brandt, *A Theory of the Good and the Right*, p. 12.
11. Again, for related discussion, see Loeb, "Full-Information Theories of Individual Good."

determine when (additional) exposure to a given item of information would affect someone's desires, but also the strength of each factor, the contexts in which it is and is not effective, and the ways in which it interacts with each other factor. Because no one even comes close to knowing all this, we have no inkling of whether most fully informed agents would want lives of knowledge, excellence, or virtue.

Indeed, as things stand, we cannot even assume that most of Brandt's fully informed agents would have *any* particular desires in common. For all we know, the sort of information that can affect what a person wants, and the sorts of effects it can have, may depend heavily on that person's individual history. As Brandt himself concedes, the power of current information to alter desires that were shaped by early childhood experiences may be quite limited.[12] This reinforces the suspicion that many who were fully informed in Brandt's sense might *not* want lives of knowledge, excellence, or virtue. And, although I shall not argue the point, it seems clear that any other informed-desire theory would be vulnerable to very similar objections.

That leaves only explanation (3), which attributes the value of knowledge, excellence, virtue, and the rest to their tendency to promote the happiness, or to satisfy the desires, *of people in general.* This is the explanation that many utilitarians would endorse.[13] But is (3)'s factual claim any better supported than those of (1) or (2)? Are knowledge, excellence, virtue, and the rest any more likely to be conducive to the happiness or desire-satisfaction of people in general than to the happiness or desire-satisfaction of their possessors alone?

In some cases, the answer is a clear yes. In stark contrast to our uncertainty about whether just and beneficent persons are either particularly happy or particularly likely to obtain the objects of their actual or informed desires, we can hardly deny that justice and be-

12. Brandt, *A Theory of the Good and the Right,* pp. 113, 137, 145. A related problem, raised by Norman Daniels, is that ideologically based desires that were produced by entrenched practices or social institutions may be "highly resistant to extinction merely through exposure to 'all the relevant facts'" (Norman Daniels, "Can Cognitive Psychotherapy Reconcile Reason and Desire?" *Ethics* 93, 4 [July 1983], p. 780).
13. Unlike the explanations considered earlier, this one implies that the value of knowledge, excellence, virtue, and the rest is far more instrumental, and far less closely linked to lives of individuals who *are* knowledgeable, accomplished, and virtuous, than many would intuitively suppose. This implication is unsettling, but I shall not discuss it further here.

neficence are highly conducive to the general welfare. We are all obviously better off when those around us are fair-minded and helpful than when they are unfair or selfish. It is equally clear that (e.g.) drug use does tremendous social harm and that scientific and technological knowledge make it possible to satisfy many wants. Thus, utilitarians are well positioned to explain why justice, beneficence, and other virtues are valuable, why crack users live bad lives, and why many forms of knowledge are worth pursuing.

But they are far less well positioned to account for the value of many other activities, traits, and relationships. These include, but are far from exhausted by, aesthetic appreciation, a refined sensibility, outstanding individual achievement, philosophical insight and other "useless" intellectual activities, and modes of interaction involving mutual understanding and shared or merged interests. On the negative side, utilitarians are hard pressed to account for the disvalue of servility, self-abasement, and coarse and indelicate activities and sensibilities. Unlike justice, beneficence, and similar virtues, these traits, activities, and forms of association do not wear their utility on their sleeve. Whether a society's degree of culture or individual attainment, or even the way its members interact, bears any relation to its level of happiness or desire-satisfaction is, in the present state of knowledge, again hopelessly obscure.

There are of course rejoinders that a utilitarian could make. He could claim, for example, that every highly developed skill can sometime be turned to practical use; that no life without art can be truly happy; or that a vulgar, boorish public culture creates a pervasive sense of unease. But these claims are again unsupported by either hard data or common sense. No less than the claims that all fully informed agents would prefer lives of accomplishment, knowledge, and virtue, they are at best shrewd speculations and at worst mere wishful thinking. Hence, in many important cases, (3)'s explanations of the value of knowledge, excellence, virtue, and the rest are no better than those of (1) and (2).[14]

14. In his *Enquiry Concerning the Principles of Morals,* Hume noted that even when a form of virtue or excellence is otherwise useless, it often tends to evoke pleasant reactions in those who encounter it. Thus, Hume wrote that "[a] certain degree of generous pride or self-value is so requisite, that the absence of it in the mind displeases, after the same manner as the want of a nose, eye, or any of the most material feature of the face or member of the body." He also wrote that "[e]loquence, genius of all kinds, even good sense and sound reasoning . . . seem immediately agreeable, and have a merit distinct from their usefulness" (David Hume, *Enquiries Concerning the Human Understanding and Concerning the Principles*

III

I am not sure whether these arguments make it irrational for a subjectivist to believe that knowledge, excellence, virtue, and the rest are
valuable. That depends on whether rationality requires only that our
beliefs not *conflict* with any relevant evidence or, more stringently,
that our beliefs actually be *supported* by some appropriate evidence.
However, either way, subjectivism will clearly undermine the authority of many specific value-beliefs.

Ironically, it also undermines the authority of a further important
class of beliefs whose natural home is precisely the deliberative
nexus to whose elements subjectivist themselves appeal. For, as
David Brink has observed,

[t]he desire-satisfaction theory says that something is valuable just in case,
and because, it would contribute to the satisfaction of actual or counterfac-
tual desires. But . . . this seems to get things just about the opposite way
around in many cases; we desire certain sorts of things *because we think these
things valuable*. . . . At least part of the explanation of my wanting to be a
professional philosopher involves my belief that philosophy is a valuable
activity; I would not have this desire if I did not think philosophy was a
valuable activity.[15]

As Brink here implies, when we must make a serious choice, our
question is often not which alternative we *do* most want – that is

of Morals, ed. L. A. Selby-Bigge, 2d ed. [Oxford: Oxford University Press, 1955] pp.
253, 263). If we read these passages as explanations of why some otherwise
useless virtues and excellences are valuable – if we take Hume to be arguing that
those excellences and virtues are valuable *because* they are pleasing to
contemplate – then his argument will invite the objection that the cited pleasures
are too trivial to bear his conclusion's weight. It will also raise the question of why
these traits *are* pleasant to contemplate – a question whose answer may well turn
on their independent value. By contrast, if Hume is saying only that in attributing
value to self-respect and skill we *express* the pleasure we get from contemplating
them, then he will not be trying to justify these attributions of value at all, but will
in effect be trying to explain them away.

15. David O. Brink, *Moral Realism and the Foundations of Ethics* (Cambridge: Cam-
bridge University Press, 1989), pp. 225–26. For related remarks, see Joseph Raz,
The Morality of Freedom (Oxford: Oxford University Press, 1986), pp. 140–42 and
300–4; E. J. Bond, *Reason and Value* (Cambridge: Cambridge University Press,
1983), especially ch. 3; Will Kymlicka, *Liberalism, Community, and Culture* (Oxford:
Oxford University Press, 1989), pp. 10–12; Michael Stocker, *Plural and Conflicting
Values* (Oxford: Oxford University Press, 1990), p. 191; and Charles Taylor, "What
Is Human Agency?" in *Human Agency and Language: Philosophical Papers 1* (Cam-
bridge: Cambridge University Press, 1985), pp. 15–44.

often already clear – but rather which alternative is most *worth* wanting. To find out, we try to look *past* our current desires and preferences to the value or disvalue of their objects. Similarly, when we actually choose among our alternatives, we often do so on the grounds that one is more worthy of choice than the others. At both stages, we commonly presuppose that some things have a value that exists prior to, and so cannot be grounded in, our current desires or choices.

But what, exactly, does this presupposition show? According to Brink, "the need for value-laden explanations of many desires shows that we think that desire-satisfaction theories are false."[16] But does it? Clearly someone who wants or chooses something because he takes it to be valuable cannot at the same time believe that it is valuable only because he *now* wants it or is *now* choosing it. But even so, he may still believe that it is valuable only because of some *other* fact about its relations to his, or other people's, desires, choices, or enjoyments. In particular, he may still take it to be valuable only because he believes that it would either (a) satisfy his other actual desires; (b) satisfy his informed desires; (c) satisfy the actual or informed desires of other people; or (d) make him or other people happy, or prevent him or them from being unhappy. And because these familiar possibilities all remain open, the beliefs implicit in deliberation may seem fully consistent with most versions of subjectivism.

But to leave things here would be to overlook the real force of Brink's observation. That I take to be not that there is any *formal* inconsistency in the idea that we might deliberate exclusively about how to promote desire-satisfaction or enjoyment, but rather that when we juxtapose this picture with ordinary, familiar instances of deliberation, we find that it distorts them almost beyond recognition. Here, in particular, are three ways in which it fails to capture the usual structure of deliberation.

First, it represents deliberation as unduly focused on causal facts. If deliberation always aimed at discovering how best to promote desire-satisfaction or enjoyment, then the choice between any two equally enjoyable or equally desired alternatives would turn exclusively on their ability to generate *further* enjoyments or to satisfy *other* desires. The crucial issue would always be what Bentham called "fecundity." Hence, when we deliberated, we would have to con-

16. Brink, *Moral Realism and the Foundations of Ethics*, p. 226.

sider only such topics as the evidence for various causal claims, the mechanisms through which various effects are produced, and the likelihood that specific causes will produce specific effects. But while these topics clearly do arise, they equally clearly do not dominate. Although we often do ask causal questions, we often ask other kinds of questions, too.

Moreover, second, even when our questions are causal, they usually are not directed at the effects that the alternatives would have on people's *mental states.* Faced with a choice between a career in (say) engineering or law, a person might well ask how each choice would affect other people. But if he did, he would most likely be asking whether (e.g.) it is more important to help people get where they are going by designing safe and reliable transportation, or to broaden access to legal services and represent unpopular but worthy causes. To recast all such questions in terms of enjoyment or desire-satisfaction would be a further and entirely gratuitous step.

The last and most important difficulty is a generalization of the first two. It is that the emerging picture systematically deflects attention from the most central topic of deliberation – namely, the alternatives themselves. If what mattered to us were only the impact of our choices on people's desires or enjoyments, we could never deliberate simply about *what we might do.* The actual alternatives – to marry or remain single, to pursue this or that career, to spend the afternoon reading or doing laundry or just lying on the beach – would enter only as so many replaceable causal vehicles. In weighing the alternatives, we would consider only their effects, but never what is attractive, valuable, or important simply about *them.* But that is not deliberation as we know it.

To add emphasis to these points, let me briefly return to Brink's example of the desire to be a professional philosopher – a desire with which many readers are no doubt familiar. As Brink correctly notes, most persons who have this desire would not have it if they did not believe that philosophy was a valuable activity. However, as Brink does *not* sufficiently stress, their belief that philosophy is valuable is also unlikely to have much to do with anyone's subjective states. That is, when an aspiring philosopher takes a career in philosophy to be worth pursuing, his deepest reason is unlikely to be either that it will promote his own or other people's enjoyment or that it will satisfy his or others' actual or informed desires.

For, first, when someone takes a career in philosophy to be worth pursuing, his reason is very unlikely to be that it will bring *other* people enjoyment or satisfy *their* desires. At least in our earlier years, we seldom confuse our future contributions to philosophy with philanthropy. And, although it may be less obvious, the aspiring philosopher's reason for considering philosophy worthwhile is also unlikely to be that a career in it will make *him* happy or satisfy *his* desires. The point here is not that an aspiring philosopher is unlikely to expect to enjoy philosophy: to the contrary, he very well may. Instead, the point is that this expectation, if he has it, is *itself* likely to be backed by a belief that philosophy is worthwhile. For people seldom enjoy spending their lives doing what they consider worthless, so if the aspiring philosopher expects to enjoy his career, he also is likely to expect to believe that it is worth pursuing while he is pursuing it. But on what basis can he expect to believe this in the future if he does not already believe it now? Nor, finally, is his current belief that philosophy is worth pursuing likely to be rooted in a conviction that he *would* want to engage in philosophical inquiry if he were (more) fully informed; for given the opacity of one's informed desires, the only plausible basis for that conviction is, again, a prior belief that philosophy has independent value which full information would reveal.[17]

IV

So far, I have argued that subjectivism has a number of implications that raise the cost of accepting it. But every theory has its weaknesses, and, for all we have yet seen, the cost of rejecting subjectivism may be even higher. Thus, before we can draw any conclusions, we must examine the main countervailing arguments *for* subjectivism.

These, unfortunately, are more often assumed than articulated. Richard Brandt is unusually forthright, but not unusually dismissive, when he writes that

[v]arious philosophers have thought that some things, different from happiness and possibly not desired by anyone or everyone, are worthwhile in themselves and worthy of being produced for no further reason, for instance: knowledge and virtue. This view, however, seems to be obsolescent, and I propose to ignore it.[18]

17. See ibid., pp. 229–31.
18. Brandt, *A Theory of the Good and the Right*, p. 246.

Because the case for subjectivism is seldom made explicit, I shall have to speculate about the sources of its appeal.

One, pretty clearly, is its ability to forge a link between value and motivation. Because subjectivists trace each thing's value to certain desires or other motivationally effective states, they seem able to provide a natural explanation of why persons have the impulse to seek the good. Their explanation is simply that value and the impulse to pursue it are always traceable to a single source. By contrast, because perfectionists do *not* trace each thing's value to any motivationally effective state, their view appears to leave the *attraction* of value mysterious.[19]

A second apparent advantage of subjectivism is its ability to explain what makes value-claims *true*. According to subjectivists, the facts that determine a value-claim's truth – facts about what people do or would want, choose, or enjoy – are, from a metaphysical standpoint, relatively unproblematic. But because perfectionism does *not* take these facts to be the sole determinants of value, it may seem to commit us to a realm of strange, nonempirical facts that are hard to reconcile with a fully naturalistic picture of the world.

And there may be yet a third reason to favor subjectivism: namely, that it alone seems capable of explaining how things *come to be* valuable. For if, with many perfectionists, we treat the value of each (kind of) good thing as just another brute fact, then we obviously cannot explain how anything *acquires* its value. We also cannot explain what different good things have in common. But if we accept some sort of desire or choice theory – though, interestingly, *not* if we accept any kind of enjoyment theory – then we may be able to explain both phenomena. To do so, it may be sufficient to observe that each good thing acquires its value precisely when, and precisely because, it *is or would be* wanted or chosen in the requisite way. Alternatively, and in a commonly used variant formula, the explanation may be that the relevant actual or possible desires or choices *confer* value on their objects.

We are now in a better position to understand the appeal of subjectivism. Unlike perfectionism, it purports to explain, at a single stroke, how value motivates, what makes value-claims true, and how different things come to be valuable. If these advantages could be sustained, they might well be decisive. However, in what follows, I shall argue that the advantages *cannot* be sustained. In each case, the

19. For relevant discussion, see Railton, "Facts and Values," especially p. 9.

proposed explanation either fails or else is available to at least some perfectionists.

V

Let us begin with the subjectivist's explanation of why we seek the good. As we saw, its crucial premise is that the very same desires, choices, or affective states that make things valuable are also sources of impulses to pursue them. But even if we accept this premise, it will not follow that the persons whom the relevant subjective states motivate are the very ones whose motivation needs to be explained. And, in fact, none of these subjective states *do* motivate just the right agents in just the right ways.

This is easiest to see when the subjective states are informed desires; for however we understand full information, we must agree that few persons actually have it. On any reasonable account, each person's informed desires are usually if not always merely hypothetical. They are usually only desires that the agent *would* have if he were far better informed than he actually is. But if an informed desire is not itself actual, then how can it supply anyone with any actual motivation? We certainly can understand how an *actual* desire can supply its possessor with an actual motive; and we can also understand how a merely hypothetical desire *would* supply such a motive if it *were* actual. But none of this explains how any merely hypothetical desire can, just by itself, give rise to any actual impulse to act. That is just as puzzling, and is puzzling for just the same reasons, as how the value of something that is *not even* hypothetically desired can supply anyone with any actual impulse to act. Hence, at least in its informed-desire versions, subjectivism is no better able than perfectionism to explain why we seek the good.

Can a subjectivist avoid this problem by focusing exclusively on *actual* desires? That depends, in part, on how he interprets actuality. On one common interpretation, the actual world encompasses everything that has happened, will happen, and is happening now. When actuality is understood in this way, the actual-desire approach attaches value to the objects of all past and future as well as present desires. It thus implies that the best way for someone to live at any given moment is to have as much as possible, not only of what he then wants, but also of what he wanted in the past and will want in the future. This way of thinking about past and future desires is not entirely unfamiliar. For example, we attach value to the objects of past desires whenever we say that a dead person's wishes give us a reason to do something now,[20] and – to borrow an example from Thomas Nagel – we attach value to the objects of *future* desires when we say that we have a reason to learn Italian now because we will want to speak it in Italy next year.[21]

Still, whatever its other merits, this version of the actual-desire theory is too inclusive to solve our current problem. The reason, quite clearly, is that just as no merely hypothetical desire can supply anyone with any *actual* motivation, no merely past or future desire can supply anyone with any *present* motivation. It is, of course, true that each past desire *has been* a source of motivation and that each future desire *will be* one; but neither fact explains how any past or future desire can be a source of motivation *now*. As long as a past or future desire does not now exist, any impulses that it did or will supply do not now exist either. Thus, even if we do attribute value only to the objects of people's actual desires, our inclusive interpretation of actuality will still prevent us from explaining what motivates people to seek much of what our theory counts as valuable.

This objection suggests the possibility of a further retreat. It suggests that to preserve his advantage, a subjectivist may have to fall back to the position that what has value is the satisfaction, not of *all*, but only of all *current*, actual desires. Although this bare-bones version of the desire theory would be implausible on other grounds,[22] it may at least seem to offer hope of forging a firm link between value and the impulse to pursue it.

But, once again, that hope is vain. The trouble this time is that although a person's current actual desires do provide *him* with a motive to seek their objects, they do *not* provide such motivation to any *other* persons. Because each desire *belongs* to only a single person, each desire can also *motivate* only a single person. Yet if each person's getting what he wants is a good thing, and if an adequate theory

20. For an attempt to explain why past events, including past desires, continue to be morally important, see George Sher, *Desert*, (Princeton: Princeton University Press, 1987), ch. 10. For an argument that it is rational to ignore one's past desires, see Derek Parfit, *Reasons and Persons* (Oxford: Oxford University Press, 1984), especially pp. 148–59.

21. Thomas Nagel, *The Possibility of Altruism* (Oxford: Oxford University Press, 1970), pp. 58–59.

22. To cite just two of many difficulties, it forces us to attach value to the satisfaction of desires based on gross misinformation and to outcomes that agents will immediately regret.

must explain what motivates us to seek the good, then the people whose motivation must be explained cannot be just those with the value-conferring desires. As I shall argue in the next section, the contexts in which desire theories are standardly advanced commit their proponents to the view that when an outcome O would satisfy X's desires, it is not only X, but also Y and Z, who sometimes have reason to pursue O. If so, however, then in addition to explaining what moves someone to pursue the things that his *own* desires make valuable, an adequate desire theory must also explain what could move anyone *else* to pursue (his having) these things. But the impulses supplied by a person's own value-conferring desires are, of course, no explanation of this.

Thus, in the end, even the most pared-down version of the desire theory cannot supply the needed explanation. Such a theory may explain why some persons seek some good things, but, like its predecessors, it cannot explain how most instances of value enter most people's motivational systems. Moreover, although it would be tedious to repeat the arguments, it seems clear that similar problems would arise if we substituted choice, enjoyment, or any other subjective state for desire.

This, of course, is not the end of the story. To explain how informed (or future, past, or other people's) desires can motivate us to pursue what they make valuable, a desire theorist (and, mutatis mutandis, a subjectivist of some other stripe) can still do any of several things. He can, in particular, still (1) postulate a universal desire for the satisfaction of all other desires; or (2) argue that even without such help, each desire can transmit its motivational impulses across possible worlds, across time, or across the boundaries between persons;[23] or (3) simply give up hope of finding any internal connection between a thing's goodness and the impulse to seek it, and concede that all such impulses are mere fortunate contingencies.[24] But as soon as a subjectivist does any of these things, he will forfeit his advantage over the perfectionist; for a perfectionist can do each of them too. He, too, can (1) postulate an all-purpose desire to promote (what he takes to

---

23. In *The Possibility of Altruism*, Nagel argues that desires *can* transmit their motivational force over time and across the boundaries between persons, but – interestingly – not across possible worlds.
24. As Philippa Foot points out in a related context, a motive can be merely contingent without being untrustworthy or easily shaken; see Foot, "Morality as a System of Hypothetical Imperatives," in *Virtues and Vices* (Berkeley: University of California Press, 1978), pp. 157–73.

have) value; or (2) argue that each thing's value is *itself* a source of motivation; or (3) construe all impulses to seek the good as mere fortunate contingencies. Thus, in the end, both sides are equally able – or equally unable – to explain why we seek the good.

VI

The second argument for subjectivism is metaphysical. It says that only subjectivists, but not perfectionists, can provide a metaphysically respectable account of what makes value-claims true. Its reasoning is that according to subjectivism the truth of each value-claim depends on some empirically identifiable state such as enjoyment or desire-satisfaction, whereas according to perfectionism it depends on a mysterious further something – "value" – which some traits, activities, and relationships have but others lack.

But, at least in its current form, this argument is confused. We certainly may grant that what subjectivists take to be valuable – desire-satisfaction, enjoyment, and the like – is, metaphysically, relatively unproblematic. But by the same token, what *perfectionists* take to be valuable – excellence, virtue, and the like – is relatively unproblematic too. This, therefore, is no reason to favor either approach. Yet neither can we favor subjectivism on the further grounds that perfectionists must not only *mention* knowledge, excellence, virtue, and the rest, but also attribute the additional property of being valuable *to* them; for here again, a subjectivist must do the same.[25] The only difference is that what a subjectivist takes to *have* this additional property is not knowledge, excellence, or virtue, but rather desire-satisfaction or enjoyment.

Or *is* this the only difference? Even if both subjectivists and perfectionists must not only single out certain parts of the world but also attribute value to them, it does not follow that the form or content of their value-attributions must also be the same. If their value-notions differ, there may indeed be room for the claim that perfectionism, but not subjectivism, has objectionable metaphysical implications. More-

25. Here I assume that subjectivism is not put forth as a reductive analysis. When subjectivism is construed as a reductive analysis, it does *not* imply the existence of any value-property over and above the relevant empirical property (though it may then become vulnerable to Moore's "open question" argument). However, by the same token, perfectionism does not imply the existence of any additional value-property when *it* is put forth as a reductive analysis.

193

over, when we examine the rhetoric of the two sides, we find some evidence that their value-notions are indeed different.

For when a subjectivist asks which things are valuable, he is most often interested in ascertaining what is good *for people*. This, at any rate, is the natural way to understand Sidgwick's assertion that informed desires determine "a man's future good on the whole."[26] Moreover, along similar lines, Rawls advances his version of the informed-desire theory as an account of "a person's good,"[27] while James Griffin defends his version in a book entitled *Well-Being*. In adopting this terminology, these subjectivists – and, I think, most others – appear to be asking not the portentous question, What sorts of things make the universe a better place? but only the more modest, What sorts of things make *people* better off?

By contrast, when perfectionists talk about value, they generally say things like this:

[W]hatever human nature turns out to be, whatever form of life satisfies people more, it would still be the case that [some forms of life] would be intrinsically superior to [others].[28]

Perfectionism holds that there are certain intrinsically valuable states of human beings, and that each of us should maximize the achievement of these states both in herself and in others.[29]

[Consider] two states of the universe equal in respect of virtue and of pleasure and of the allocation of pleasure to the virtuous, but such that the persons in the one had a far greater understanding of the nature and laws of the universe than those in the other. Can anyone doubt that the first would be a better state of the universe?[30]

What is most striking about these passages is that they do *not* assimilate value to benefit or well-being. The logical form of their value-predicate appears to be not "——— is good for X," but rather "——— is good *simpliciter*." Moreover, as the last quotation illustrates, what perfectionists want to know is often *exactly* which traits and

---

26. Sidgwick, *Methods of Ethics*, p. 111.
27. John Rawls, *A Theory of Justice* (Cambridge, Mass.: Harvard Universtiy Press, 1971), especially p. 424.
28. Vinit Haksar, *Equality, Liberty, and Perfectionism* (Oxford: Oxford University Press, 1977), pp. 3–4.
29. Thomas Hurka, "The Well-Rounded Life," *Journal of Philosophy* 84, 12 (December 1987), p. 727.
30. W. D. Ross, *The Right and the Good* (Oxford: Oxford University Press, 1930), p. 139.

activities make the universe a better place. To capture the distinction between claims about what is good for persons and claims about what is good *simpliciter,* I shall call the first sorts of value-claims *person-relative* and the second sorts *impersonal.*[31]

Can a subjectivist exploit this distinction to revive his metaphysical argument? To do so, he needs to establish both that (1) perfectionists, but not subjectivists, must take some things to be impersonally valuable, and that (2) attributions of impersonal value are metaphysically objectionable while attributions of person-relative value are not. But whatever we say about premise (2) – and, for the record, I am not convinced that attributions of impersonal value *are* metaphysically objectionable – there are two reasons to reject premise (1). For, first, despite their rhetoric, perfectionists are no less able than subjectivists to understand value in purely person-relative terms; and, second, despite *their* rhetoric, even most subjectivists cannot avoid taking some things to be *impersonally* valuable.

My reason for saying that perfectionists are no more committed to attributions of impersonal value than subjectivists is simply that the two distinctions cut across each other. It is one thing to disagree about which things *are* (noninstrumentally) valuable, and quite another to disagree about whether noninstrumental value is best understood as goodness for persons or goodness *simpliciter.* Hence, there is no deep reason why a perfectionist must couch his theory in terms of impersonal value. Instead, he can say – in the manner of Aristotle himself – that knowledgeable, excellent, and virtuous lives are good precisely *for persons.* This person-relative form of perfectionism, though weaker than its impersonal counterpart, is *not* weaker than an equally person-relative form of subjectivism. Thus, even if we entirely reject the notion of impersonal value, the dispute between perfectionists and subjectivists will live on as a dispute about what is best for persons.

But, further, the notion of impersonal value is not so easy to reject. Indeed, my second point is precisely that even most subjectivists cannot altogether avoid relying on it. In saying this, I do not mean

31. My distinction between person-relative and impersonal values is related to, but should not be confused with, the more familiar distinction between person-relative and impersonal *reasons.* As the latter terms are usually defined, a person-relative reason is one that has force only for certain persons, whereas an impersonal reason has force for everyone. These definitions imply that there can be impersonal reasons to promote what in my terms are person-relative values. In particular, such reasons will exist whenever everyone has a reason to promote a certain person's good.

that it is theoretically impossible to regard desire-satisfaction or enjoyment as good only for persons. My point, rather, is that this cannot be what most subjectivists have meant *in the contexts in which they have typically advanced their views.*[32]

The most familiar of those contexts is utilitarianism. As many have observed, the principle of utility has two components. It asserts, first, that desire-satisfaction or enjoyment is the sole good – this is subjectivism – and, second, that each person ought to *maximize* this good. Hence, when we interpret the principle's first, subjectivist component, we must do so in a way that is compatible with its second, value-maximizing component.

But suppose we took the subjectivist component to assert only that (say) the satisfaction of each person's desires is a good thing *for him.* In that case, the only person who would have a reason to pursue the satisfaction of any desire would be precisely the person who had the desire. Because the relevant form of goodness would be only goodness *for him,* the goodness of the satisfaction of his desire would not give anyone *else* a reason to seek it. But if no one even had a reason to *seek* the satisfaction of anyone else's desires, then a fortiori no one would have a reason to *maximize* the satisfaction of desire. And, hence, the person-relative reading of the subjectivist component of the principle of utility seems incompatible with that principle's value-maximizing component.

Could someone resist this conclusion by contesting the inference from "the satisfaction of each person's desires is good only for him" to "no one has a reason to seek the satisfaction of anyone else's desires?" At first glance, this may indeed seem possible; for it could be maintained that what gives one person a reason to seek the satisfaction of another's desires is precisely the fact that the satisfaction of those desires *would* be good for the other person. According to this suggestion, the fact that something would be good for a given person just *is* a reason for others to seek it. And so it may be; but if it is, then a person's having what is good for him must itself be a good thing in some further sense. Moreover, if that further sense is only person-relative – if the claim is only that each person's having what is good for him is itself good *for him* – then the same problem will only arise again. To keep it from reappearing, the rejoinder must instead be that each person's having what is good for him is a good thing *simpliciter.*

---

32. For more ambitious arguments against the view that all value is person-relative, see Larry Temkin, *Inequality* (Oxford: Oxford University Press, 1993), ch. 9.

However, on this interpretation, the rejoinder will itself reintroduce the very notion of impersonal value that it was introduced to exclude.

Whatever his official line, the logic of the utilitarian's position compels him to regard something – either desire-satisfaction or enjoyment or, one level up, well-being – as impersonally valuable. But many subjectivists are *not* utilitarians, so it is important to note that the same point holds when subjectivism is affirmed in a variety of other contexts. It holds, for example, whenever subjectivism is combined with any principle of beneficence or nonmaleficence; for these principles, too, imply that persons sometimes have reason to seek the satisfaction (or prevent the frustration) of others' desires. And, even more important for us, the point also holds whenever the value of a person's happiness, or of the satisfaction of his desires, is advanced to justify some action that might be taken by the state or its agents. Here again, if the person's enjoyment or desire-satisfaction were good only *for him* – if it were valuable only in the sense that it increases his well-being – then its value would *not* give the state any reason to act. Thus, to hold that its value does provide such a reason, one must again take the person's enjoyment or desire-satisfaction either to be good *simpliciter* or to contribute to something else, such as his well-being, which has that status in its turn.[33]

VII

The last of the three arguments for subjectivism – that unlike perfectionism, it offers an explanation of how various things *come to be* valuable – can be dealt with more briefly. The two points that need to be made are, first, that there is far less to this explanation than meets the eye and, second, that what little there is is also available to some perfectionists.

The main problem is that the explanation rests on a series of metaphors: that desires *confer* value on their objects, that things *acquire or*

---

33. In saying this, I do not mean to imply that every reference to value in an argument about how government should act must construe value as impersonal. To the contrary, Eric Mack has argued that the case for deontic restraints on governments turns precisely on the *rejection* of impersonal value: see Eric Mack, "Moral Individualism: Agent-Relativity and Deontic Restraints," *Social Philosophy and Policy* 7, 1 (Autumn 1989), pp. 81–111. My point is only that we cannot avoid construing the value of desire-satisfaction or happiness as impersonal when we invoke it to justify some action *by* the state. I take such justifications to be very common.

inherit value by being chosen, that value flows from desires or choices *to* their objects, and so on. But by themselves, these expressions explain little. To shed any real light, a subjectivist must not only *represent* desires or choices as (somehow) creating value, but also tell us how they *accomplish* that feat. He must, in other words, either specify the (causal, metaphysical, or normative) *mechanism through which* wanting or choosing a thing transforms it into something worth having, or else tell some other convincing story about how the transformation occurs. But, at least up to now, no adequate story has been forthcoming.[34]

Nor, if one were, would the resulting explanation necessarily distinguish subjectivism from all forms of perfectionism. It would indeed give subjectivism an edge over those versions of perfectionism that merely attribute intrinsic value to diverse arrays of activities or traits; but not all forms of perfectionism are so radically pluralistic. As defined, perfectionism also encompasses theories that ground the value of diverse traits and activities in certain very general goals that characterize the human species. These species-specific goals, no less than goals that are peculiar to individuals, may be said to confer value on their objects. Hence, these versions of perfectionism may inherit all the advantages of the dynamic metaphors. And, not coincidentally, the theory I shall advance in the next chapter is of precisely this sort. Though recognizably perfectionist, it shares the subjectivist's assumption that what counts as a good life for us is somehow rooted in our mental makeup. This allows it to preserve the subjectivist's main insight while avoiding his errors.

---

34. Compare E. J. Bond: "The theory . . . that an end's merely being desired is a sufficient condition of its worth for the desirer . . . is . . . often taken as self-evident and seldom argued for. There are various desired ends, it is assumed, and there are means to their achievement. The value of the end is simply left unquestioned. The desire *confers* it" (*Reason and Value,* p. 43).

Chapter 9

Perfectionism: A theory

The perfectionist theory that I shall defend is pluralistic in one sense but monistic in another. It is pluralistic in the sense that it attaches value to a number of irreducibly different activities, traits, and types of relationship, but monistic in that it traces the value of each to a single source. Thus, in the terms of a distinction made earlier, mine is a theory of inherent rather than intrinsic value. To develop the theory, I shall proceed in three stages. First, I shall present a list of candidate goods that seems initially plausible. Next, I shall sketch a unifying account that, if defensible, would justify each entry on the list. Finally, I shall defend that unifying account on independent grounds.

I

As I argued in the preceding chapter, there are various traits and activities about whose value most would agree. For example, few would deny that it is good to possess knowledge and insight, to excel at what one does, to display various virtues, and to stand in close and loving relations. But many other claims about the good are far more controversial. Some regard promiscuity and homosexuality as abominations; others attach great value to aesthetic appreciation; still others locate the good in direct civic participation; and others again think it best to live in harmony with nature. In each case, many strongly disagree. Similarly, many people do, but many others do not, attach special value to intellectual activity, physical activity, self-expression and spontaneity, self-control, balance, and excess. And, at the less reputable end of the spectrum, we find all manner of beliefs that persons of this or that race, or this or that religion or cultural background, are superior or inferior to others.

Given this mixture of agreement and disagreement, any attempt to list the constituents of a good life is bound to be contentious. Jonathan Glover speaks for many when he attributes his own aborted impulse to provide such a list to a "[t]emporary loss of a sense of the absurd."[1] Nevertheless, various others have been less inhibited, and I intend – bravely or foolishly – to join their ranks.

One well-known list of goods was put forth by W. D. Ross. Writing in 1930, Ross suggested that

[f]our things . . . seem to be intrinsically good – virtue, pleasure, the allocation of pleasure to the virtuous, and knowledge.[2]

Other things, Ross argued, are good only because of their relations to these. But Ross's contemporary G. E. Moore believed instead that

[b]y far the most valuable things, which we know or can imagine, are certain states of consciousness, which may be roughly described as the pleasures of human intercourse and the enjoyment of beautiful objects.[3]

Moore differed from Ross both in assigning intrinsic goodness only to states of consciousness and in maintaining that knowledge has "little or no value by itself"[4] (though he conceded that it "is an absolutely essential constituent in the highest goods, and contributes immensely to their value").[5]

Others have taken different positions again. For example, David Brink has recently suggested that

reflective pursuit and realization of agents' reasonable projects and certain personal and social relationships [are] the primary components of valuable lives.[6]

And another contemporary, John Finnis, writes that in addition to life itself, the basic forms of human good include knowledge, play,

1. Jonathan Glover, *Causing Death and Saving Lives* (Harmondsworth: Penguin, 1977), p. 52.
2. W. D. Ross, *The Right and the Good* (Oxford: Oxford University Press, 1930), p. 140.
3. G. E. Moore, *Principia Ethica* (Cambridge: Cambridge University Press, 1903; reprint, 1962), p. 188.
4. Ibid., p. 199.
5. Ibid.
6. David O. Brink, *Moral Realism and the Foundations of Ethics* (Cambridge: Cambridge University Press, 1989), p. 231.

aesthetic experience, sociability, practical reasonableness, and "religion."[7]

Whatever their differences, all four of these thinkers clearly endorse the lists they propose. However, ironically, the list that I find most convincing is advanced by somone who does *not* endorse it. Although Derek Parfit neither accepts nor rejects perfectionism – he calls it "the objective list theory" – he illustrates it by suggesting that

[t]he good things might include moral goodness, rational activity, the development of one's abilities, having children and being a good parent, knowledge, and the awareness of true beauty.[8]

This list combines (versions of) the most popular and appealing elements of each alternative list. But how can it, or any other list, be defended?

II

Here it helps to recall what was said earlier about moral epistemology. In Chapter 6, I briefly argued that a claim is justified when and only when it coheres, or hangs together, with enough other relevant beliefs. I also argued that even when a claim is normative, the beliefs with which it must be shown to cohere include both normative *and* nonnormative convictions. But if justification is in this way holistic, then we never need say, with Finnis, that the value of a good such as knowledge "is self-evident, obvious. It cannot be demonstrated, but equally it needs no demonstration."[9] Instead, there will always be indefinitely many deductive, probabilistic, explanatory, and analogical relations from which to (try to) fashion a justificatory argument. Nor, if we require coherence with nonnormative as well as normative beliefs, need we aspire only to eliminating or explaining away the inconsistencies among our normative beliefs. Instead, we may appeal to the natural affinity, or "fit," between specific value-claims and (what we take to be) specific facts about the world. Moreover, among the relevant facts, we may legitimately include various facts about human psychology and human nature.

---

7. John Finnis, *Natural Law and Natural Rights* (Oxford: Oxford University Press, 1980), chs. 3 and 4; the quotation marks around "religion" are his.
8. Derek Parfit, *Reasons and Persons* (Oxford: Oxford University Press, 1984), appendix I, p. 499.
9. Finnis, *Natural Law and Natural Rights*, p. 65.

In what follows, I shall propose an argument of this general sort. Tracing a well-worn path, I shall argue that certain human capacities are especially fundamental, and that their links to certain traits or activities are what make the latter inherently valuable. Like anyone else who takes this line, I must be careful about the term "fundamental." My argument would be circular if I maintained both that what makes an activity inherently valuable is that it exercises a fundamental capacity and that what makes a capacity fundamental is that its exercise is inherently valuable. To avoid this circularity, I need some independent and well-motivated criterion for when a capacity is fundamental. For reasons that will become clear, I shall impose two distinct but jointly sufficient requirements: first, that to be fundamental, a capacity must be one that virtually all humans possess, and, second, that it must be one whose exercise its possessors either cannot avoid at all, or else can avoid only intermittently and with great difficulty. Thus, on my account, a fundamental capacity will be one whose exercise is both near-universal and near-inescapable.

This criterion plainly makes it harder to show that a capacity is fundamental. But, at the same time, doesn't it make it easier – indeed, far *too* easy – to show that individuals live good lives? For if what has inherent value is just the exercise of a fundamental capacity, and if a capacity is only fundamental if virtually no one can avoid exercising it, then won't it follow immediately that virtually *everyone* lives a good life?

This inference, if sound, would make short work of my account. But, in fact, the inference is *not* sound, and the reason for its failure is instructive. The key fact is that many fundamental capacities are teleological: as we shall see, many are essentially directed at particular goals. Moreover, at least in the cases that interest us, the achievement of those goals is far from automatic. Despite our best efforts, we can and often do fail to achieve them. Thus, to avoid the absurd implication that virtually all lives are good, I need only insist that what has inherent value is not the mere exercise of a fundamental capacity, but rather its *successful* exercise as measured by the achievement of its defining goal.

This suggestion raises many new questions. To flesh it out, I must explain both which capacities *are* fundamental and how various traits, activities, and relationships are bound up with their goals. More deeply, I must explain why we should *accept* the argument-schema "virtually all persons find it virtually impossible to avoid pursuing X, so X is good in itself." Because the two questions are so closely connected – because the argument-schema's viability depends in part on its interpretation, which in turn depends in part on its rationale – it does not matter much where we start. However, for purposes of exposition, it will be best to start with some illustration. Thus, to begin, I shall explore the relations between a number of fundamental capacities and the value-claims I take them to support. And it is just here that Parfit's list comes into its own; for each of its entries is especially closely linked to the goal of some fundamental activity.

III

In some instances, the connection is obvious. For example, despite our manifest differences, each of us has both a native capacity to understand the world and an inescapable tendency to try to exercise that capacity. We seek such understanding not only when we propose a scientific hypothesis or try to predict the stock market, but when we idly read the newspaper, engage in conversation, or simply look about us. We seek it, too, when we ponder, wonder, muse, conjecture, speculate, or reflect. In each case, our mental activity centers on some proposition, or some structured set of propositions, that has engaged our attention; and in each case, our guiding question is whether these propositions are true. Even when we try to avoid all truth seeking, our success is temporary at best. As any insomniac knows, it takes a special effort to avoid all processing of information that aims at true belief. This effort can only be sustained for brief periods of time. Thus, if what has inherent value is the successful exercise of fundamental capacities, it would be very surprising if reason-based true belief – or, in other words, knowledge – were not inherently good.[10]

As thus developed, my argument does not distinguish important from trivial knowledge. It does not imply that it is any better to know *why* a fact holds than merely to know *that* it does. However, in fact, the latter sort of knowledge does seem far more valuable. As Ross correctly observed, "[k]nowledge of mere matters of fact (say of the number of stories in a building), without knowledge of their relation to other facts . . . seems to be worth much less than the knowledge of

---

10. For related discussion, see Charles Fried's illuminating treatment of the wrongness of lying in his *Right and Wrong* (Cambridge, Mass.: Harvard University Press, 1978), pp. 59–69.

general principles, or of facts as depending on general principles."[11]
But why, on my account, should this be so?

The answer lies, I think, in a more precise articulation of what we unavoidably seek. For when we process information, our inescapable aim is not merely to amass an ever greater number of unconnected true beliefs, but is also to understand the subsumptive, explanatory, and justificatory relations among the true propositions we believe. We are inescapably driven to ask not only what the facts are but also how they fit together. Moreover, these inescapable goals are nested: the aim of understanding the relations among different facts encompasses, and so is more ultimate than, the aim of merely knowing each one. Thus, if our fundamental goals determine what has inherent value, it is not at all surprising that general knowledge seems to be worth far more than knowledge of unconnected facts.

Nor, further, is it surprising that successful *practical* activity appears to be valuable; for just as we cannot avoid trying to understand the world, we also cannot avoid thinking about how to act in and upon it. As practical agents, we are unavoidably implicated in a complex sequence of activities whose goal and characteristic tendency are the performance of reason-based actions. The elements of this sequence include at least identifying different plans of action that we might adopt, surveying the reasons for and against each plan, weighing these reasons against one another, choosing the plan that we take to be backed by the strongest reasons, intending to carry out the chosen plan, and actually doing what we have chosen and intended. The sequence can, of course, be foreshortened or extended in many ways; but we can no more consistently avoid it than we can avoid processing different reasons for belief. Hence, just as knowledge belongs on our list of inherent goods, the formation and execution of reason-based plans – what Parfit tersely designates "rational activity" and Brink more elaborately calls the "reflective pursuit of agents' reasonable projects" – appear to belong there too.

But here again there is a complication – this time, that the reasons for acting seem far less well behaved than the reasons for belief. For when the question is what to believe, there are few barriers to assessing all reasons on a single scale. By contrast, when the question is what to *do*, our ability to weigh competing reasons is much less clear. Practical reasons include, among others, reasons of prudence, aes-

11. Ross, *The Right and the Good*, p. 139.

thetic reasons, and reasons grounded in personal relations and individual commitments and projects. They also include any reasons provided by nonmoral values and, of course, the important reasons of morality. Whether these types of reason are all commensurable is notoriously controversial. If some are not, then practical reason will not always speak with a single voice.

Yet even so, we can hardly avoid *trying* to decide on the basis of our strongest reasons; for that is just what practical deliberation *is*. When we are unsure which combination of reasons is strongest, we either decide on the basis of our best estimate or else set the question aside on the grounds that it is more important to reach some sort of closure than to reach a finer appreciation of what is best. Either way, we display a commitment to exercising rather than abdicating our practical rational capacity. Thus, whether or not all relevant practical reasons are *in fact* commensurable, anyone who deliberates must at least try to bring them into mutual contact. As I shall henceforth put this point, basing one's decision on one's weightiest combination of reasons is the *generic aim* of all practical deliberation.

Of course, if some practical reasons are in fact incommensurable, then we cannot fully achieve this generic aim. Yet even if we cannot, some decisions are likely to come closer to achieving it than others. For one thing, even if practical reason certifies no action as best, it may still rule some out as definitely *not* best. More important, even if some practical reasons are incommensurable, the overall balance of reasons may still decisively favor a single action. This may be so because all the incommensurable reasons that are relevant happen to support the same action; because all the relevant reasons happen not to *be* incommensurable; or – perhaps – because even incommensurable reasons can be compared ordinally. And as long as practical reason can get this much of a grip, we need not worry about our argument-schema's ability to account for many autonomy-related goods.

It also can account for the value of a third item on Parfit's list – namely, a generalized version of what he calls "having children and being a good parent." I say "a generalized version" because I see no reason to focus exclusively on parental relations. Rather, much that can be said about them can also be said about the bonds between sexual partners, ties of friendship, and even professional and collegial relations. Moreover, in each case, a good deal can be said. It is true that efforts to form and sustain social bonds are less unremitting than theoretical or practical deliberation. We can avoid (noninstrumental) social interaction far longer than either efforts to arrive at true beliefs or efforts to decide what is best to do. Still, over the longer term, our efforts to form social bonds do seem close to inescapable. At the very least, we all have very powerful urges to seek out, communicate with, and care for and be cared for by other human beings. The occasional solitary notwithstanding, we appear to be essentially social creatures.

Even by themselves, these truisms are illuminating. At a minimum, they explain why our list of inherent goods must include some interpersonal relations. But unless we can specify *which* social goals persons cannot avoid pursuing, our explanation will lack precision. It will tell us only that *some* kinds of relationship have value, but not which ones these are. There is, of course, no real mystery here: we clearly should assign little value to interpersonal relations that are (e.g.) manipulative, exploitative, coercive, or destructive. However, if the proposed account is left unrefined, it will provide these judgments with no theoretical backing.

To arrive at the needed refinement, we must return to a theme that was sounded earlier. In Chapter 7, I argued that society's role in constituting the self implies neither that individuals are morally secondary nor that society is an independent source of value. But even if society's contribution to the self has no such global implications, it may still have important implications about which forms of relationship are most valuable. For when people interact, they seek not only love and companionship, but also something akin to the social identity that communitarians have stressed. As many have noted, each person defines himself through the eyes of others. To regard ourselves as persons in the full sense, we must recognize others as recognizing us as rational and affective agents with a perspective of our own. This quest for mutual recognition has been noted by thinkers from many traditions, and it suggests a natural (though highly schematic) explanation of why relationships differ in value.

The explanation is simply that not all relationships are equally successful in *achieving* mutual recognition. Although efforts to achieve it are inescapable, these may fail because one or both parties pay insufficient attention to the other's perspective, because one or both have mistaken beliefs about the other's beliefs and attitudes toward them, and – no doubt – in other, far more complex ways. The paradigm of one such failure is the master–slave relation as analyzed by Hegel:[12] the master, in failing to acknowledge the slave as a separate and independent agent, is cut off from the recognition he craves but which the slave cannot confer because his standpoint has not been acknowledged in turn. Although I cannot here argue the point, I would conjecture that each other mode of interaction that we consider valueless or disvaluable – manipulation, exploitation, and so on – owes its lack of value to some similar failure of mutual recognition.

If anything like this is correct, the proposed argument-schema will account for three of Parfit's six entries. It will enable us to explain the value of knowledge, rational activity, and close personal relations by pointing out that each is the internal goal of some fundamental human capacity. But what, next, of Parfit's other three entries? What of moral goodness, the appreciation of true beauty, and the development of one's abilities? Unlike the first three entries, these surely are *not* fundamental human goals; for even if we all have the capacity to pursue each, our exercise of those capacities is far from unavoidable. We all know people who willingly dissipate their talents, who act immorally, and who spurn or destroy what is beautiful. Thus, my ambitious claim of a few pages back – that each of Parfit's entries is intimately linked to some near-universal and near-inescapable goal – may seem obviously false.

IV

But, in fact, it is not; for even if no *further* capacities are fundamental, the ones already identified may allow us to complete the argument. This is possible because the internal goal of a single fundamental capacity may be suitably related to more than one type of activity.

Consider first what Parfit calls "the development of one's abilities." Of all his entries, this one comes closest to the notion of excellence that gives perfectionism its name. Moreover, at least in broad outline, its connection to fundamental goals is clear. The key facts are, first, that developing any ability improves some set of cognitive, practical, or social skills, and, second, that each skill contributes to the achievement of various goals, including various fundamental ones. The skills we thus employ are of course diverse – we call on one

12. See G. W. F. Hegel, *The Phenomenology of Mind* (1807), tr. George Lichtheim (New York: Harper and Row, 1967), B, IV, A, pp. 228–40.

set when we write an essay, another when we fix a drain, and still another when we comfort a distressed child, or work out a family disagreement – but, crucially, they are rarely innate. Even comforting a child or resolving a dispute requires delicate judgment and self-restraint that improve with practice. And, in general, almost every successful attempt to achieve a fundamental goal relies on, and would be impossible if the agent lacked, many previously developed abilities.

The harder question is how to fit this fact into the proposed argument-schema. It will not do to say that because developed abilities increase our chances of achieving fundamental goals, developing those abilities is therefore *also* a fundamental goal. Given our definition of "fundamental" – to warrant this appellation, a goal must be near-universally and near-unavoidably pursued – this inference would fly in the face of plain facts. But what we can say, and what seems sufficient for our purposes, is that when developing an ability would greatly increase our chances of achieving fundamental goals, the goal of developing it is a direct consequence *of* our fundamental goals. Though not a goal that we *do* near-universally and near-unavoidably pursue, it is a goal that we *should* all pursue because of its relation to other goals that *are* near-universal and near-unavoidable. It is, in this sense, a *derivatively* fundamental goal.[13]

Of course, this argument only tells for the inherent value of developing abilities that will contribute to the achievement of fundamental goals. It thus falls short of establishing that developing *any and all* abilities is good in itself. Yet just because of this, the argument can meet the familiar objection that self-realization theories either lack content or else beg the crucial question of which of our innumerable abilities we should develop. To this question, our theory offers the answer "develop whichever of your abilities would contribute the most to the achievement of your fundamental goals." Moreover, which abilities these are is in principle not hard to discover. This depends partly on the general usefulness of different skills and partly on the details of each agent's (present and future) aims and projects. Also, because even strenuous efforts to develop an ability will be ineffective if one lacks native talent, it depends partly on each agent's particular constellation of strengths and weaknesses. While

---

13. Although I shall not develop the point, I think similar arguments apply to other traits that are often taken to be good in themselves – for example, health, intelligence, and such virtues as ingenuity, drive, and persistence.

each criterion raises obvious practical difficulties, each seems conceptually straightforward.

It would be pleasing if some analogous argument(s) could establish the inherent value of Parfit's final two entries. Unfortunately, becoming morally better or more aware of beauty generally does *not* make us more able to achieve our fundamental goals. In the main, persons who are evil or aesthetically insensitive do not seem less able than others to understand the world or carry out complex plans. It is true that some moral flaws preclude close personal ties; but even this connection often does not hold. By tightly compartmentalizing their lives, many quite despicable people manage quite satisfactory relationships.[14] Hence, to establish the inherent value of moral goodness or the appreciation of beauty, we will have to try another tack.

To reorient the discussion, let us now focus not on all three of the cited fundamental capacities, but only on the capacity for practical activity. Also, instead of focusing on the late stage of practical activity at which decisions are implemented and skills exercised, let us now focus on the earlier stage at which decisions are *reached*. As we saw, each agent's generic aim at this early stage is precisely to reach whatever decision is supported by the strongest reasons. Hence, to achieve his generic aim, a deliberating agent must be receptive to any and all reasons that apply. Moreover, of the applicable reasons, the very weightiest are often said to be moral. Moral considerations are often said either automatically to override all others or else to be so important as usually to have this effect.

But if moral reasons *are* always very weighty, then no deliberating agent can fully achieve his generic aim without *assigning* them great weight. Hence, simply by avoiding any decisions that morality forbids, and a fortiori by making any that morality requires, an agent will at least partly achieve his generic aim. Thus, by our familiar argument-schema, a morally good decision will (almost) always be inherently better than a morally bad one. Of course, this does not mean that all morally good decisions are *equally* valuable, since any decision's inherent value will depend on the agent's success in evaluating nonmoral as well as moral reasons. Still, even if we grant this, moral goodness will remain one important determinant of inherent value.

14. Here I have in mind not only a willingness to trample others in pursuit of financial gain (which is quite compatible with genuine regard and affection for one's family and friends), but also the parochialism that classifies people as "us" or "them," and that denies that "they" are full members of the moral community.

Here, then, is a way in which our argument-schema does seem to tell for the value of morally good acts. Yet just because the argument focuses exclusively on particular acts, it may *not* seem relevant to the value of morally good *traits of character*. This omission may seem serious because many who attach value to moral goodness are concerned precisely with moral virtue. Yet on any reasonable view, the performance of morally good acts and the possession of a virtuous character are themselves closely linked. On one account, the moral virtues are simply dispositions to behave as morality requires; on another, they are dispositions to behave in those ways *because* morality requires it; on still another, they are distinct states that give rise to one of these dispositions. Whichever account we favor, having a consistently effective disposition to act for a given moral reason is at least sufficient for having the corresponding virtue. Hence, by demonstrating the inherent value of each act that is performed for a given moral reason, we will also demonstrate the inherent value of the pattern that constitutes the corresponding virtue.[15]

A second objection may seem more troubling. In arguing that agents cannot achieve their generic deliberative aim without treating moral reasons as very weighty, I have assumed that moral reasons always *are* very weighty. However, this assumption looks a lot like my conclusion that acting morally is inherently valuable. Thus, in making the assumption, haven't I in effect begged the question?

That depends on how the assumption is itself justified. Because I am arguing for the inherent value of acting morally, it obviously *would* beg the question to base the claim that moral reasons are always very weighty on the inherent value of the acts they support. But of the important answers to the question, Why be moral? none in fact take this line. Instead, they appeal to such distinct considerations as the requirements of self-interest or the common good, the allure of the impartial perspective, or the universalizing demands of practical reason. Whichever such answer we accept, there is nothing circular about invoking the reasons for acting morally that it provides to

15. Although this argument shows why it is inherently valuable to be consistently responsive to moral reasons, it does *not* show why it is inherently valuable simply to have (say) charitable or honest impulses or dispositions. Thus, there may remain a version of the claim that moral goodness has inherent value which my argument does not justify. However, I am not sure what charitable or honest impulses or dispositions would amount to if separated from all awareness of moral reasons; and neither, therefore, am I confident that such impulses or dispositions would *be* inherently valuable. Also, even if the proposed argument does not tell the whole story, it may of course be correct as far as it goes.

show that acting morally *also* has inherent value. Of course, not everyone believes that moral reasons always *are* very weighty: many believe instead that they are only weighty when they stem from an agent's actual commitments or desires. I disagree but cannot argue the point here. Thus, I shall observe only that most who take this position would also deny that acting morally *is* inherently valuable. Because of this, their stance if anything suggests that an argument like mine may well be what establishes the inherent value of acting morally *if any argument does*.

Might a similar argument justify Parfit's final entry, the awareness of true beauty? Might aesthetic reasons, too, be so weighty that not responding to them means failing to achieve a fundamental goal? This suggestion is even more problematic than its predecessor, both because aesthetic reasons are even less well understood than moral ones[16] and because aesthetic reasons seem more likely to be grounded in (aesthetic) *values*. Still, as long as aesthetic value remains distinct from the value of responding *to* it – as long as the values that are embodied *by* artworks are not the same as the value of a life that is engaged *with* them – there is nothing circular about invoking the reasons that aesthetic value supplies to account for the further value of aesthetic awareness. Also, whatever we say about aesthetic reasons, anyone who rejects their force is unlikely to regard aesthetic awareness as inherently valuable either. Thus, here again, the proposed argument may well be what justifies the claim that aesthetic awareness is inherently valuable if any argument does.[17]

16. One problem about aesthetic reasons is that there is so little current agreement about the aims or proper content of art. Although Parfit's phrase suggests the traditional view that artists seek to create beauty, many contemporary artists describe their enterprise in quite different terms. For discussion, see David T. Schwartz, "Can Intrinsic-Value Theorists Justify Subsidies for Contemporary Art?" *Public Affairs Quarterly* 9, 4 (October 1995), pp. 331–43.

17. Indeed, by advancing an argument along these lines, we may be able to justify or explain not only the view that it is inherently good to be *aware* of beauty, but also the view that it is inherently good to *create* beauty. To do so, we need only add that aesthetic reasons themselves have a practical dimension. This claim is, of course, controversial – as Raz observes, "some people hold that some kinds of values, e.g. aesthetic ones, provide no reasons for action: that they are relevant merely to appreciation" (Joseph Raz, *The Morality of Freedom* [Oxford: Oxford University Press, 1986], p. 397) – but its denial appears to distort both contemplation and aesthetic reasons. Genuinely to contemplate an artwork, we must selectively direct our attention to the work's different elements and the relations among them. This selective directing of attention requires concentration and will and, when successful, responds to the same aesthetic reasons that manifestly were practical when they guided the artist in creating the work. These in turn are no

V

I have now tested my argument-schema against all six of Parfit's entries. Despite many unanswered questions, the schema may well justify, and failing that may well explain the appeal of, many if not all the entries on his list. In good coherentist fashion, I conclude both that the list's initial appeal enhances the argument-schema's credibility and that any independent defense of the argument-schema will lend additional support to the list's entries.

Given this conclusion, the obvious next move is to provide the promised independent defense. But before I do that, I want to examine two possible ways of extending Parfit's list. My aim here will be, first, to shed further light on the argument-schema's resources and limitations and, second, to make closer contact with the perfectionist underpinnings of some actual political proposals.

The first additional claim to be discussed is that decency and good taste are valuable in themselves. This claim was briefly advanced earlier, and it has considerable appeal. Even Joel Feinberg, who opposes all coercive attempts to raise a society's level of taste, candidly includes both "lower standards of manners and the spread of morally graceless conduct" and "general ugliness, depressing drabness, and the like" in his list of "free-floating evils" (i.e., things that are bad whether or not they cause harm or offense). Elaborating on this classification, Feinberg writes that

[i]t is possible . . . to imagine gradual changes in our standards of manners in objectively undesirable directions – changes that threaten to take the grace and civility out of our encounters with strangers. If such changes were little noted nor long regretted, people would take them in stride, and develop immunity to any harm from them. Nevertheless, the change might be regrettable.[18]

He also writes that "[n]egative judgments about the look of the south Bronx are not like expressions of dislike for brussels sprouts."[19]

I anticipated my defense of these claims in Chapter 3 when I suggested that a coarse, vulgar public culture desensitizes us to cer-

different in kind from the aesthetic reasons that guide innumerable other practical activities from planning a city to matching the colors of one's clothes. Thus, if the proposed argument shows that internal, private responses to aesthetic reasons often have inherent value, it should show the same about overt, public responses.

18. Joel Feinberg, *Harmless Wrongdoing* (Oxford: Oxford University Press, 1988), p. 42.
19. Ibid.

tain important considerations. To that suggestion I can now add, first, that the considerations to which we are desensitized are important precisely because of their connections to fundamental goals and, second, that coarseness and vulgarity desensitize us to them by impoverishing our categories of thought and analysis. For when we are barraged by images of casual sex and routine violence and when our manners are unrestrained, our streets filthy, and our language imprecise and undiscriminating, the cumulative effect is to degrade our capacity to discern, and a fortiori to respond to, many of the subtle reasons that our situations provide. As a result, our efforts to achieve our fundamental goals are systematically thwarted and our lives correspondingly worsened.

Let me be more specific about what I have in mind. When critics deplore the coarseness of our culture, their main emphasis is usually aesthetic. They say – and I agree – that an endless diet of punk rock or sitcoms leaves one ill-equipped to appreciate the music of a Mozart or the prose of a Jane Austen.[20] But as damaging as these effects are, the interpersonal effects of coarseness and vulgarity are far worse yet. The main elements of our public culture – its stories, stereotypes, taboos, concepts, vocabulary – all profoundly influence our sense of what goes on within and among people.[21] They shape our understanding of how others see both themselves and us – our understanding of the nested structures of belief, feeling, and conditional intention that each person directs at other people and *their* beliefs, feelings, and conditional intentions. Hence, if our stories, stereotypes, and the like are crude, one-sided, or distorted, then our ability

20. In saying this, I do not mean to deny that crude humor, sexual titillation, and depictions of violent action can engage us at a primal level. Still less do I wish to deny that themes of sex and violence can be treated with great subtlety and depth. However, I *do* want to say that a constant diet of unchallenging, lowest-common-denominator fare – the reader can fill in his own examples – cannot promote, and may actively reduce, one's sensitivity to nuances of plot, language, character, line, color, and composition. Such fare also seems apt to foster a preference for the comfortably sentimental over the astringent, unsettling, and ambiguous. In these and other ways, a coarse, vulgar public culture seems bound to reduce responsiveness to important aesthetic and moral reasons.

21. Compare Alasdair MacIntyre: "It is through hearing stories about wicked stepmothers, lost children, good but misguided kings, wolves that suckle twin boys, youngest sons who receive no inheritance but must make their own way in the world and eldest sons who waste their inheritance on riotous living and go into exile to live with the swine, that children learn or mislearn both what a child and what a parent is. . . . Deprive children of stories and you leave them unscripted, anxious stutterers in their actions as in their words" (MacIntyre, *After Virtue* 2d ed. [Notre Dame, Ind.: University of Notre Dame Press, 1984], p. 216).

to recognize what goes on within and among people will be crude, one-sided, or distorted, too. And this cannot but diminish our ability to attain a whole range of fundamental goals.

For, first, if we misinterpret others' intentions and expectations, we will not fully understand what they say, think, or do. This will impede our efforts both to know and to be known by them. Hence, we will fall short of achieving fundamental cognitive and interpersonal goals. Also, others' intentions and expectations give us important reasons for *acting* – reasons that often have a recognizably moral cast – so our failure to decode them can also lead us to misunderstand what we owe to specific others. For example, an exhortation to one's wife or husband to do what she or he finds difficult – refrain from smoking, or confront a troublesome colleague – may be just what is owed in a marriage defined by one set of mutual understandings, but may be an intolerable intrusion in a marriage defined by a second set, and, perhaps, may be both what is owed *and* an intolerable intrusion in a marriage defined by a third. Again, whether failing to invite a friend to dinner constitutes a snub depends partly on the prevailing conventions, but partly also on the nature of that particular friendship – a nature that is again determined precisely by the parties' mutual expectations, their beliefs about the other's expectations, and so forth. In these cases and innumerable others, our success in understanding what we have most reason to do, and hence in achieving our generic deliberative aim, requires just the kinds of discernment and imagination to which a coarse, vulgar environment is antithetical.

So far, I have tried to account only for the disvalue of coarseness and vulgarity in a public culture. But many also believe that individual indecent *acts* are disvaluable. Many hold that public nudity and self-exposure, public defecation, public sexual displays, and the like are bad for reasons quite independent of any general coarsening effects. In their view, the world is simply a better place if persons do not "make love to animals in public, or eat [their] excrement in public, or . . . masturbate in public."[22] Because it is not obvious that these acts frustrate any fundamental capacities – indeed, if anything, some seem to represent the unfettered *exercise* of certain natural capacities – my argument-schema may seem not to apply to them.

22. Vinit Haksar, *Equality, Liberty, and Perfectionism* (Oxford: Oxford University Press, 1977), p. 267.

Hence, just here, we may seem to have reached the limits of our ability to justify what many perfectionists believe.

But although we will reach those limits soon, I think we are not there yet. To show this, I now want to combine one aspect of my earlier discussion – its account of the value of close relationships – with an account of what privacy contributes to a relationship. That contribution has been perceptively analyzed by Charles Fried. The nub of Fried's analysis is that privacy secures for a person control over certain information about himself, and thus allows him to decide with whom to share the information and from whom to withhold it. Such control is important, Fried argues, because the voluntary sharing of personal information is a constitutive element of all significant close relationships:

> Love and friendship . . . involve the initial respect for the rights of others which morality requires of everyone. They further involve the voluntary and spontaneous relinquishment of something between friend and friend, lover and lover. The title to information about oneself conferred by privacy provides the necessary something. To be friends or lovers persons must be intimate to some degree with each other. Intimacy is the sharing of information about one's actions, beliefs, or emotions which one does not share with all, and which one has the right not to share with anyone.[23]

Because privacy "creates the moral capital which we spend in friendship and love," it "is the necessary context for relationships which we would hardly be human if we had to do without."[24]

But capital that can be spent wisely can also be squandered; and one clear implication of Fried's account is that indecent behavior *is* wasteful. It is wasteful because it dissipates an agent's limited stock of privileged information about himself. When someone behaves immodestly, he makes this information available to all, and so devalues both its prior and its subsequent bestowal on those about whom he cares. This renders him less able to form and sustain precisely the close relationships at which he unavoidably aims. His self-exposure is thus indecent in just the way that *all* waste is indecent. Moreover, it retains that status even when it extends only to "conventionally designated areas of privacy"[25] such as excretion; for in-

23. Charles Fried, *An Anatomy of Values* (Cambridge, Mass.: Harvard University Press, 1970), p. 142.
24. Ibid.
25. Ibid., p. 145.

formation about such functions has great "symbolic importance."[26] By behaving immodestly, a person devalues the information whose selective bestowal is a requirement of real intimacy, and so becomes less able to achieve one of his fundamental goals.[27]

The claim that taste and decency are good things is not terribly controversial. However, in defending it, I may seem to have edged into a further topic – the status of homosexuality – that is controversial indeed. One obvious connection between the preceding discussion and homosexuality is that some oppose homosexual behavior precisely on the grounds that it *is* indecent. Another is that my premise about the inherent goodness of achieving one's fundamental goals is at least superficially similar to the further claim – also often advanced against homosexuality – that it is inherently bad to act against one's *natural* goals. For both reasons, I want to end this section by asking what my account does imply about homosexuality. The answer, I shall suggest, is "very little."

Consider first the claim that homosexuality is disvaluable because it is indecent. This claim draws no support from either of my arguments for the value of decency. It draws no support from the links between a tasteful, decent public culture and receptivity to important aesthetic, moral, or cognitive reasons for the simple reason that nothing about homosexuality *diminishes* such receptivity. Neither individual homosexual acts nor a public culture in which they are tolerated or even affirmed can plausibly be said to have this effect. Indeed, given the prominence of homosexuals in literature and the arts, the reverse if anything seems true. Nor are particular homosexual acts indecent in the further sense of dissipating what ought to be privileged information; for in themselves, such acts are no less private, and no less discerning in their revelations, than heterosexual ones. It is true that one mode of homosexual activity – promiscuous and impersonal coupling – does diminish one's ability to bestow personal information selectively (as well as exposing participants to obvious health risks). However, even here, the problem is not that

26. Ibid.
27. This argument might be challenged on the grounds that its analysis of important relations is historically or geographically parochial. While I cannot evaluate the claim that there are societies in which important relationships involve no sharing of privileged information, I must confess to some skepticism: I suspect this claim derives whatever appeal it has from its resemblance to the truism that different cultures privilege different *sorts* of information. But rather than pursue this reply, I shall simply note that even if the objection goes through, my argument will still show that, and why, tasteful and decent lives remain better than others *for us now.*

the coupling is homosexual but that it is promiscuous and impersonal.

Thus, whatever else we say, we cannot assimilate homosexuality to either of the cited forms of indecency. But neither, second, can it be said to frustrate natural goals, or to be "against nature," in any sense that is relevant to my argument-schema. Unlike some who reject the "argument from nature," I do not deny that there is an important sense in which homosexuality is less natural than heterosexuality.[28] To the contrary, I would agree that it is less natural in two related senses: first, in that it plays no functional role in the perpetuation of the species and, second, in that it is (therefore) not straightforwardly explainable in terms of natural selection. I would agree, further, that there is consequently a sense in which homosexuality does frustrate a natural goal; for it does not yield the outcome – reproduction – to whose typical production in the past our sexual organs owe their current existence.

But when the frustrated goal is understood in this way, its irrelevance to my argument-schema quickly becomes apparent; for whatever else is true, this goal is clearly not one that almost all persons near-unavoidably seek. Indeed, on the most straightforward reading, the goal is not one that *persons* seek at all. Instead, it is attributable only to organs that in turn usually *belong* to persons (though on occasion they may belong to such nonpersons as anencephalic or brain-dead human beings). And because reproduction is the goal only of certain bodily organs – because it is attributable only at the biological and not at the personal level – the claim that homosexuality frustrates it is patently irrelevant to my own contention. That contention, to repeat, is only that it is inherently good that persons achieve *their* fundamental goals.[29] Nor, further, does anything change if the natural goal of reproduction is (secondarily) attributed to persons in virtue of their *possession* of sexual organs; for even then, its pursuit by persons remains far from unavoidable. Despite their physical organization and the evolutionary history of the species, most people can easily avoid trying to have children, and many have

28. One author who tries to rebut the argument on the grounds that there is no such sense is Burton Leiser in *Liberty, Justice, and Morals,* 2d ed. (New York: Macmillan, 1979), pp. 52–59.

29. Significantly, when Michael Levin advances his version of the argument from nature, he defends his contention that "it is advisable to use your organs for what they are for" by maintaining that "you will enjoy it" (Michael Levin, "Why Homosexuality Is Abnormal," *Monist* 67, 2 [April 1984], p. 259). Here Levin in effect acknowledges the need to link natural goals to the goals of persons.

no interest in reproducing at all. When someone lacks such interest, it is hard to see how his using his sexual organs to reproduce would make the world a better place or him better off.

VI

Much more obviously could be said, both about how the proposed argument-schema relates to each entry on Parfit's list and about the prospects for augmenting that list (yet) further. But instead of pursuing either topic, I now want to return to a more basic question that was raised earlier but then deferred. This is, of course, the question of why we should accept *any* inference of the form "X achieves a near-universal, near-inescapable human goal, so X is inherently valuable." Because I am concerned only with live practical and political options, I shall, as before, take this question to require not a refutation of value-nihilism or value-skepticism, but only a defense of one nonskeptical theory over others.[30]

Because the theory to be defended assigns inherent value to a variety of traits, activities, and the like, but traces the value of each to a single source, one nonskeptical alternative is an even more thoroughgoing pluralism. According to this sort of maximal pluralism, various traits, activities, and types of relationship are all valuable in themselves, but their value has no deeper source and admits of no unifying explanation. The valuable entries share no feature that *makes* each of them worth having: instead, the intrinsic value of each is simply a brute, ground-level fact.

Because brute facts are just facts that cannot be explained, a maximally pluralistic theory may seem incapable of rational defense. This charge, if it could be sustained, would tell heavily against such theories. But even if we should reject maximal pluralism – and in the end I think we should – explaining why a value-claim holds is surely not the only way to justify it. A different justificatory strategy, which can be equally effective, is to offer a convincing explanation of which that value-claim is a *premise*. This, indeed, is precisely the strategy of those who argue that their lists of intrinsic goods make the best

30. For these purposes, we need not take the nonskeptical alternatives to include any version of noncognitivism. Although some noncognitivists do take their theories to have substantive implications – Allan Gibbard, for example, writes that his expressivism "has worth . . . chiefly if it does help us with normative inquiry" (Allan Gibbard, *Wise Choices, Apt Feelings* [Cambridge, Mass.: Harvard University Press, 1990], p. 9) – those implications remain largely undeveloped.

overall sense of our specific value-judgments. And because I believe that such arguments often have real weight, I also believe that the maximally pluralistic form of perfectionism cannot be dismissed out of hand.

Still, even if it cannot, it is inevitably a fallback position. It is what we get if, on the one hand, we find it reasonable to say that various different things are valuable just in themselves, but, on the other hand, we see no plausible way of tracing these judgments to any single source. If a maximally pluralist and a unifying theory have equally plausible implications – if, for example, two theories agree about *which* things are valuable but one adds a satisfying story about *why* those things are valuable – then the unifying theory, which explains the phenomena at a deeper level, will clearly be preferable. And this is significant because I have already argued that my own unifying theory *does* imply a variety of important value-judgments. Thus, if that theory is otherwise plausible, it should be preferable to any fully pluralistic account.

VII

The harder question, of course, is whether the theory *is* independently plausible (and, if so, whether any other unifying theory is more plausible still). To prepare for our discussion of this question, let us selectively survey a number of competing unifying theories.

The available positions can be organized around two cross-cutting distinctions. First, when someone tries to trace all of the elements of a good life to a single source, he may locate that source either within or outside the subjectivity of the person whose life is involved. I shall call a theory of the first sort *subjective* and one of the second *objective.* But, second, on either account, the unifying property or relation may or may not be directed at a goal. I shall call a theory of the first sort *teleological* and one of the second *nonteleological.* By combining the two distinctions, we get four classes of theories, which I shall discuss in order.

Consider first theories that are subjective and nonteleological. In principle, there are many nonteleological features of experience that might sustain an account of value; but by far the best-known theories of this type are variants of hedonism. A hedonistic theory asserts that each thing's value depends on the amount of pleasure or enjoyment that it brings minus any attendant pain or suffering. Hedonistic theories are nonteleological because (or to the extent that) pleasure, enjoyment, and their opposites are purely qualitative; they are subjective because (or to the extent that) pleasure, enjoyment, and the rest are located entirely within experience.

Yet just because pleasure, enjoyment, and the rest do seem to be entirely experiential, hedonistic theories have implications that many find repugnant. As Robert Nozick has noted, they imply that it might be best to spend one's life hooked up to a machine that produces just the experiences that one finds most enjoyable. As Nozick also notes, this seems to ignore such crucial determinants of a life's goodness as what someone actually does, what sort of person he actually is, and the degree to which he is in contact with reality.[31] Mutatis mutandis, the same objections should apply to any other unifying theory that is both subjective and nonteleological.

Might an *objective* nonteleological theory do better? Can we isolate some nonteleological property P, such that (1) P belongs, not to our *experience* of each intrinsically valuable trait, activity, and so on, but to all and only such traits and activities themselves, and (2) P's belonging to each trait or activity provides a plausible explanation of *why* it is intrinsically valuable? Here one influential candidate is the property of *being part of a person's essential (human) nature*. According to Thomas Hurka, this property "is of sufficient depth and generality to be in itself the basis of all moral claims."[32] Building on this idea, Hurka argues that "what is good, ultimately, is the development of human nature"[33] and that "[t]he best perfectionism . . . equates human nature with the properties essential to humans and conditioned on their being living things."[34] Hurka argues, as well, that the relevant essential properties should not be understood as purposive or functional: such teleological interpretations are "just an accretion to perfectionism considered as a morality."[35]

One problem with Hurka's unifying approach, to which I shall return, is that claims about essential properties are notoriously problematic. Other things being equal, it is surely best to avoid reliance on premises this strong. Here, however, I want to make only the nar-

---

31. Robert Nozick, *Anarchy, State, and Utopia* (New York: Basic Books, 1974), pp. 42–45.
32. Thomas Hurka, *Perfectionism* (Oxford: Oxford University Press, 1993), p. 32.
33. Ibid., p. 3. As Hurka notes, many philosophers have sought to ground the human good in some aspect of human nature: his list includes Plato, Aristotle, Aquinas, Marx, Hegel, Spinoza, Leibniz, Kant, Bradley, and Nietzsche.
34. Ibid., p. 17.
35. Ibid., p. 24.

rower point that if the human essence is conceived nonteleologically, then it is unclear how any resulting theory of the good can possibly be action guiding. The problem lies in the nature of essential human properties: because these are properties that every human already has (and, indeed, would have in any world in which he existed at all), their possession by humans is not something that anyone can bring about or prevent. And, for this reason, no theory that identifies the human good with their possession seems capable of telling us anything about what anyone should *do*.

At first glance, this objection may seem to overlook the fact that essential properties can admit of degrees. A person can, for example, be either more or less theoretically or practically rational. Thus, given Hurka's view that theoretical and practical rationality are essential human traits, he may seem entitled to reply that humans can develop their nature more fully, and so improve their lives, by becoming more rational.[36] But in what sense can becoming more rational be developing one's nature more fully? If an agent is already human when he is rational only to degree D, then the property of being rational to some higher degree *cannot* be essential to being human. Instead, human nature, conceived as the full complement of essential human properties, must be as fully realized when someone is rational only to degree D as when he is rational to any greater degree. And because of this, someone who increases his rationality beyond D cannot be developing his nature in the sense of acquiring any new or more complete essential property. Instead, if he can be said to be developing his nature at all, he is doing so only in the sense of acquiring more of a property whose possession to some lower degree is part of his essence. But if we can develop our nature only in this highly attenuated sense, then it is not at all clear why a property's being essential to our nature should give us any reason to acquire any more of it than we already possess.

Because this difficulty would not arise if our essential properties were teleological – because our actions could then be directed, not at increasing the degree to which we *have* essential human goals, but rather at *achieving* those goals – I am unconvinced that the best essentialist unifying theories are nonteleological. But before we turn to theories that locate the human good in the achievement of essential

36. Although Hurka does not quite make this reasoning explicit, he clearly is committed to something like it.

human goals, let us consider an objective nonteleological theory whose unifying property is *not* essential.

Interestingly enough, the best-developed theory of this sort of which I know traces each thing's intrinsic value, not to any of its monadic properties, but rather to a certain relation among its elements. This theory, again advanced by Robert Nozick, asserts that "[v]alues are organic unities; something is intrinsically valuable in accordance with its degree of organic unity."[37] Organic unity is conceived as a function of both the complexity of the material being ordered and the tightness of the ordering imposed upon it. Thus,

[h]olding fixed the degree of unifiedness of the material, the degree of organic unity varies directly with the degree of diversity of that material being unified. Holding fixed the degree of diversity of the material, the degree of organic unity varies directly with the degree of unifiedness (induced) in that material.[38]

In Nozick's view, this theory accounts not only for aesthetic value – its original and most natural domain – but also for the value of types of organism ("people above other animals above plants above rocks"),[39] scientific theories, and many other things.[40] Indeed, Nozick resolves to "proceed on the assumption that the degree of organic unity is the basic dimension of intrinsic value, accounting for almost all differences in intrinsic value."[41]

I cannot here summarize the 170-odd dense pages that Nozick devotes to this view. Yet even without detailed discussion, we may observe that organic unity seems ill-suited to account for the goodness of a person's *life*. It seems too abstract and formal to be the basic value-element in the messy, engaged business of *living*. To overcome this objection, Nozick must show us how the value of various traits, activities, and types of relationship can plausibly be attributed to the amount of organic unity that each one displays; and part of his discussion is an attempt to do just that. He argues that a number of

37. Robert Nozick, *Philosophical Explanations* (Cambridge, Mass.: Harvard University Press, 1981), p. 446.
38. Ibid., p. 416.
39. Ibid., p. 417.
40. Because this suggestion locates a thing's value in its relational properties, it may seem incapable of showing why anything is *intrinsically* valuable. However, as long as the relevant relation is *internal* to the thing – as long as it holds exclusively among the thing's elements, and not between the thing and something else – its polyadicity will not prevent it from being a source of intrinsic value.
41. Nozick, *Philosophical Explanations*, p. 418.

valuable aspects of people's lives, including knowledge, autonomy, and value-seeking itself, all display high degrees of organic unity. Unfortunately, his criteria for assigning degrees of organic unity are never carefully spelled out. This makes it hard to assess such casual but crucial remarks as "autonomously accepting value, choosing that there be value, establishes a tighter linkage between the person and value, and so a more valuable linkage, than some non-autonomous relationship."[42] Conversely, it is hard to assess the prospects for showing that even very orderly seeming evils – for example, complexly organized totalitarian regimes and meticulous schemes for the infliction of suffering – actually rank low in organic unity.

By itself, this omission is not decisive. Despite his failure to show us *how* different goods rank high in organic unity, Nozick might still be able to show us *that* they do by making a powerful independent case that organic unity is uniquely worth seeking and having. But despite the length of his discussion, I do not think he has made such a case. He does argue that organic unity uniquely satisfies a number of desiderata for a unifying source of value – for example, "that the basic dimension of intrinsic value establishes an ordering, that V-ing [i.e., prizing, seeking, etc.] values is valuable, [and] that the existence of values and of a basic dimension of value is valuable."[43] However, many of his arguments are themselves built on the assumption that organic unity is valuable, as when he tries to explain why V-ing value is valuable by maintaining that the V-ing relation is itself highly unified. Because these arguments themselves presuppose that we have criteria for assigning degrees of organic unity, they can hardly be used to remedy the absence of such criteria.

Nor, more importantly, does Nozick convincingly explain why organic unity would be uniquely worth seeking and having if it *did* uniquely satisfy his conditions. As he himself acknowledges, it remains hard to see how even facts that satisfy the cited conditions – facts about organic unity or anything else – could possibly add up to *values*. Why, as Nozick strikingly asks, doesn't even a universe that contains these facts remain merely *dark*? But when Nozick tries to answer this question, he invokes a mysterious existential choice that somehow transmutes facts about organic unity *into* values.[44] Just how the choice is supposed to work the transformation is not made

42. Ibid., p. 565.
43. Ibid., p. 436.
44. Ibid., pp. 552–70.

clear. Also left unclear is why, if choices can transform facts about organic unity, they cannot similarly affect facts of other sorts.[45]

By allowing the value of organic unity to depend on choice, Nozick introduces a teleological element that threatens to swallow up the rest of his theory. Yet even if this move is dialectically unwise, the impulse behind it may well be sound. As long as we consider only nonteleological properties, we will have great difficulty explaining how any of them can give rise to value. At least to this extent, the fact–value gap remains a serious problem even for coherentists. But things may improve when we turn to teleological properties; for because the pursuit of any goal implies a norm of success – because anyone who achieves a goal must ipso facto satisfy the norm that it supplies – there is a recognizable sense in which teleological properties already straddle the fact–value gap. Perhaps for this reason, many prominent unifying theories of value have in fact been teleological.

VIII

Like their nonteleological counterparts, teleological theories can be either subjective or objective. When they are subjective, they trace all value to goals embedded in (actual or hypothetical) desires or choices;[46] when objective, they trace it to goals of other sorts. Because we have already devoted a good deal of attention to subjective teleological theories, we need not linger over them here. As we saw, such theories do offer an explanation of how some traits, activities, and types of relationship can be more valuable than others: namely, they may be more conducive to the satisfaction or implementation of the relevant desires or choices. However, as we also saw, subjective teleological theories shed far less light on *which* traits, activities, and the like are more and less valuable. To draw any specific conclusions, we would need far more information about what in fact satisfies actual

45. Nozick also acknowledges, but fares no better in answering, the closely related question of why value is (even potentially) *attractive* to us. He observes that value has an "allure" that *calls* for an explanation, but he stops (just) short of trying to show how identifying value with organic unity *provides* the explanation (ibid., pp. 436–41).
46. Although desires do not always issue in action, their classification as teleological states seems warranted by their strong tendency in this direction. As G. E. M. Anscombe has put the point, "[t]he primitive sign of wanting is *trying to get*" (*Intention* [Oxford: Basil Blackwell, 1957], p. 67; emphasis in original).

or informed desires and choices than we now have or can reasonably expect to acquire. Thus, no such theory can convincingly account for our considered judgments that knowledge, excellence, virtue, and the rest are elements of good lives. Also, because deliberation seeks to establish what is *worth* desiring and what we *should* choose, any theory that grounds all value in what individuals *do or would* desire or choose will distort if not invert its structure. These considerations, I argued, suggest that an individual's desires and choices are not the fundamental determinants of how well he lives.

Might that depend, finally, on the achievement of more objective goals? Might the goodness of our lives depend on how well they fulfill goals that are embedded, not in the attitudes or choices of specific individuals, but – somehow – in reality itself? To explore the variants of this final alternative, let us briefly consider attempts to extract objective goals from three possible sources: our essential nature, evolution, and homeostatic systems.

OUR ESSENTIAL NATURE

The first suggestion, that our essential nature provides us with objective goals, was of course Aristotle's view. On his account, each entity has a built-in end, or *telos,* that specifies the functions that are essential to entities of its type. For humans, these essential functions involve certain activities and the corresponding virtues. We flourish when we engage in the relevant activities and when we display the relevant virtues. Commentators may disagree about the exact content of these activities and virtues, and in particular about whether they are predominantly practical or theoretical, but such questions need not concern us here. For present purposes, what matters is only the view that *some* goals are essential to our nature.

For despite Aristotle's vast influence, it has never really been made clear why we should accept this view. Why regard *any* goal or mode of functioning as essential, either to any particular person or to the whole human species? When Aristotle advanced his essentialist conception of human nature, it was part of a much larger world-picture that was teleological throughout. But it is hard to see how that picture can itself be defended, and few today accept it. Even Alasdair MacIntyre, the most influential contemporary defender of a return to Aristotelian ethics, has conceded that "any adequate generally Aristotelian account must supply a teleological account which can replace Aristotle's metaphysical biology."[47] Yet when claims about essential goals are advanced *without* metaphysical backing, their content and justification become obscure. To make them at all plausible, we seem forced to reinterpret them as, for example, reports of linguistic usage, conjectures about what persons typically want or enjoy, or disguised assertions about how it is best to live.[48] But as soon as we do any of this, their inadequacy as unifying bases of value becomes transparent.

EVOLUTION

A second possible source of objective goals is the process of evolution.[49] Natural selection, which favors traits conducive to survival and reproduction, can be viewed as a teleological process whose "goal" is the perpetuation or improvement of either the whole species or certain genetic subpopulations. These goals are objective in the required sense: they are clearly independent of any individual's desires or choices. Yet just *because* they are so remote from particular individuals, the goals seem ill-suited to determine how well individuals live. Even the flourishing of a nonhuman organism appears to depend more on its own traits or activities than on its number of offspring or its success in perpetuating its genes. A fortiori, whatever the *human* good involves, its determinants, too, must be traits or activities *of the person himself.*[50]

By itself, this objection may not be fatal. To meet it, someone might agree that how well an individual lives depends on his own traits

47. MacIntyre, *After Virtue*, p. 163.
48. One recent attribution of essential traits that is pretty clearly value-based is Martha Nussbaum's suggestion that we would become "less than fully human" if we lost our sense of play or our respect for nature; see Martha Nussbaum, "Aristotelian Social Democracy," in R. Bruce Douglass, Gerald M. Mara, and Henry S. Richardson, eds., *Liberalism and the Good* (New York: Routledge, 1990), pp. 203–52.
49. One locus classicus of "evolutionary ethics" is the work of Herbert Spencer; but his theory of value also has an important hedonistic component. He writes, for example, that "taking into account immediate and remote effects on all persons, the good is universally the pleasurable" (Herbert Spencer, *The Principles of Ethics*, vol. 1 [Indianapolis: Liberty Classics, 1978], p. 66). More recently, some sociobiologists and philosophers influenced by them have raised the possibility of grounding ethics in evolution: see, for example, E. O. Wilson's *On Human Nature* (Cambridge, Mass.: Harvard University Press, 1978), and Michael Ruse, "The Morality of the Gene," *Monist* 67, 2 (April 1984), pp. 167–99.
50. Thomas Hurka makes a similar point against the view that the properties that figure in evolutionary explanations are part of our essence; see Hurka, *Perfectionism*, p. 49.

and activities, but might then add that what *makes* a given trait or activity valuable is precisely *its* contribution to evolutionary goals. In support of this claim, one might adduce the contention, advanced by E. O. Wilson and others, that altruism and related virtues have survival value.[51] Still, whatever we say about altruism, the goals associated with evolution – survival, reproduction, biological fitness – seem far too crude and undifferentiated to account for much else of what seems good. To cite just two examples, these goals provide no obvious reason to value either rational activity or aesthetic awareness as highly or unconditionally as we do.

HOMEOSTATIC SYSTEMS

One other sort of objective goal warrants brief mention. In an important discussion of moral realism, Richard Boyd has suggested that

There are a number of important human goods, things which satisfy important human needs. Some of these needs are physical or medical. Others are psychological or social. . . . Under a wide variety of (actual and possible) circumstances these human goods (or rather instances of the satisfaction of them) are homeostatically clustered. . . . Moral goodness is defined by this cluster of goods and the homeostatic mechanisms which unify them. Actions, policies, character traits, etc. are morally good to the extent to which they tend to foster the realization of these goods or to develop and sustain the homeostatic mechanisms upon which their unity depends.[52]

Boyd's homeostatic clusters are in effect teleological systems. They are ordered collections of elements that tend to persist, or to reestablish themselves, in certain states under certain ranges of disturbing conditions.[53] For this reason, they can be said to seek the goal of perpetuating themselves *in* the relevant states. This goal, no less than the goals supplied by evolution or Aristotle's natural teleology, is objective in the sense of being independent of any individual's desires or choices. Moreover, unlike Aristotle's essential goals but like the goals supplied by evolution, it can be attributed without

---

51. See Wilson, *On Human Nature*, ch. 7.
52. Richard Boyd, "How to Be a Moral Realist," in Geoffrey Sayre-McCord, ed., *Essays in Moral Realism* (Ithaca: Cornell University Press, 1988) p. 203.
53. For two important discussions of this notion, see R. B. Braithwaite, *Scientific Explanation* (New York: Harper and Brothers, 1953), ch. 10, and Ernest Nagel, *The Structure of Scientific Explanation* (New York: Harcourt Brace and World, 1961), ch. 12.

metaphysical excess. Conversely, unlike the goals supplied by evolution but like Aristotle's essential goals, it may be complex enough to account for many actual value-beliefs.

Yet if Boyd's homeostatic clusters are to supply the goals in whose achievement value consists, the reason cannot be *merely* that these goals are objective, empirically discoverable, and complex; for many similar goals share all three traits. Many other teleological systems, from thermostats to guided missiles, are directed at goals that are equally objective, equally empirically discoverable, and equally complex; yet their achievement has no particular moral standing. A nuclear-tipped missile's ability to correct course in midflight does not confer value on its arrival on target, and the self-perpetuating nature of a neurotic dependency or an oppressive social system can actually make it worse.[54] Thus, before we can accept any theory of the proposed sort, we must understand how Boyd's homeostatic clusters differ morally from other teleological systems.

Although Boyd does not explicitly address this question, an answer is implicit in his discussion. The difference seems to be that unlike other teleological systems, his homeostatic clusters are composed of elements that are themselves valuable. This answer is suggested both by Boyd's language – as we saw, he refers to what satisfies a need as a good – and by the content of his list of needs. These include "the need for love and friendship, the need to engage in cooperative efforts, the need to exercise control over one's own life, the need for intellectual and artistic appreciation and expression, the need for physical recreation, etc."[55] This list is pretty clearly shaped by Boyd's independent moral commitments.

There is, of course, nothing wrong with this. Given Boyd's holistic view of justification – a view I also endorse – he is fully entitled to call on his background moral theory to isolate the needs whose satisfactions count as goods. He is also entitled to attach additional value to the stable clustering of those goods, and to invoke the value of both the goods and their stable clustering to modify his original background theory. But what does seem doubtful – yet what is required if Boyd's homeostatic clusters are to sustain a unified account of value – is that the goals supplied by these clusters can explain why the clustered elements are goods in the first place. If we cannot even

54. Arthur Kuflik makes this point in his essay "Critique of Moral Realism" (in progress).
55. Boyd, "How to Be a Moral Realist," p. 203.

228

identify a homeostatic cluster as a system whose goal is value-conferring without first assuming that the cluster's elements are themselves valuable, then we can hardly go on to explain why those elements *are* valuable by citing the goal of that very cluster. Hence, if we interpret Boyd's theory as providing a unifying account of value – an interpretation that he himself might well reject – it is no more satisfying than its predecessors.

IX

This completes my review of the different types of unifying theories of the good. Bearing them in mind, let me now return to my own proposal: that what unifies the diverse elements of a good life is their connection(s) to near-universal, near-unavoidable goals. Given its reference to goals, this proposal is obviously teleological; given its insistence that the goals be near-universal, it is also objective. Hence, to make the case for it, I must show, first, that we should accept some sort of teleological theory and, second, that this one is preferable to its (subjective and objective) competitors.

One main reason to favor some kind of teleological theory is that only such a theory can imply that there are both experiential and nonexperiential goods. As I have repeatedly stressed, the elements of a good life include knowledge, rational action, close relationships, and various other forms of contact with the world. This means that whether someone lives a good life cannot depend exclusively on the quality of his experience. But neither is the quality of his experience irrelevant. We can hardly deny that happiness, pleasure, and enjoyment are among life's goods, so any satisfactory unifying theory must appeal to a property or relation that is capable of belonging to experiential as well as nonexperiential states. However, of the available nonteleological theories, each appeals to a property or relation that seems capable of belonging only to one of these types of state.

Thus, consider first *subjective* nonteleological theories. As we saw, the most famous theory of this type is hedonism, which traces each thing's value to the degree to which it is pleasant or enjoyable. While hedonism explains why pleasant and enjoyable experiences are valuable in themselves, it cannot similarly explain how any *non*experiential occurrences could have that status. It cannot explain this because being pleasant and enjoyable are properties only *of* experience. We do, of course, also call meals, conversations, and football games

pleasant; but when we do, we mean only that they do, or will, produce pleasant experiences in us or others. Because any other subjective and nonteleological theory would be vulnerable to the same
objection, any such theory will imply that nothing *except* certain
kinds of experience is good in itself.

By contrast, objective nonteleological theories face a converse
difficulty: according to them, it is *pleasant experience* whose value is
hard to explain. As we saw, some such theories, such as Hurka's,
equate the human good with the (full) realization of essential human
properties. However, these essential properties cannot plausibly be
taken, and standardly are *not* taken, to include the property of expe-
riencing pleasure. This could hardly be part of the human essence
because many individuals who are unquestionably human experience little pleasure and some especially unfortunate humans may
experience none. Thus, as Hurka acknowledges, a pure version of his
theory must claim that "satisfaction has no value."[56]

And so, albeit for different reasons, must a theory like Nozick's.
Because Nozick holds that each thing's intrinsic value depends on its
degree of organic unity, and because artworks, organisms, and actions can all be assessed along this dimension, Nozick has no trouble
explaining how things of these sorts can be intrinsically valuable.
However, he is far less well positioned to explain how *pleasant experiences* can be intrinsically valuable. He is of course aware that "some
have held that feelings of satisfaction, pleasure, and contentment are
intrinsically valuable, even when these are unstructured, not 'intentional' or directed at an object";[57] but he is also aware that to account
for the value of these feelings, he would have to show that they, too,
display high degrees of organic unity. And, in fact, Nozick *cannot*
show this. He cannot show that pleasure or contentment elegantly
unites diverse elements for the simple reason that pleasure and contentment do not *consist of* diverse elements. Being purely qualitative,
they are homogeneous throughout. And because of this, Nozick
rightly concedes that "[t]he view of value as degree of organic unity
. . . will not explain what is valuable about [these feelings]."[58]

Of course, even if no current nonteleological theory can attribute

56. Hurka, *Perfectionism*, p. 27.
57. Nozick, *Philosophical Explanations*, p. 418.
58. Ibid.

intrinsic value to both experiences and nonexperiential occurrences, some future theory still may. But because experiences and nonexperiential occurrences are so different – because nonexperiential occurrences are located in space as well as time and are in principle intersubjectively accessible, whereas experience is (arguably) nonspatial and, in its qualitative aspect, is accessible only to those who have it – the stock of suitably ecumenical properties may well be small.[59] Moreover, even if that stock is large, the record to date does not inspire confidence.

By contrast, the *teleological* unifying approach raises no such difficulties; for desires, choices, and the rest can unproblematically be directed at either experiential *or* nonexperiential states. The features that give them this flexibility will be examined later; but, for now, the crucial fact is simply that they all have it. Because they do, they all can avoid the current difficulty. To cite just two examples, a desire theorist can account for the value of both experiential and nonexperiential states by pointing out that most people want and seek them both; while I can do the same by augmenting my earlier account of the value of knowledge, close relationships, and the rest with the observation that no one can altogether suppress his impulses to pursue pleasant sensations and escape unpleasant ones. And, indeed, because this last suggestion is independently plausible, the theory I am proposing promises not only to capture what is true about hedonism but also to explain *why* it is true.

Even by themselves, these considerations would strongly support the teleological approach. But that approach also draws support from a further argument – an argument that exploits certain striking parallels between the structural features of teleological states and the implications of value-claims.

One relevant structural feature of teleological states is their intentionality. Just as anyone who holds a belief or makes an assertion must believe or assert something, anyone who has a desire or makes a choice must want or choose something.[60] No less than beliefs,

---

59. Berkeley, for one, seems to have thought that *no* properties are this ecumenical: one of his famous arguments rests on the dictum "an idea can be like nothing but an idea" (George Berkeley, *Essay, Principles, Dialogues* [New York: Scribner's, 1929], p. 128).

60. It is not entirely clear whether nonteleological and teleological intentional states always take the *same* sorts of intentional objects. Beliefs, clearly, always take propositional objects – we believe *that* it is raining, or *that* the cat is on the mat – but the objects of desire are less clear. On the one hand, we speak as naturally of wanting a banana as we do of wanting to have or eat one; but, on the other hand,

utterances, and conjectures, desires, choices, and other teleological states are always directed at intentional objects. Moreover, in each case, the state's intentional object – the thing that *is* believed, asserted, wanted, or chosen – need not actually exist. Beliefs can be false, and desires unsatisfied, without thereby ceasing to *be* beliefs or desires. Thus, when a state takes an intentional object, its object is only a kind of further state whose instances *would* be especially appropriate to it if any of them *were* to exist.

This is important because attributions of value have very similar implications. Like the claim that something is wanted or believed, the claim that something is valuable does not imply that it actually exists. Indeed, when a thing's value provides a reason to bring it *into* existence – and value often does just that – then what is valuable *cannot* already exist. Hence, also like claims about intentional states, claims about value must be understood as singling out types of occurrences whose instances would have some special status, or would in some way be especially appropriate, if they *did* exist. Of course, unlike claims about intentional states, claims about value do not make it clear *to what* the valuable things would be especially appropriate if they existed. Yet just because the second term of this relation is so unclear, its identity is itself something that an adequate theory of value must explain.

And given what has been said, a plausible explanation is close at hand. To provide it, we need only identify the factual bases of value – the factual states that *give* valuable things their special status – with (some of) the intentional states that we already know to confer special status on other states. Because intentional states are firmly anchored in the natural world, yet can reach beyond it to single out other states that are merely possible, they are the obvious – we might almost say the only – factual candidates for the role of sources of value.[61] Moreover, by endorsing their candidacy, we can draw on our understanding of them to fill in what is mysterious about the special status of what is valuable. In particular, to the question, To what would a valuable thing be especially appropriate if it were to

wanting a banana may always *reduce* to wanting to own, eat, or do something else with one.

61. There has, of course, been much controversy about how naturalists can best account for intentional content; but the very urgency of the controversy (and the unattractiveness of the eliminative alternatives) suggests that they must accommodate it somehow.

exist? we can answer: To whatever intentional state is the basis of its value.

This move is clearly an important step forward. However, by itself, it does not tell us whether to equate the factual bases of value with *teleological or nonteleological* intentional states. Hence, it gives us no more reason to ground value in (e.g.) desires or choices than in (e.g.) beliefs or conjectures. Thus, if the former intentional states are the better candidates – as, intuitively, they surely are – the reason must lie elsewhere.

It lies, I suggest, in a difference in the direction of the adjustments that are called for when the objects of the two classes of intentional states do not exist. For when the object of a *non*teleological intentional state does not exist – when, for example, a belief is false – what is assumed to be defective, and hence to require revision, is not those parts of the world that fail to conform to the intentional state. Instead, because a belief seeks accurately to represent some portion of reality that is assumed to be held fixed, what the discrepancy calls for is just a revision of the belief itself. Here the world is the independent variable and the intentional state the dependent one. But just the reverse is true of teleological intentional states such as desires and choices. Instead of treating the world as fixed, these states treat the nonexistence of their intentional objects as defects or failings *in* the world. When a desire is unfulfilled or a choice unrealized, what the desire or choice calls for is not its own alteration to conform to the world, but rather the world's alteration to conform to it.[62]

And with this observation, the argument's last step falls into place. Its central premise is simply that in this final respect, the implications of value-claims match the demands of teleological intentional states but not of nonteleological ones. That is, when we attribute value to something that does not exist, we do not imply that the world's failure to contain a thing of the valuable type requires that any person revise any of his attitudes (except, of course, if what would be valuable would just be his *having* a certain attitude). Instead, we imply that the world's failure to contain a thing of the valuable type requires that *it* be altered to bring a thing of that type *into* existence. Like unsatisfied desires but unlike false beliefs, attributions of value to nonexistent states call for adjustments of the world rather than of

62. For an important early discussion of this difference in "direction of fit," see Anscombe, *Intention;* for a very recent treatment, see Michael Smith, *The Moral Problem* (Oxford: Basil Blackwell, 1994), ch. 4.

persons. And because they do, the only intentional states that could possibly qualify as their factual grounds are ones that make similar demands – that is, *teleological* intentional states. Thus, just as we previously saw that intentional states are better suited to be the factual bases of value than nonintentional ones, we can now see that teleological intentional states are better suited to this role than non-teleological ones.

X

But to *which* teleological states should we assign that role? My own theory, which favors near-universal, near-unavoidable goals, is plainly a compromise; for though objective, it is less robustly so than its essentialist or evolutionary competitors. Thus, to defend it, I must show that it is preferable both to less and to even more objective accounts.

Let me begin by specifying certain requirements that any adequate teleological theory must satisfy. There are, I think, at least two requirements, each traceable to a different aspect of the question, What makes a person's life good? First, because the question concerns the goodness of *a person's life,* any relevant goal must stand in some appropriate relation *to the person himself.* If person and goal are not appropriately related, then the goal's achievement will have no bearing on how well the person lives. To capture the thought that any relevant goal must belong *to* a person in some suitably deep sense, I shall call this *the depth requirement.*

But, second, because the question concerns the *goodness* of a person's life, any relevant goal must also stand at enough distance from him to afford a critical perspective on his life. To provide a standard of assessment, a goal must be distinct from whatever is being assessed – including, significantly, the goal seeker's own actual desires and choices. To capture this second requirement, I shall refer to it as *the distance requirement.*

Although neither requirement has been carefully formulated, each can be seen to underlie a common objection to the simpler desire and choice theories. One such objection is that many of a person's desires and choices – for example, his whims, impulses, and spur-of-the-moment decisions – are too superficial to have much bearing on how well he lives. This objection plainly appeals to the depth requirement. Also, many would agree with Michael Sandel that "if my conception of the good is simply the product of my immediate wants and desires, there is no reason to suppose that the critical standpoint it provides is any more worthy or valid than the desires it seeks to assess."[63] This objection clearly depends on what I have called the distance requirement.

It is less clear that both requirements tell against the more sophisticated desire and choice theories. Indeed, some such theories can be understood precisely as attempts to accommodate one or another of the requirements. Thus, when subjectivists trace the goodness of a person's life to the degree to which it satisfies his *informed* desires or choices, part of their reasoning may be that because informed desires and choices are merely hypothetical, they are far enough removed from actuality to provide the needed critical distance. And, again, when subjectivists focus on goals that agents have internalized, goals with which agents strongly identify, or goals through which agents define themselves, they can be seen as trying to isolate the subset of each agent's goals that are most deeply his own. In this way, they may be trying to accommodate the depth requirement.

It is, however, unlikely that either maneuver can succeed; for precisely by moving closer to satisfying one requirement, a subjectivist will also move further away from satisfying the other. Thus, what enables informed desires and choices to satisfy the distance requirement is that they are merely hypothetical rather than actual. But merely hypothetical goals do not belong to agents at all and so, a fortiori, cannot belong to them in a deep enough sense to affect the goodness of their lives.[64] Hence, the very feature that enables informed desires and choices to satisfy the distance requirement also prevents them from satisfying the depth requirement. Conversely, when an agent internalizes or fully identifies with a goal, the very intimacy of the connection that enables it to satisfy the depth requirement also lends special urgency to the question of whether the goal

63. Michael J. Sandel, *Liberalism and the Limits of Justice* (Cambridge: Cambridge University Press, 1982), p. 165.
64. This helps to explain why certain consequences of informed-desire theories seem so counterintuitive. Suppose, for example, that someone would have loved the opera, and would have wanted to attend as many performances as possible, had he been given suitable musical training; but suppose, further, that he was not given the training and so now finds opera excruciating. If we take seriously the idea that the good life for a person is just the life he would have wanted if fully informed, we will have to say that it is best that he sit through endless hours of opera. Our reluctance to say this attests to our reluctance to believe that any merely hypothetical desire can be deeply an agent's own.

was worth internalizing, or, having been internalized, is worth retaining. Because no theory that treats internalized goals as supplying the standard of goodness can answer such questions, the same feature that allows these theories to satisfy the depth requirement also prevents them from satisfying the distance requirement.

This of course is not the end of the story. To arrive at a more defensible view, a subjectivist might opt for a hybrid theory that combines the full-information and internalized-goal approaches. Alternatively, he might try some other tack, such as exploiting the distinction between higher- and lower-order desires or choices. But these maneuvers, too, are problematic, and the overall outlook does not seem bright.[65] Thus, all things considered, the most promising strategy is simply to move beyond subjectivism.

To do that, we must look to goals that are independent both of all actual desires and choices *and* of all hypothetical ones. Of course, if the only remaining goals are ones that do not belong to agents at all, then any resulting theory will again violate the depth requirement. But even if a goal is independent of an agent's *desires and choices*, it need not similarly be independent of *the agent himself.* Instead of not belonging to him at all, it may belong to him so deeply that it lies beneath, or is presupposed by, all of his specific desires and choices. Such goals, if they exist, will simultaneously satisfy both the distance *and* the depth requirement.

In what follows, I shall argue that near-universal and near-unavoidable goals are of just this sort – that they provide just the right combination of distance and depth. But before I make my argument, I want to mention, in order to dismiss, a less adequate way of arriving at the same conclusion. At first glance, it may seem that a

---

65. A theory that combined the full-information and internalized-goal approaches would say that in order to determine what would make a person's life good, a goal must be both actually internalized by him *and* capable of surviving informed scrutiny. The trouble, though, is that there is no guarantee that any goals *will* pass both tests. If someone has taken a wrong path in life, none of the goals he has internalized may be capable of surviving informed scrutiny. If so, the proposed hybrid theory will offer us the options of (1) favoring the agent's actual internalized goals over his hypothetical informed ones; (2) favoring his hypothetical informed goals over his actual internalized ones; or (3) conceding that for such an agent, there is simply no answer to the question "What sort of life would be best?" Of these options, none seems palatable. Nor is it promising to identify the determinants of a good life with a person's second-order desires and choices – with his desires to desire or choices to choose. The obvious problem here is that because these desires and choices, too, must remain open to evaluation, this strategy would only reraise all the problems associated with the distance requirement.

goal can satisfy the depth requirement simply in virtue of its near-unavoidability and the distance requirement simply in virtue of its near-universality. It may seem, in other words, that near-universal and near-unavoidable goals satisfy both requirements because (1) any goal that an agent cannot avoid pursuing is ipso facto his in a suitably deep sense, and (2) any goal that an agent shares with virtually all others is ipso facto distant enough from him to license evaluations of his purely personal goals.

However, on closer inspection, neither suggestion can be sustained. If we accepted (1) and held that every goal that an agent cannot avoid pursuing belongs to him in a suitably deep sense, then we would have to agree that even the most pathological of compulsions – even irresistible urges to steal locks of people's hair, eat grass, or sodomize young children – all satisfy the depth requirement. This is highly implausible. And if we accepted (2) and held that a goal stands at a suitable distance from a given agent whenever enough other people also pursue it, then we could never criticize any goals that were sought by large enough groups of people. However, even if virtually everyone were to seek (e.g.) salvation or wealth, we surely could still ask whether those goals are really worth seeking. Of course, at present, no single culture is dominant everywhere so no goal supplied by any culture is truly universal; but the need for critical assessment would hardly disappear if some single culture did achieve complete dominance.

Given these difficulties, any attempt to show that all near-universal, near-inescapable goals satisfy the distance and depth requirements must take a different form. Instead of linking the satisfaction of each requirement to one of the goals' features, we must somehow show that both features contribute to the satisfaction of each requirement. However, at least initially, the prospects for showing this do not seem bright.

For consider, first, the claim that all near-universal, near-inescapable goals satisfy the depth requirement. As we just saw, some goals that are merely near-unavoidable (e.g., pathological ones) do *not* appear to satisfy the depth requirement. Thus, on the current proposal, the failure of these goals to belong deeply enough to their possessors must somehow be attributable to the fact that they are not widely shared. But how, exactly, could this be so? How could the depth of a goal's relation to any one person possibly depend on the number of others who also cannot avoid pursuing it?

I think this question can be answered, and that its answer reveals something important about the interplay between near-universality and near-unavoidability. The key fact is that if virtually no one can avoid pursuing a certain goal, then any given agent's inability to avoid pursuing it is *not a fluke.* This is not a fluke in that it is not an artifact of that agent's particular traits, genetic makeup, or personal history. It cannot depend on any of these features, or on any other feature that might easily have been different, because persons with so many other traits, genes, and histories are equally unable to avoid pursuing the goal. Thus, whatever the person happens to be like, he still would have been unable to avoid pursuing the goal if he had been different in a wide variety of ways. And this does provide a plausible explanation of how such a goal can belong more deeply to its possessor(s) than any mere idiosyncratic compulsion; for when a near-unavoidable goal is also near-universal, it belongs deeply to each agent not only in the sense that he is (virtually) unable to avoid pursuing it, but also in the sense that his inability to avoid pursuing it is *itself* (virtually) unavoidable.[66]

Thus, the combination of near-universality and near-unavoidability does enable a goal to satisfy the depth requirement. But what, next, of the *distance* requirement? As we saw, the mere fact that all the members of a society, or every society, happen to pursue a goal does not eliminate the question of whether that goal is worth pursuing. Hence, near-universality alone does not satisfy the distance requirement. So, on the current proposal, what places a near-universal goal beyond evaluation is just the additional fact that its pursuit is also near-unavoidable. But how, again, can this make the difference?

The answer, pretty clearly, is that when a near-universal goal also *is* near-unavoidable – when it is a goal that virtually no one can *avoid* pursuing – then questions about whether any or all of those persons ought to pursue it, or whether it is worthy of their pursuit, *simply do not arise.* Unlike a goal that is supplied by a pervasive culture, and so is just as open to criticism as that culture itself, a goal that is both near-universal *and* near-inescapable is a fixed feature of our lives.

66. Because agents *are* unable to avoid pursuing these goals under so many possible conditions, even the rare persons who *can* avoid pursuing them must remain close to being unable to do so. They remain close to this in the sense that they *would have* been unable to avoid pursuing the goals under almost all alternative conditions (under which they could live at all). And this is important because it gives content to the idea that even someone who can avoid pursuing one of these goals may live a better life if his activities in fact conform to it.

Because something about our constitution makes our pursuit of it inevitable, there is simply no point in asking whether it is worthy of pursuit or whether we ought to continue pursuing it. Thus, such a goal is indeed a suitable touchstone for the evaluation of all other goals, including all other near-universal ones, whose pursuit is not similarly fixed.

All in all, a goal that is both near-universal and near-inescapable does seem to satisfy both the distance and the depth requirements. Moreover, in each case, the goal's two components – its near-universality and its near-inescapability – work in tandem to secure this result. Thus, we may reasonably conclude that the proposed theory represents the smallest philosophically acceptable departure from subjectivism.

XI

However, it is one thing to argue that the theory lies closer to subjectivism than any other acceptable alternative, and quite another to argue that it is the *best* alternative. To take this last step, we must compare the theory to its even more stringently objective competitors, the evolutionary and Aristotelian approaches.

Its advantage over evolutionary theories is easily stated: they violate the depth requirement as it does not. As we saw, natural selection can be viewed as a teleological process whose goals are the survival and reproduction of the species. However, as we also saw, it does not follow that these goals are pursued by all (or even any) *members* of any species. Because the sexual urge is quite different from the desire to reproduce, and because natural selection works through genetic mutations over which individuals have no control (and of which they are almost never aware), the goals of evolution cannot be attributed to individuals in any straightforward sense. If they are the goals of any entities at all, the far more natural candidates are the species or the "selfish gene." Hence, unlike goals that almost all persons unavoidably seek, these evolutionary goals are far too tenuously connected to individuals to be plausible determinants of how well they live.

The more interesting comparison is between my own proposal and a teleological essentialism; for that view, too, satisfies both the distance and the depth requirements. If even near-universal, near-inescapable goals can belong deeply enough to agents to determine how well they live, and hence can satisfy the depth requirement, then so a fortiori can any essential goals. Indeed, an essential goal, without which someone would not be the individual (or kind of individual) he is, would belong to him in the deepest possible sense. And, similarly, if even near-universal and near-inescapable goals are far enough removed from all specific desires and choices to satisfy the distance requirement, then so too, again a fortiori, would be any essential goals. Indeed, a person's essential goals would stand at a still greater distance from any of his specific desires and choices for two distinct reasons: first, because they would be intersubjective in an even stronger sense – they would, after all, belong to all *possible* humans – and, second, because their pursuit would (therefore) be even less susceptible to manipulation or open to choice.

These remarks shed new light on my own theory, for they bring out its striking resemblance to essentialism itself. Indeed, my theory is perhaps best viewed as an empirical substitute for a teleological essentialism – a kind of poor man's Aristotelianism. Because the substitute comes at a far lower metaphysical cost, there is a strong presumption in its favor. Still, before we can accept it, we must ask whether there is any countervailing reason to insist that the relevant goals be necessary.

If so, the reason is apt to be that only essential goals are sufficiently beyond our control; for as long as any goal's pursuit is merely contingent, there must be some genetic or environmental factors *upon which* it is contingent. If we knew what these features were, we theoretically could alter the goal by manipulating them. This gives at least theoretical sense to the question, Would our lives be better or worse if the goal were altered? Yet if a given goal's achievement is just what *determines* whether our lives are better or worse – or if it is a central enough component of what determines this – then the question of whether our lives would be better or worse if the goal itself were altered will have no determinate answer. Thus, in the end, it may seem that only essential goals can completely satisfy the distance requirement.

This, however, is not an argument that teleological essentialists can comfortably press; for despite their claim that the pursuit of certain goals is necessarily bound up with being human, they do *not* hold that human existence is *itself* necessary. Their essentialism does not rule out the possibility of a nuclear holocaust or the earth's collision with a stray comet. For that matter, it does not even imply that we must always pursue the goals that currently make us human. Instead, it implies only that if we ceased to pursue those goals, we would also cease to *be* human. And, hence, even teleological essentialism leaves room for the question, Would altering the goals that make us human make our lives better or worse? Of course, in asking this question, we cannot be asking whether the alteration of these goals would make the lives *of humans* better or worse; for by hypothesis, ceasing to pursue the goals would mean ceasing to be human. However, we can still be asking two closely related questions: namely (1) Is it better that there be humans or biologically similar organisms who lack the goals that humans necessarily pursue? and (2) If such biologically similar beings existed instead of humans, would their lives be better or worse?

The cogency of these questions undermines the effort to make a case for teleological essentialism by invoking the distance requirement; for it suggests that if near-universal and near-inescapable goals do not provide enough critical distance to satisfy that requirement, then neither do essential goals. Of course, merely to generalize the objection is hardly to rebut it; but once we realize that its implications are this far-reaching, we may suspect that something has gone awry.

And so, indeed, something has; for the objection rests on an inappropriately strong reading of the distance requirement. In fact, when we say that a value-conferring goal must stand at a suitable distance from every aspect of a person's life that is open to evaluation, we need not take the evaluable aspects of a person's life to include every goal whose alteration is even theoretically possible. There are some goals – the clearest examples are those whose alteration would require the extinction of all life – that are inseparable components of any world in which we could conceivably take an interest. Even if their alteration *is* theoretically possible, it cannot be a live option for us. However, if not, then a theory's inability to evaluate it will surely not violate the distance requirement.

The interesting question is whether there are also goals whose elimination lies permanently beyond the horizon of our interests even though eliminating those goals would *not* mean the destruction of all life. Is this true, in particular, either of any goals that humans might necessarily pursue or of any goals whose near-universal and near-unavoidable pursuit is a contingent fact? Where teleological essentialism is concerned, the question is hard to answer because so many different goals might be said to be essential; but because I am not interested in defending teleological essentialism, I need not canvass all the possibilities. Instead, I must establish only that at least where our *contingently* near-universal and near-unavoidable goals are concerned, the result of any significant changes would indeed be a world in which we could not take any real interest.

To see that this is so, we need only consider in more detail what such a world would be like. Humans who lacked the goal of knowing what the world is like would simply not care if their beliefs were true, and so would have no inclination either to seek evidence for their beliefs or to make correct inferences from them. Humans who lacked any interest in doing what they have most reason *to* do would feel no pressure to deliberate or plan, and so would never inhibit their immediate impulses. Humans who lacked the goal of achieving mutual understanding and care would be utterly indifferent to all others of their kind. Given the interpenetration of thought, action, and affection, even one of these changes, and a fortiori all of them, would produce a world that was at best unutterably alien and at worst simply unintelligible. Such a world would contain neither communication nor any of the activities that make it possible, would lack both cooperation and meaningful competition, and would be barren of the shared understandings that now confer meaning on even the most mundane of interactions. This picture, surely, is not one that can hold any interest for us.

Thus, properly understood, the theoretical mutability of near-universal, near-inescapable goals does not threaten their ability to satisfy the distance requirement. And because it does not, we may safely decide between the proposed theory and teleological essentialism on the boring but nonetheless crucial grounds of methodological conservatism. For barring a return to a broadly teleological world-view, there is little a priori reason to believe that any particular goals are essential to humans,[67] but much a posteriori evidence that various goals are at least near-universal and near-unavoidable. This evidence is supplied by introspection, by our own and others' verbal and nonverbal behavior, and by many relevant background theories. Though always contestable, our attributions of near-universal, near-unavoidable goals are at least no more so than any other empirical claims. Thus, by settling for the proposed account, we can preserve the benefits of teleological essentialism while avoiding its metaphysical excesses.

67. However, for arguments that various *properties* are essential to humans, see Hurka, *Perfectionism*, sec. I.

XII

This concludes my attempt to sketch a defensible conception of the good life. The view that has emerged unites various strands of perfectionist thought but also leaves various loose ends. Without discussing these in detail, let me end by mentioning some questions that a more complete account would address.

A first unanswered question is whether what has been proposed is only a theory of value and its absence, or also a theory of *disvalue.* This question is important because many of the perfectionist arguments that are advanced in public life are most naturally understood in terms of disvalue. In particular, when someone argues that the state should restrict or forbid a certain activity because it is degraded, abhorrent, or unworthy of its participants, he generally means to assert not merely that that activity is less good than others, but rather that it actually has negative value. Thus, any proponent of my account must either water down such claims at the cost of greatly reducing their force – it is not very persuasive to say that an activity should be forbidden merely because the agent could do so much better – or else explain how any mere failure to achieve a near-universal and near-unavoidable goal can add up to positive badness. It is some consolation, but only some, to note that analogous problems confront all other teleological accounts.

A further question concerns my account's distributive implications. The issue here is whether the account tells us only which traits and activities are inherently good (and, perhaps, bad), or whether its implications also extend to their distribution. That is, given its conclusion that (say) knowledge and excellence make each person's life better, does the account also tell us whether it is best if a relatively small number of people are exceptionally knowledgeable and accomplished or if the general level of knowledge and excellence is higher but no one is outstanding? It seems safe to predict that the account will not favor the first, more Nietzschean alternative, but whether it actively endorses the second or is simply silent on the question is considerably less clear.

If it is merely silent, then anyone who opts for the second alternative must hold that there is *independent* value in the relatively equal distribution of what makes lives good. This claim would deflate my theory's pretensions by highlighting its inability to provide a complete account of value. Yet some deflation is inevitable anyhow, both because of the theory's exclusive concentration on the goodness of human lives – its inability to account for the apparent intrinsic value of species and other natural objects has already been noted – and because my earlier arguments appealed to independent aesthetic and moral reasons. Thus, a third unanswered question concerns the number and kinds of independent values for which the theory cannot account.

And that question leads directly to a fourth: namely, can the theory be augmented to produce a yet more unified account? There are, indeed, two different questions here. One, which concerns elements internal to the theory, is whether the different near-universal, near-inescapable goals to which it appeals can themselves be brought under some single rubric; while the other, which concerns the theory's relation to other theories, is whether its account of a good life can be woven into a more comprehensive scheme that also includes (say) distributional and aesthetic values.

However unified the theory turns out to be, it will remain pluralistic at least to the extent of attributing inherent value to a number of different aspects of human life. Thus, a final question is what, if anything, can be said about trade-offs among these goods. If all the theory tells us about (say) knowledge and aesthetic appreciation is that each is inherently valuable, then it will provide no guidance when they conflict. It will not help us to choose *between* knowledge and aesthetic appreciation when we cannot promote them both. Of course, this absence of priority rules is neither unique to perfectionism nor a serious handicap in practice: we regularly face trade-offs between merely instrumental goods. Such conflicts do not prevent us from making reasoned decisions about how to balance health care and national defense, or economic growth and the suppression of inflation, and there is no reason to expect them to be more problematic here.[68] Still, from a theoretical perspective, it would be satisfying to understand what if anything underlies the trade-offs we are inclined to make. Thus, a final unanswered question is whether some extension of the theory can set reasoned priorities among its elements.

68. Compare William Galston: "it is possible to talk of an intelligible structure of trade-offs among heterogeneous elements of the good even if no abstract principle can be stated that 'explains' that structure. Moral deliberation in particular cases can yield shared judgments that quantity X of good A is more important than quantity Y of good B. . ." (Galston, *Liberal Purposes* [Cambridge: Cambridge University Press, 1991], p. 181).

Chapter 10

Conclusion

All the elements of my argument are now in place. In the book's first part, I rejected the view that governments must remain neutral toward competing conceptions of the good, while in the second, I defended one conception as superior to others. There is, I argued, a strong case for the traditional perfectionist view that, for example, knowledge, excellence, and virtue make people's lives better, and that the best lives contain them in abundance. The obvious conclusion, and the one that in fact I want to draw, is that governments and individual political agents often have ample reason to promote such lives.[1]

---

1. This formulation conceals an awkward problem which I can mention but not fully resolve: namely, that because the proposed case for perfectionism is so involved and arcane, and because it presupposes so much philosophical background, it is bound to remain foreign to most who invoke perfectionist values in politics. It is a dissociated fantasy to suppose that any public figure will couch his reasoning in terms of notions such as teleology, essentialism, or the fact–value gap; and it is no less dissociated to expect these notions to inform the private deliberations of many political agents. But if the proposed arguments are rarely available to political agents – if as far as those agents are concerned, their commitment to perfectionism is already (close to) bedrock – then in what sense do the arguments provide reasons *for* their actions?

   I can envision two sorts of response, neither entirely satisfactory. One is to sever or weaken the connection between having a good reason and knowing what that reason is. On this account, all that is required for an agent to have a good reason is that it be in some sense *possible* for him or someone else to produce that reason. The other response preserves the connection between having a reason and being aware of it but denies that the relevant arguments *are* incapable of being known. It emphasizes that even theories too abstruse to achieve general currency may create or reinforce movements of thought that will eventually filter into the wider culture.

   Although both responses raise deep issues that I cannot address, the obvious objections to the first center on the relevance of reasons of which agents are not aware, while the obvious objections to the second concern the plausibility of its causal claims. These objections may or may not be tractable; but either way, the

In saying this, I mean to imply neither that perfectionist values are the *only* proper grounds for political decisions nor that they should dominate all others. We often legitimately use politics to further our private interests, as when we vote for candidates who will create jobs in our district or protect our health insurance; and even when voters or legislators take a larger view, their reasons need not be perfectionist. They may instead act to maintain order, to further the provision of public goods, or to increase the efficiency, justice, or humaneness of the state's arrangements. In addition, legislators may support policies whose wisdom or justice they question in deference to their constituents' wishes or in order to secure the support of fellow legislators on more important issues. Such familiar reasoning is the stuff of political decision making, and is compatible with many conceptions of the good. My point is only that these do not *exhaust* the legitimate reasons for political action: when a government can elevate its citizens' tastes, characters, aspirations, and modes of interaction, these too fall within its legitimate aims.

But if we should not expect perfectionist values to dominate, we also should not consign them to a marginal role. We may be tempted to do this if we concentrate too exclusively on a few stock examples, such as the criminalization of pornography and prostitution, which are indeed tangential to most people's main concerns. But when we review the goods that emerged in the preceding chapter – when we recall that these include the quality of people's relationships, the civility of their interactions, their levels of knowledge, accomplishment, and aesthetic awareness, and the content of their characters – we realize that they are potentially relevant to virtually every aspect of human life. Thus, once perfectionist considerations are admitted at all, they can be expected to play a role in many areas of political decision making. They are, for example, often relevant to decisions about public assistance, educational policy, the criminal and civil justice system, the prison system, city planning and land use, transportation policy, the tax code, support for cultural institutions, regulation of the entertainment industry, investment incentives, and the structure of institutions such as the military – to name just a few of the more obvious candidates. If perfectionist reasons rarely exclude others, they are also rarely absent from any list of relevant factors.

difficulty is hardly restricted to my account: once again, precisely the same problems arise when political agents appeal to nonperfectionist values, to justice or rights, or even to self-interest.

Indeed, in one important respect, this characterization of their scope is still too narrow; for while the cited topics can all be addressed within the current political framework, we also can engage in perfectionist reasoning about that framework itself. As we saw, Rawls has recently drawn back from the comprehensive neutrality of *A Theory of Justice*. He now allows that conceptions of the good may properly influence what we might call ordinary policy questions while continuing to insist that they not influence our thinking about "constitutional essentials or basic justice." But if my argument has been correct, then even this more moderate form of neutrality cannot be sustained. At least in theory, perfectionist reasoning may properly influence not only ordinary policy decisions but also decisions about the constitution and basic structure of society.

Is this *only* a theoretical possibility, or are there plausible perfectionist grounds for altering or retaining aspects of the basic structure? Although this question is beyond my scope, the idea of such reasons is far from absurd. Indeed, to find a live specimen, we may not have to look further than Rawls's own discussion; for his arguments for the design of the basic structure are themselves rooted in an ideal of the person that many consider perfectionist. Moving beyond Rawls, it is not implausible to connect those aspects of our legal system which have increasingly defined social problems in terms of conflicts of rights, and so have encouraged their resolution through litigation, with the atrophy of civility and common sense in our interpersonal relations. If this connection can be sustained, we may argue for change on the grounds that it is best not to be the sort of person whom the current system creates and rewards. Along similar lines, Marxists have long mounted perfectionist arguments against capitalism. We can also put a perfectionist cast on the reasoning behind many recent efforts to amend the U.S. Constitution – for example, efforts to outlaw abortion or protect or mandate school prayer.

Indeed, in principle, one might go further yet. It is quite possible to envision perfectionist arguments against freedom of speech and religion, majoritarian decision making, or even racial equality. Moreover, despite their lack of cogency, we have no guarantee that these arguments will not gain adherents or even prevail. But if their inferiority is not enough to defeat them, then adding an additional layer of argument against even considering them is not likely to do so either. Even if that additional layer is somehow incorporated into our political arrangements, any structure that has been created for one reason can be dismantled for another. In the end, we have no choice but to trust the rational faculties of those who will decide. There is, I have argued, nothing to be gained, and much to be lost, by imposing artificial limits on the reasons they may consider.

Index

Index

Index